ENVOY TO NEHRU

Escott Reid and Nehru

ENVOY TO NEHRU

ESCOTT REID

DELHI
OXFORD UNIVERSITY PRESS
TORONTO OXFORD
1981

Oxford University Press
OXFORD LONDON GLASGOW
NEW YORK TORONTO MELBOURNE WELLINGTON
NAIROBI DAR ES SALAAM CAPE TOWN
KUALA LUMPUR SINGAPORE HONG KONG TOKYO
DELHI BOMBAY CALCUTTA MADRAS KARACHI

© Oxford University Press 1981

Printed in India by P. K. Ghosh
at Eastend Printers, 3 Dr Suresh Sarkar Road, Calcutta 700 014
and published by R. Dayal, Oxford University Press,
2/11 Ansari Road, Daryaganj, New Delhi 110 002

TO RUTH

CONTENTS

Preface		ix
Acknowledgements		xi

PART ONE: PROLOGUE

1	I Choose India	3
2	The Special Relationship between India and Canada, 1947–1952	14

PART TWO: THE SPECIAL RELATIONSHIP IN OPERATION

3	Introduction to Indian Diplomacy—and Villages	29
4	The Armistice in Korea	43
5	China	53
6	Indo-China	69
7	Lester Pearson's Visit	86

PART THREE: THE EROSION OF THE SPECIAL RELATIONSHIP

8	American Arms for Pakistan	99
9	Kashmir	117
10	Krushchev–Bulganin Visit	133
11	Hungary and Suez	144
12	Krishna Menon	181

PART FOUR: CONCLUSION

13	Some Public Figures	193
14	India's Prospects	208
15	Nehru	220
16	Reconsideration: Epilogue	236

ANNEXES:

A	The Poorest Forty per cent of the People of India	283

Contents

B A New Partnership between Rich Countries
   and Poor Countries   286
Notes   289
Index   295

PLATES

Frontispiece
Escott Reid and Nehru

(*Between pages* 88 *and* 89)

Escott Reid presenting his credentials to Rajendra Prasad, President of India. Looking on is R. K. Nehru.

S. Radhakrishnan, Vice-President of India, Escott Reid and Ruth Reid.

Escott Reid and Krishna Menon at New Delhi Airport.
('If the Canadian government want to protest, let them protest.')

Escott Reid and Mrs Pandit.

L. B. Pearson in conversation with N. R. Pillai of External Affairs when the former called on him in New Delhi.

At the Canadian High Commissioner's dinner in honour of Louis St Laurent. *Left to right*: Escott Reid, Indira Gandhi, St Laurent, Madeleine O'Donnel (St Laurent's daughter), Nehru, Ruth Reid, Jean Paul (St Laurent's son).

Waving farewell at New Delhi Railway Station.

PREFACE

I was Canadian High Commissioner in India from 1952 to 1957 when there was a special relationship between Canada and India and when the Prime Minister and the Foreign Minister of Canada, Louis St Laurent and Lester Pearson, worked closely with Jawaharlal Nehru on many issues which threatened the peace of the world. This book is not based on memory which is errant. It is based on the reports which I sent at the time to the Canadian Government. The book is thus a personal account of a critical period in the history of independent India. It is also a study of some aspects of the foreign policy and diplomacy of India, Canada, the United States and Britain when the cold war was being waged, when the Soviet Union and China were allies and when the Commonwealth had, in Alastair Buchan's words, 'a vitality which gave it many of the characteristics of alliance'.

The epilogue to the book was written in 1979 following a visit which my wife and I made to India in the winter of 1978-9.

When I look back on my stay in India I realize how fortunate I was in being posted to India at that particular time. Nehru was then at the pinnacle of his power in India and of his influence abroad. India had emerged out of the terrible time of troubles which had followed the partition of the Indian Empire between India and Pakistan and, for the first time in three decades, production was increasing more rapidly than population. Canada under St Laurent and Pearson was conducting a foreign policy and diplomacy which were more active and more positive than in any five-year period since then. St Laurent and Pearson attached great importance to working with Nehru on foreign policy particularly on questions relating to Korea, Indo-China, and the newly established Communist regime in China.

During most of the period from 1952 to 1957 the relations between the United States and India were bad. They were worse than they needed to have been and for this each side was to blame. I had this chiefly in mind when, after three years in India, I wrote to my three children who were then at university:

Often governments are criticized for pursuing foreign policies based on national self-interest. I am coming more and more to believe that more often the valid basis for criticism is that the foreign policy is not based on national self-interest but on irritation, resentment, anger. Foreign policy might be more realistic if foreign ministers every day recited a litany of: 'In my decisions on foreign policy today, Good Lord deliver me from envy, hatred, malice, pride and vain-glory.' It would be too much to ask that they also request deliverance from uncharitableness and hypocrisy.

There is much in this book to support this thesis.

My wife, Ruth, was my partner in India. Much of what I perceived clearly there I perceived through her eyes. Our children, Patrick, Morna and Timothy, who were with us for part of our time in India, helped both of us to understand India better. This year Ruth and I celebrate fifty years of marriage. This book is dedicated to her.

Ste. Cécile de Masham,
Québec, January 1980

ACKNOWLEDGEMENTS

The Department of External Affairs of Canada gave me permission to consult the archives of the Department in order that I might refresh my memory of my reporting from India when I was High Commissioner there. The Historical Division of the Department helped me to locate documents in the Department's archives. Geoffrey Pearson gave me permission to quote from letters to me from his father, Lester Pearson, and from his father's journal of his visit to India in 1955. The Canada Council gave me a grant towards my expenses in writing the book. Ernestine Hopkins, who was for a time my secretary in New Delhi, typed and retyped the manuscript with accuracy and intelligence. Professor Michael G. Fry and Dr Nancy Jetly collected material for me to use in Chapter Eleven on Hungary and Suez. Friends and former colleagues read drafts of the whole or of parts of the epilogue and made helpful comments. The Oxford University Press helped me greatly by their suggestions for tightening up the manuscript and by their editing. To all these I am most grateful.

I am grateful to Granada Publishing Ltd. for permission to quote from Doris Lessing's *The Four-Gated City* at the beginning of Chapter Eleven and to the Oxford University Press for permission to quote from Sarvepalli Gopal's *Jawaharlal Nehru: A Biography*.

An expanded version of Chapter Fourteen was published in the *India Quarterly*, April–June 1965, under the title 'Nehru's India'. Chapter Fifteen is substantially the same as my essay 'Nehru: An Assessment in 1957' which appeared in the *International Journal*, Summer 1964.

PART ONE
PROLOGUE

CHAPTER ONE

I CHOOSE INDIA

The first time I saw Nehru was in October 1949. He spoke at the Country Club near Ottawa at a dinner given for him by the Canadian Prime Minister, Louis St Laurent. I was then second-in-command of the Department of External Affairs and, along with other senior government officials, was constantly attending such official dinners in honour of visiting dignitaries. The food and wine and the company at these dinners were excellent but we had to pay for them by sitting through long platitudinous speeches: first the toast by the Canadian prime minister or foreign minister to the visitor and his country and then the reply by the visitor. Some of my colleagues used to enliven the proceedings by making bets on how long the two speeches would be. Usually the most pessimistic would win.

Douglas LePan, poet, economist and foreign service officer, had written a speech for St Laurent. St Laurent had the lawyer's capacity to absorb a brief. He spoke without notes but what he said was very much what LePan had written. It was gracious in its references to India's greatness and to Nehru's contribution to the struggle for independence, and it showed respectful sympathy for the problems and challenges which confronted India and its prime minister. The references to India's struggle for independence under Gandhi and Nehru so irritated the British High Commissioner that he came up to me after dinner to splutter a protest.

Nehru had come to Ottawa from his first visit to the United States. The visit had been a failure and he knew it. The fault lay on both sides. Influential Americans had rubbed Nehru the wrong way. Nehru had rubbed influential Americans the wrong way. Dean Acheson, then Secretary of State, was one of them. Acheson had arranged that Nehru and he would meet by themselves after an official dinner to have a private talk. The talk lasted for two and a half hours but Acheson afterwards complained that Nehru had talked to him as if he were a public meeting and, as a result of the talk, Acheson concluded that Nehru and he 'were not destined to have a pleasant personal relationship.... He was one of the most difficult men with whom I have ever had to deal.'[1] Nehru probably reciprocated the sentiment.

Nehru found in Ottawa a more congenial ambience than he had found in Washington and New York. The ambience in Ottawa at that time was markedly British and Nehru in mind and spirit was at least half British. St Laurent was deferential to him for St Laurent was modest about himself and he was modest about Canada when he was talking to the prime minister of a country which, he kept reminding himself, had over twenty times the population of Canada. Nehru had already met St Laurent and Lester Pearson at meetings of Commonwealth prime ministers and he had come to like and respect them.

It was clear from the first sentences of Nehru's speech at the official dinner in reply to St Laurent that St Laurent's speech had touched him. Nehru spoke without notes. He spoke, it seemed, on the inspiration of the moment. We felt he was paying us the tribute of sharing with us his agony at discovering when he became prime minister that the choices he had to make were so seldom between good and evil but were so often between the greater evil and the lesser evil. His audience was touched in a way I have never before or since seen an audience of that kind at that kind of official function touched, and I must in my time have sat through a hundred or so such functions.

As soon as I got to the office the next morning I asked one of the other External Affairs officers who had been present at the dinner to prepare an account of Nehru's speech to be sent to our high commissioner in New Delhi. He returned the following day to tell me that he and his colleagues who had been at the dinner had been so moved by the speech that they could not remember what Nehru had said.

Three years later I discovered what Nehru had said in his after-dinner speech in Ottawa. I was then High Commissioner in India and I was attending the opening in New Delhi in January 1953 of a Unesco seminar on the Gandhian outlook.

When Nehru made the opening speech I experienced a shock of recognition. The speech was much the same as the one he had given in Ottawa. In my report to Ottawa I said:

Neither speech was, I think, prepared. In both, Mr Nehru was thinking aloud about some of the problems which seem constantly to perplex him as a political leader, particularly the necessity of the political leader leading 'the multitude who has made him what he is', but at the same time not getting so far in front of them that 'one loses touch, one is cut off from those one works for and works with, . . . one is isolated'. This means that the political leader 'always has to think in terms either of compromises or of a choice of evils and he has to choose what he considers the lesser evil lest the greater overwhelm'. The way of the political leader 'who cannot and who is not capable of acting like a prophet or like the ultimate man of truth' must therefore differ from the way of the prophet—'the man of truth wedded to truth whatever happens'. 'The prophet usually meets his doom in crucifixion and it was in the fitness of things that Gandhiji met his doom in that way. . . . But we are not prophets and we are humbler folk and, if we have responsibility cast upon us as politicians and the like, we have to deal with human material which is very far from perfect.' . . . But at the same time 'ends should never be subordinated to means. If you adopt any means you like, well, your ends disappear; you don't arrive at the end [you have aimed at] because you have taken the wrong path and it leads you somewhere else.'

The second time I heard Nehru speak was at the meeting of Commonwealth foreign ministers held in Colombo, Ceylon, in January 1950. On the preceding day, Malcolm MacDonald, then the British Commissioner-General for South-East Asia, had given the conference an account of the visit which he had made to Indo-China six weeks before. At that time Bao-Dai was Emperor of Vietnam. Malcolm MacDonald said that he had been impressed by Bao-Dai's personal character; he was a sincere nationalist and patriot and no tool of the French; he seemed to have a good grasp of political problems, an independent mind and a good judgement and, with experience, and above all with success, he was likely to develop into a popular national leader. (A couple of years later one of Malcolm MacDonald's colleagues said to me, 'The trouble with Malcolm's judgement is that all his geese are swans.') MacDonald went on to say that the military situation seemed to be turning in Bao-Dai's favour and against Ho Chi Minh and that Bao-

Dai's influence in Vietnam was at least equal to that of Ho Chi Minh and was steadily increasing. (This was one of those tragedy-laden faulty assessments of the situation in Vietnam by well-intentioned and intelligent representatives of western governments—French, British and American—which bedevilled western policy on Vietnam for almost thirty years after the end of the Second World War.)

At the meeting of the Conference the next morning Nehru was asked to open the discussion of the situation in Indo-China with special reference to the question whether, as the British foreign minister, Ernest Bevin, had suggested, the governments of the Commonwealth should accord *de facto* recognition to Bao-Dai's regime. I can still hear the first sentences of Nehru's statement. He spoke slowly; he spoke hesitantly; he paused as if in search of the right word so that when the word came out, it came out with greater emphasis. He spoke with studied moderation. He demonstrated his mastery of the traditional diplomatic language of understatement. When he differed from British policy, he expressed his difference of opinion firmly but politely. My recollection of his statement on Indo-China is that it began somewhat as follows: 'I have listened with great interest to Mr Malcolm MacDonald's account of his [pause] visit to Indo-China. The Indian Government has, of course, its own sources of information on what is happening in Indo-China and the accounts which we have received from our sources [pause] differ [pause] markedly from the [pause] impressions which Mr MacDonald received. According to our information Bao-Dai has little influence over the bulk of the population of Vietnam.' Nehru then went on to demolish the case which MacDonald had made for *de facto* recognition of the Bao-Dai government. Bao-Dai's own personal record, Nehru said, hardly fitted him to be an effective or powerful national leader. 'He may be a nice man but he has had a strange career', co-operating, for example, with the Japanese during the Second World War. Nehru doubted whether the Bao-Dai experiment was likely to succeed. He added that he found it difficult to believe that *de facto* recognition of Bao-Dai's regime would lead to any happy results. In his opinion the French had, during the previous three and a half years, made a mountain of mistakes in dealing with Indo-China. He thought that the French should encourage Bao-Dai to come to terms with Ho Chi Minh on the basis of holding free elections for a constituent assembly which might devise means of establishing a new single government for Vietnam. His advice was that the governments of the Commonwealth should at this stage take no definite action in relation to Indo-China but that the situation should be watched carefully in order to determine what action should be taken in the future. One phrase which constantly recurred in Nehru's statement was a formula used by British civil servants in memoranda to their ministers, 'It is a matter for consideration whether'.

Here was not the philosopher-statesman of the Country Club speech in Ottawa. Here was the experienced, suave, international diplomat. My interest in Nehru and my admiration for him increased.

After the Colombo meeting the Canadian contingent at the meeting went on to New Delhi. We stayed in the former palace of the viceroys where Chakravarti Rajagopalachari resided as the last Governor-General of India. I saw something of the beauty of India. I learned a little about its poverty and its problems. A year after I returned to Ottawa I was made chairman of the first interdepartmental committee to be established by Canada on international aid to poor countries. At that time our aid was restricted to India, Pakistan and Ceylon.

In December 1946 Mackenzie King, then Prime Minister, had asked me to be the first Canadian High Commissioner to India. I was flattered. This was a signal honour. I was only forty-one and I had been in the Department of External Affairs for less than eight years. But in the previous nine years my wife and I and our three young children had lived in too many places for too short a time—Toronto, Halifax, Toronto, Washington, Ottawa, Washington, Ottawa—and we had been back in Ottawa for only eight months. We had just bought a farm in the Gatineau hills twenty-five miles north of Ottawa as a summer and week-end home. We wanted our children to strike roots in Canada—to feel that this farm was their home. We were looking forward to settling down in Ottawa for four or five years.

I was in New York at the time attending the U.N. General Assembly. I consulted St Laurent, who was heading the Canadian delegation. He advised me to write a personal letter to the Prime Minister explaining my situation and asking him if he could withdraw the invitation. I awaited his reply with some trepidation. Mackenzie King undoubtedly considered that he had conferred a great honour on me—as he indeed had. Prime ministers don't like having their conferments of honour rejected. Perhaps he would hold this refusal against me, and my career in the Canadian foreign service would be damaged. The reply came back almost by return mail:

> Had it been possible for you to accept the post in India, I am sure you would have found it fascinating and would have filled it to the satisfaction of all concerned. However, were I circumstanced similarly to yourself . . . I think my decision would have been the same as yours. One thing about the Department of External Affairs is that posts are likely always to be available for its most efficient members.

Here was King at his best—sympathetic, understanding, reassuring, flattering.

Five years later I was offered a choice between being ambassador to Japan and ambassador to the Netherlands. I knew that the post in India would be vacant in about six months. I said that India was the post I wanted. My wish was granted.

I was forty-seven when I went to India in the autumn of 1952 as Canadian High Commissioner. I had been in the Department of External Affairs for almost fourteen years, since January 1939; and ever since about 1943 I had been obsessed with what seemed to me to be a clear and present danger that a third world war might break out within the next ten years or so and I was determined that I would do my best to ensure that Canada did its best to reduce the chances of this happening.

In August 1947, a year and a half before the North Atlantic Treaty was signed, I put my arguments in a lengthy top-secret departmental memorandum which was circulated to St Laurent, who was then foreign minister, to Lester Pearson, who was then under-secretary for external affairs, and to the senior officers of the Canadian foreign service. I said that to diminish the possibility of war the western powers should maintain an overwhelming preponderance of force relative to that of the Soviet Union and that they should use the threat of this force to hold back further extensions of Soviet power. They should not provoke the Soviet Union into any desperate gamble but they should 'pursue a firm, patient and fair-minded policy' towards it. They should 'organize in advance an alliance which would become immediately effective if the Soviet Union should commit aggression' against the states of western Europe. In this alliance each member state 'would undertake to pool all its economic and military forces with those of the other members if any power should be found to have committed aggression against any member'. The western powers should maintain their armed forces at a level which was 'reasonable in relation to the armed forces of the Soviet world'. But more than this was required to create an overwhelming preponderance of force. Economic assistance should be given to western Europe in order to restore stability, prosperity and hope, and thus to lessen the possibility of pro-Soviet elements capitalizing on discontent in their efforts to gain power. The western world should make rapid progress in granting self-government to colonies and in removing racial discrimination. Otherwise,

the western powers may have the great majority of the colonial and coloured peoples hostile or unfriendly to them in the event of war with the Soviet Union or at least doing their best to fish in troubled waters. In this context the term 'colonial peoples' may well include a considerable section of Latin America, as well as the whole of Asia and Africa and the South West Pacific. . . . There are dangers in giving colonial peoples self-government before they are ready for it. But the dangers in not giving them self-government quickly are probably greater, since the longer independence is delayed the greater are the chances that the colonial independence movements may come under Soviet influence or control.

I ended my memorandum of August 1947 as follows:

No curtain, even of iron, is impenetrable. No two civilizations have, in the past, been able to live side by side without becoming more and more like each other. The longer, therefore, that the Soviet and western worlds live side by side in peace, even if it is an uneasy peace, full of conflicts and crises, the more similar to each other they will become. The more similar they become the more manageable will become the conflicts and crises which will arise between them, for the less will each have to fear from the triumph of the other's way of life, and the less will each want to impose its way of life on the other.[2]

When my appointment as High Commissioner to India was announced, someone (I do not now remember who) said: 'Reid's appointment is not surprising. Mr Nehru will find him a most congenial spirit in the field of anti-imperialism.' The comment, though malevolent, was shrewd. My views, when I went to India as envoy to Nehru, of what should be done to make the world safer and saner, were much the same as Nehru's. During my stay in India a number of my colleagues in the Department of External Affairs in Ottawa used to complain that I almost never found fault with Nehru's views on foreign affairs (though I often found fault with his diplomatic methods). They might more justly have complained that I never found fault with the views I had expressed in my departmental memorandum of 30 August 1947.

I called on Lester Pearson on 9 September 1952 to say goodbye before leaving for India. My note on the interview reads as follows:

Pearson said that one difficulty which I would face in India was that the Indians tend to exaggerate our influence in international affairs. They are also convinced of our great goodwill and he hoped that in this their views were not exaggerated. The Indians also tend to exaggerate our freedom of action in international affairs and fail to realize the limitations imposed upon us because of our position between the United States and the United Kingdom. In addition, India tends to expect more assistance from Canada [under the Colombo Plan] than it was likely we would be able to give. . . . It was natural that the Indians wanted more from Canada since they had a great programme [of economic development] and were in a hurry to get it completed. . . . India is a great power and is subject to the temptations of a great power. It will be interesting to see over the next fifty years whether, as India becomes more conscious of its position as a great power and becomes more powerful, it may make the same kind of mistakes in foreign affairs as the rest of us. . . . One of the jobs of a Canadian in New Delhi would be to help to disabuse Indians of their more extreme prejudices against the United States.

A few days later my wife, Ruth, our eighteen-year-old daughter, Morna, and I left Ottawa for India. Our two sons stayed behind. The older, Patrick, was in his final year at the University of Toronto. The younger, Timothy, who had been at Lisgar Collegiate in Ottawa, was about to begin two years at Ridley College. We proceeded by slow stages: Washington and New York where I had talks with Indian officials and officials of the State Department; by sea to London where I again had talks, this time with Indian officials and with Lord Salisbury, then the foreign secretary in the Conservative government which had come to power a year before, and with some of his officials. Norman Robertson, Canadian High Commissioner in London, arranged for us to meet at dinner at his house Sir Raghavan Pillai who was about to take up his appointment as Secretary-General of the Ministry of External Affairs in New Delhi. This was the beginning of a deep lifelong friendship. Then after London, a holiday by the sea in Devon and by P.&O. ship to Bombay.

En route we heard that Adlai Stevenson had been defeated by Eisenhower for the presidency of the United States, and that the Republicans had a majority of one in the Senate and nine in the House of Representatives. I had worked with Adlai Stevenson in London in the autumn of 1945 on the executive committee and preparatory commission of the United Nations and at the General Assembly of the U.N. in New York in the autumn of 1946 and had been greatly impressed and charmed by him. When we were passing through Washington we had listened over the radio to one of his election speeches and had been deeply moved by it. He had, as the Chatham House survey of international affairs for 1952 put it, 'by personality and by television ... persuaded both general and expert opinion that his chances [of election] were about as good as those of his famous opponent'. His defeat depressed me. Acheson had shown little understanding of Nehru, India or Asia. The Republicans were likely to show even less.

We arrived in Bombay on 14 November, an auspicious day for an envoy to Nehru, for it was his birthday. We stayed in Bombay for two days as guests of the governor of Bombay state, Sir Girja Bajpai, whom I had known in Washington during the Dumbarton Oaks conference (which he called at the time the Dumbarton hoax conference) and at the Chicago conference on international civil aviation. He had retired recently as secretary-general of the External Affairs Ministry in New Delhi. Bajpai told me that Chester Bowles, the American Ambassador, had just been staying with him. He said that Bowles had been successful in India because he had based his actions on four beliefs: India's foreign policy was its own affair; United States help to India was not charity but was in the interests of the United States; when India differed from the United States on foreign policy, it was not necessarily being perverse; the way to detach China from the Soviet Union was to woo it. Bajpai said that he had heard a rumour (which fortunately turned out to be unfounded) that Pillai was not going to be the secretary-general of the External Affairs Ministry but would take a post in Europe, possibly because of the bad relations between his wife and the wife of R. K. Nehru, who was now temporarily in charge of the ministry. R. K. Nehru was the son of a first cousin of the Prime Minister. Bajpai did not express an opinion of Pillai but his views of the senior officers in the External Affairs Ministry were uncomplimentary: one was deaf and dumb, another he had little respect for, and a third was sound, had views and was willing to express them, but was not capable of filling the highest posts.

Nor were his opinions of Nehru's cabinet high. There were, in his opinion, only three men of ability in the Cabinet, in addition to the Prime Minister: Gopalaswami Ayyangar (the Minister of Defence), C. D. Deshmukh (the Minister of Finance), and T. T. Krishnamachari (the Minister of Commerce and Industry). No successor to the Prime Minister was in sight. Deshmukh had many of the necessary qualities but he had no political experience and no following in the Congress Party. The Prime Minister was not attempting to build him up as a possible successor or to build anyone else up.

On this visit to Bombay I did not meet the Chief Minister of the state of Bombay, Morarji Desai. This would have been inappropriate since I had not yet presented my credentials to the President of India. I had, however, news of him. Bruce Rankin, the Canadian Trade Commissioner in Bombay (whose post corresponded to that of a consul-general), was giving a reception for my wife and me the day after our arrival in Bombay. He had invited Bajpai and his wife. Bajpai told me the evening before the reception that Morarji Desai had just called on him to tell him that he would be breaking the recently enacted prohibition law of the state of Bombay if he attended the reception, since alcoholic drinks were to be served and he was not a permit holder. Bajpai said that he had had a tussle with Morarji Desai about this and that at one point in the conversation he had had to say that he would have to report the matter to the President, whose representative he was. Bajpai and I reached the simple solution that no alcohol would be served during the first half hour of the reception and that he would come during this 'dry' period. In any case he did not come. He telephoned me just before the reception to say that his wife was most unwell and he begged to be excused; his daughter would come with us.

The next day we left by train for New Delhi where we arrived on 17 November.

CHAPTER TWO

THE SPECIAL RELATIONSHIP BETWEEN INDIA AND CANADA, 1947–1952

In 1952 when I went to India, Canada was in the second half of what I was later to call the golden decade of Canadian foreign policy. It was not in fact a decade; it was closer to fourteen years, from 1943 to 1957. After the collapse of France and the occupation of most of western Europe in 1940 and the entry of the United States into the war in 1941, Canada was the third most important country in the western alliance—very much, of course, a low third, since the United States and Britain were so much more powerful. Canada remained the third most important country in the West until the middle fifties. By then countries such as France, Italy and Germany, which, because of defeat or occupation, had lost their normal influence, had got much of it back.

As the result of hard, creative, imaginative work by Cabinet ministers and government officials, the Canadian Government was able to take advantage in international affairs of the opportunities which its position of temporary prominence gave it. It was, for example, a member, along with the United States and Britain, of the inner groups of three which prepared the first drafts of the international agreements establishing the Food and Agriculture Organization, the United Nations Relief and Rehabilitation Agency, the International Monetary Fund, the World Bank, the International Civil Aviation Organization and the North Atlantic Treaty.

The Canada of 1952 had, therefore, become accustomed to pursuing an active foreign policy. This was a fundamental change from the period between the two world wars when Mackenzie King, Prime Minister for about two-thirds of the period, pursued a deliberately inactive foreign policy. King sought a foreign policy that divided Canada the least. Louis St Laurent, who had become Prime Minister in 1948, and Lester Pearson, who had almost simultaneously become foreign minister, sought a foreign policy that united Canada the most. Both were keenly interested in foreign affairs—they liked dealing with foreign affairs, they were good at it, and they believed that Canadians could not be free, prosperous and secure in a disorganized and frightened world. They were supported by a small, skilled, homogeneous group of senior civil servants with like-minded beliefs—in the Department of External Affairs, the Department of Finance and the Bank of Canada. Until the Suez crisis in 1956 St Laurent and Pearson could count on almost unanimous support for their foreign policy in the House of Commons and general support for it in the country.

In 1947 and 1948 a fundamental change took place in the membership and the nature of the Commonwealth when India, Pakistan and Ceylon became independent and decided to remain in the Commonwealth. This created a Commonwealth of nine independent nations representative of almost the whole of the democratic world. Its older members comprised what was then the greatest nation in western Europe, two Australasian nations, one South African nation, one North American nation and Ireland (until 1949). Its new members comprised the second most populous nation in Asia, one of the two most populous Muslim states in the world, and a Buddhist state. The new Commonwealth included representatives of every continent except South America.

During 1947 and 1948 the government and people of Canada became conscious that the British empire had evolved into something new, and that this something new was interesting and, indeed, exciting. Many Canadians regretted India's decision in 1949 to become a republic; virtually all, however, welcomed India's decision to remain in the Commonwealth even though it had become a republic. Many found that the membership of a republic in a Commonwealth the head of which was a king, was another of those paradoxes which added to the fascination of the new Commonwealth.

The first Canadians to become enthusiastic converts to a belief in the importance to Canada of the new Commonwealth were those who attended meetings of representatives of the new

Commonwealth. Some of these meetings were informal, such as those held weekly during the General Assemblies of the United Nations. Others were formal, such as the meetings of Commonwealth prime ministers, foreign ministers and finance ministers. But, whatever the type of meeting, the Canadians who participated came back from the meetings with a sense of pleasant surprise at how illuminating the discussions had been. I remember how impressed I was by the conference of Commonwealth foreign ministers which I attended at Colombo in Ceylon in January 1950 as adviser to Lester Pearson. It was partly that the meetings were small, only eight countries. It was partly that, since the foreign ministers all spoke English fluently, there was not that barrier to comprehension which exists when people have to communicate through interpreters. It was also that all the participants had been trained politically on the basis of British rules of parliamentary discussion and within the framework of constitutional structures closely allied to the British parliamentary system. This meant that Commonwealth meetings could get down to business more quickly than could U.N. meetings and that they could do their business more speedily.

This was one reason why those of us who attended meetings of the eight-nation Commonwealth in the late forties and early fifties found them such a relief after U.N. meetings. But there was a more profound reason why we found these Commonwealth meetings so helpful.

In the years from 1947 to 1952 we in Ottawa became increasingly conscious of the fact that every view of the world suffered from some distortion, and that the view from Ottawa was no exception. As the new members of the Commonwealth began to play a greater part in Commonwealth consultations, we began to comprehend how advantageous it was for us in Ottawa to have chances of seeing the world through the eyes of other countries situated in different parts of the world and with different traditions, different concepts of national interest, different emotional reactions to world events. We began to understand that this helped greatly to correct distortions in our view of the world from Ottawa.

As more and more nations in the years immediately after the Second World War emerged in Asia and Africa, as the demands of those new nations for national freedom, economic improvement and the removal of racial discrimination became more pressing and more vocal, we in Ottawa also became conscious of the great value of the new Commonwealth as a bridge between the old democracies of the West and the new democracies of Asia and Africa.

All these things became increasingly clear to us in Ottawa in the five years before I went to India, the years from 1947 to 1952. This made us attach to the new multiracial Commonwealth a new and special importance as a means of assisting us to achieve the principal objective of Canadian foreign policy, the creation and maintenance of an international order in which Canadians might be able to be free, prosperous and secure.

We in Ottawa were not alone in the importance which we attached to the new Commonwealth. Alastair Buchan wrote in 1973 that in the five years or so from 1952 on, 'The American relationship occupied only part of the British horizon, for, after the absorption of India, Pakistan and Ceylon under a new style Commonwealth, this gained for a while a vitality which gave it many of the characteristics of alliance.'[1] Alastair Buchan's conclusion that the Commonwealth in the five years or so from 1952 on (the period of my stay in India) had many of the characteristics of alliance applies with even greater force to the period of the five years before 1952. In October 1948 at the first meeting of Commonwealth prime ministers in which independent India, Pakistan and Ceylon were participants, Nehru and the prime ministers of Pakistan and Ceylon declared, according to the official record of the meeting, 'that their governments were anxious for close consultation in defence matters' with other Commonwealth governments. They also agreed that Britain's entry into the Brussels treaty (the forerunner of and pattern for the North Atlantic Treaty concluded six months after the Commonwealth meeting) 'was in accordance with the interests of the other members of the Commonwealth, the United Nations, and the promotion of world peace'.

Another indication of the unity of the new Commonwealth in its early years was Nehru's statement at the meeting of Commonwealth prime ministers in April 1949:

Free democracy as it obtained in the United Kingdom was a form of government worthy of imitation. All the peoples of the world should be able to see that it was infinitely preferable to the regime established by the Soviet Government.... Democracy was ... threatened at the present time from two directions—first, by a direct onslaught by communism; and secondly, by an internal weakening, largely due to unfavourable economic conditions.

An example of the influence of the new Commonwealth on Canadian foreign policy was Canada's participation in the Colombo Plan for Co-operative Economic Development in South and South-East Asia. This Plan was conceived at the meeting of Commonwealth foreign ministers at Colombo in January 1950. Ever since the end of the Second World War Canada had been giving economic aid in various forms to Britain and to west European countries. Nevertheless if anyone had asked me before I left Ottawa for the Colombo Conference whether it was practical politics to suggest that Canada should agree to make a gift of $25 million a year to the countries of South Asia to help them speed up the pace of their economic development, I would have replied that it certainly was not. Yet by 1951 we were making such a gift. How did it happen? Why did it happen when it did? Part—perhaps the greater part—of the explanation lies in the revelation which had come to us in Ottawa of the value to us and to the world of the new Commonwealth.

Lester Pearson found it extremely difficult to persuade the Cabinet in 1950 to recommend to parliament that the tax payers of Canada give money to the governments of South Asia. At first he had only one supporter in Cabinet, Robert Mayhew, who had accompanied him for much of his round-the-world tour early in 1950. It would not, I think, have been possible for Pearson to sell the proposal to the Prime Minister, St Laurent, and then with his help get it through Cabinet, if it had not been that the Colombo Plan was a Commonwealth concept, that the countries to which gifts were to be made were Commonwealth countries (India, Pakistan and Ceylon) and that the presence of these nations in the Commonwealth had struck the imagination of the government and people of Canada.

In many ways the decision of the Canadian Government to participate in the Colombo Plan was the most revolutionary of the four revolutionary changes in Canadian foreign policy which took place from 1947 to 1952. In those years Canada for the first time in its history entered in peacetime into a military alliance, the North Atlantic alliance, built up large defence forces (increasing its defence expenditure, in terms of 1950 U.S. dollars, from $500 million in 1950 to $1750 million in 1952) and sent troops and airmen to join the forces of the alliance in western Europe. But alliances and armament races are familiar patterns in history. Organized regular aid from the governments of wealthy countries to the governments of poor countries for the purpose of helping them speed up their economic development is an unfamiliar pattern in history.

Non-self-governing India had been the brightest jewel in the British crown. Independent India was, in 1952, the keystone of the arch of the new Commonwealth. For in 1952, a Commonwealth without India would not have been the kind of new Commonwealth which could capture the imaginations of so many people. It was the consciousness of this which led to Canada playing a leading role in working out a formula in 1948 and 1949 which would reconcile India's desire to remain in the Commonwealth with its decision to become a republic. The formula was that India accepted 'the king as the symbol of the free association of the independent nations of the Commonwealth and as such the head of the Commonwealth'.

To help make independent India feel at home in the new Commonwealth, the Canadian Government took steps to remove discrimination in Canadian law against Indians. The first step was taken as the result of a formal request from the interim government of India, the government in which Nehru was in charge of external affairs and Commonwealth relations. In December 1946, only three months after this government had been formed, it requested the Canadian Government to persuade the Government of British Columbia 'to confer the franchise on the small Indian community in that province and thus rectify the present anomalous position which is a source of humiliation to Indians'. By April 1947 this had been accomplished and Nehru sent a telegram of thanks to Ottawa. Four years later Canada removed a second 'source of humiliation to Indians' by terminating the immigration regulation under which Indians (along with other 'Asiatics') were barred from entry to Canada as immigrants unless they were wives or unmarried children under eighteen of Canadian citizens legally resident in Canada. In place of this Canada made an agreement with India providing for the admission to Canada as immigrants not only of the 'close relatives' of citizens of Canada resident in Canada—and this was a wider group than wives or unmarried children under eighteen—but also of a hundred and fifty other Indian citizens a year. It had been my responsibility to recommend what the size of the quota should be. I knew that what the Indian Government wanted was not the admission of Indians to Canada as immigrants but the symbolic gesture of removing a legal discrimination. I therefore recommended the token numbers of a hundred and fifty a year from India, a hundred from Pakistan and fifty from Ceylon. This was agreed to. The symbolic agreement with India was deliberately concluded on a symbolic day, 26 January 1951, the first anniversary of the day on which India had become a republic. Nehru, in a message to St Laurent, called this agreement 'another step in the developing friendship between our two countries'.

In the autumn of 1947 the Canadian Government supplied a ton of crude uranium oxide to India. This constituted the beginning of co-operation on atomic energy between Indian and Canadian scientists and was another step in the development of a special relationship between India and Canada. The Indian Government had requested this uranium oxide for the Bose Institute in Calcutta for fundamental studies in atomic physics and the possible use of atomic energy for industrial purposes. The ultimate object of the research, the Indians told us, was the use of uranium extracted from Indian rocks and minerals for the construction of an atomic reactor. One reason Canada granted the Indian request was the possibility that Canada might wish to secure thorium from India.

During the first five years of Indian independence which preceded my arrival in India, the years 1947 to 1952, tumultuous developments in Asia presented the nations of the world with many problems and challenges. The Indonesian struggle against the Dutch for self-government which began in 1945 did not terminate until 1950. In Malaya and Burma there were communist insurrections and Burma also had civil wars. In Vietnam the French fought against Ho Chi Minh. (When I went to India, France still had 175,000 members of its armed forces in Indo-China and these included twenty-six per cent of all French officers and thirty-seven per cent of all French noncommissioned officers.) The communists secured control of the whole of continental China and drove Chiang Kai-shek to take shelter in Formosa. The United States remained in occupation of Japan until 1952. In the summer of 1950 the Korean War broke out. The Korean War, as Alastair Buchan has put it, 'marked the beginning of the bipolar era, ... a system dominated by the antagonism of two diverse coalitions that aggregated around the United States and the Soviet Union'.[2] These developments (plus the popular support in the United States for Senator Joseph McCarthy's witch hunts) strained the unity of the North Atlantic powers. Some of these developments, notably the United States attitude to the Communist Government in China, General Douglas MacArthur's bellicosity and Senator McCarthy's witch hunts, widened the gulf between the United States and India. It is thus not surprising that, during these five tumultuous years from 1947 to 1952, Asian affairs loomed large in Canadian foreign policy.

In October 1948 Nehru attended his first meeting of Commonwealth prime ministers. The official account of the discussions contains a clear statement by him of his approach to Asian problems.

Asia was now going through the phase which Europe had passed through three generations ago. Nationalism was now a very great force to be reckoned with. There had been three competing ideas—nationalism, imperialism and communism. Originally, communism had supported nationalism, as championing the underdog against imperialism; and it had then been welcomed in Asia by many people who lacked any general understanding of its economic doctrine or its international implications. When, however, imperialism was removed in a country which had attained its independence, communism then came into conflict with nationalism; and when this conflict became apparent, communism had no hold on Asian peoples.... An anti-communist appeal was not likely to succeed with Asian peoples in view of the extent to which communists had in the past supported legitimate nationalist aspirations. Asian peoples had, however, no sympathy for Russian expansionist policies; and publicly drawing attention to the dangers of Russian encroachment upon Asia would be much more likely to be effective [than an anti-communist appeal]. ... Communism might carry weight if it came in support of nationalism and the underdog; but there would be no welcome for slavism and communism of a specifically Russian brand. As long as there were other forces championing nationalism and the betterment of living conditions, the ground would be cut from under the feet of the communists.

Nehru's advice to the western democracies was that they should ally themselves with the forces of nationalism in Asia and that they should realize that 'in Asia, where many thousands of people were without the primary necessities of life, the best defence against communism was to raise living standards'.

Within a year of this meeting of Commonwealth prime ministers a communist government under Mao Tse-tung was proclaimed in Peking. At subsequent Commonwealth meetings Nehru urged that it was essential to realize that the important fact was not so much that a communist government had come to power in China but that after thirty years of revolution and war China had a strong and powerful central government. Communist China was emerging as a great power in the world and this was changing the whole balance of power in Asia and indeed in the world.[3] China was proud, sensitive and resentful of any reflection on its new-found strength and self-respect. Mao Tse-tung and Chou En-lai were hard, able and experienced men who knew China well. Nehru would say that he did not know which way China would go—whether it would become more communist or more Chinese. He could not, however, conceive of China as being a camp follower of the Soviet Union. He thought that for a time it would probably appear to the Chinese Government that it would be profitable for them to co-operate with the Soviet Union in international affairs but eventually they would go their own way. The Indian Government considered that its recognition of the Communist Government in Peking would maintain the possibility of India influencing developments in China. Recognition without some measure of friendliness would be fruitless. India was shaping its policy towards China in such a way as to make clear to China that the Soviet Union [which was then China's ally] was not the only possible friend to whom China could look. India was therefore doing its best to adopt a cautiously friendly attitude towards China, while maintaining careful security precautions and while disapproving of some of the actions of the Chinese Government.

When Nehru put these arguments forward he found a sympathetic audience in St Laurent and Pearson. They, indeed, agreed with virtually everything he said. They also accepted him, as the State Department under Dean Acheson was most reluctant to do, as the most influential statesman in noncommunist Asia and as a useful, if not indispensable, intermediary between the western powers and the Government of China in Peking. If the Korean War had not broken out in the summer of 1950 Canada would, in 1950, have recognized the government in Peking and it would probably have supported the seating of its representatives in the U.N. Thus by 1952, when I went to India, Canada had established a special relationship with India in the framing and conduct of its foreign policy on Asian questions.

In January 1950 Senator Joseph McCarthy had begun his campaign against 'communists' in high places in the United States Government, especially those who he asserted were responsible for the victory of the communists in China. In this he was supported by the China lobby, which was anticommunist, pro-Chiang Kai-shek and anti-Indian. The strength of McCarthyism in the United States aroused distaste and contempt in the democratic world. When it became clear that McCarthyism was strengthening forces within the Democratic administration which wished to pursue what seemed to us in Ottawa dangerous policies in Asia, to distaste and contempt were added mounting apprehensions about the willingness and ability of the United States to pursue wise policies in Asia.

We welcomed (and were surprised by) President Truman's decision in June 1950 to resist the invasion of South Korea by North Korea, but as the Korean War went on we became more and more worried. General Douglas MacArthur, the United States commander in the Korean War, was for month after month permitted by the United States Government to pursue impatient and provocative policies which finally resulted in an unnecessary war with China. The United States Government insisted on forcing through the U.N. General Assembly a resolution which we considered unwise (but for which we reluctantly voted) authorizing the United Nations forces in Korea to cross the border into North Korea. (At that time the United States could usually force resolutions through a sixty-nation Assembly if it was determined to do so.) Then, when the Chinese attacked the U.N. forces coming close to their border with North Korea, the United States Government forced another resolution through the General Assembly which we also considered unwise (but for which we also reluctantly voted) indicting China as an aggressor. If Truman had not finally dismissed MacArthur in April 1951 he would probably have pursued policies which would have led to war with the Soviet Union. What was especially disturbing to us in Ottawa was the emotional convulsion which Truman's dismissal of MacArthur touched off in the United States. This convulsion demonstrated how deep, widespread, irrational and dangerous was the public and congressional support in the United States for MacArthur and his views on United States policy in the Far East.

As American casualties in the fighting against the Chinese in Korea mounted, bitterness in the United States against China mounted. One result was that the United States argued that the decision by the U.N. to give China the status of an aggressor ruled out any discussion by the U.N. of China's demands that its representatives be seated in the U.N. as representatives of China and that China's claim to Formosa be recognized. At the same time the display of Chinese strength in the Korean War resulted in a great increase in prestige for the Chinese Government.

Apprehensions about United States policies in Asia dominated thinking in the Department of External affairs in Ottawa from the autumn of 1950 until my departure from India in 1957 and for many years afterwards, just as they dominated thinking in the foreign offices of the other democratic North Atlantic allies of the United States. The authoritative survey of world affairs in 1952 published by the Council on Foreign Relations in New York spoke of 'an astonishing insensitivity to American wishes [on attitudes to China] on the part of this country's allies and associates'.[4] The allies and associates of the United States likewise found astonishing the insensitivity of the United States to their views on China.

It was the depth and intensity of our apprehensions in Ottawa about United States policies in Asia which convinced us more and more, in the first half of the fifties, of the necessity of Canada maintaining a special relationship with India in which India would try to moderate Chinese policy and we would try to moderate United States policy. How special the relationship between India and Canada was during the successive Korean crises is made clear in Lester Pearson's memoirs. He reports how he constantly emphasized in talking to the State Department the importance of acting in such a way as to command the approval of the Asian members of the U.N. and especially India; the use of the atomic bomb in the Korean War 'would dangerously weaken the links that remain between the western world and the peoples of the East'. He was constantly sending messages to Nehru, some of them in his own name, some in St Laurent's name, some for transmission to Peking. He worked closely with the Indian representative, Benegal Rau, in the three-man cease-fire committee of the U.N. General Assembly in its abortive search in December 1950 and January 1951 for a settlement of the war in Korea. In 1952 and 1953 he worked closely with Krishna Menon in the negotiations which led to an armistice in Korea.[5]

In June 1951 I attended a small unofficial Canadian–American conference on foreign affairs. It had been precipitated by the emergence, in the previous twelve months since the outbreak of the war in Korea, of markedly divergent views between the United States and Canadian Governments on the most prudent policies to be followed in the Far East. It was held under the joint auspices of the World Peace Foundation, the Carnegie Endowment for International Peace and the Canadian Institute of International Affairs. The American delegation included Christian Herter, Spruille Braden, Benjamin Cohen, Lincoln Gordon and Kenneth Galbraith. Many of the American delegates were bitterly critical of Nehru and of India and they deprecated the significance which Canada attached to India's role in Asia and to Nehru's views. This provoked me to a forceful and, I was told, eloquent intervention in which I defined and defended the special relationship between Canada and India. I said:

Canada in the past few years has made a conscious effort in framing its foreign policy to take fully into account the views of India and Pakistan. Canada will continue to take these views fully into account. Canadians do not think that the United States is the embodiment of the wisdom of the West. It is also not true [as had been stated by an American member of the conference] that in Canada's opinion 'wisdom walks with a sedate step in New Delhi'. Mr Nehru is a man of very great intellectual ability, highly articulate and of great personal charm. He is also, like other great men, sensitive and complex. A plea has been made at this conference that Canadians should understand the peculiar difficulties which confront United States leaders in their efforts to pursue a sound foreign policy. Canadians have pleaded for a similar understanding from Americans for their difficulties. The difficulties of Americans and Canadians are, however, not to be compared with the difficulties faced by Mr Nehru and other leaders in India. Canadians plead that the United States should not only be conscious of Mr Nehru's difficulties but should also not expect him to behave as if he were a North American politician. It is important not to alienate Mr Nehru by treating his suggestions as second-class advice from a third-class friend. Democratic leadership in Asia can be developed only if the western powers deal with Asian leaders as equals, seeking their counsel and occasionally deferring to their opinions. Americans at this conference have charged that Canadians seem to be somewhat lacking in a sense of the immediate danger. Might it not be that Americans are somewhat deficient in a sense of the continuing danger that we must face for the next generation?

Benjamin Cohen, who spoke immediately after me, said he was inclined to agree with what I had said: Mr Nehru was not perfect but 'would that we had a Nehru in China, a fifty per cent Nehru in Korea and even a twenty-five per cent Nehru in Indonesia'.

Pearson, in his memoirs written in 1972 after he had served as prime minister or foreign minister for fourteen years, told the story of his work twenty years before as President of the U.N. General Assembly on the issue of Chinese prisoners of war. He wrote: 'I have never in my life worked so hard on any negotiation as I did to get a resolution [on Chinese prisoners of war] acceptable to India and her uncommitted Asian friends and satisfactory to the United States.'[6] The search for policies acceptable to India and satisfactory to the United States was one of the principal features of Canadian diplomacy under St Laurent and Pearson. It was the essence of the special relationship which then existed between Canada and India. After I had been in India for six months I wrote in a despatch to Ottawa, 'My impression is that there is perhaps no western democratic country whose foreign policy is closer to that of India than Canada.'

PART TWO

THE SPECIAL RELATIONSHIP IN OPERATION

CHAPTER THREE

INTRODUCTION TO INDIAN DIPLOMACY—AND VILLAGES

Five days after my arrival in New Delhi I plunged into discussions with the Indian Government on the issue of Chinese prisoners of war in Korea. This was helpful to me because it meant that in my first two and a half months in New Delhi I had occasion to discuss important official business with Nehru himself, with the two top officials in the External Affairs Ministry (Raghavan Pillai and R. K. Nehru) and with Mrs Vijayalakshmi Pandit and V. K. Krishna Menon when they returned in January to New Delhi after having attended the U.N. General Assembly in New York. Mrs Pandit had been the head of the Indian delegation to the Assembly; Menon had been the Indian spokesman on Korea. The business I had to discuss arose from Lester Pearson's efforts as President of the Assembly to get through the Assembly a resolution on Chinese prisoners of war in Korea which would be acceptable to India and its uncommitted Asian friends and satisfactory to the United States. In these efforts Pearson was working hand-in-glove with Krishna Menon so that my task was to facilitate cooperation between my country and the country to which I was accredited—always a pleasant task for an ambassador, particularly pleasant for an ambassador who has just arrived at his post.

Krishna Menon had, by the middle of November, completed the drafting of a resolution on Chinese prisoners of war. Dean Acheson strongly objected to it. Pearson persuaded Menon to amend it to make it easier for the Americans to accept. Acheson was not satisfied with the amendments and brought great pressure to bear on the British, French and Canadians to demand further amendments. On 21 November, Pearson, Paul Martin (the head of the Canadian delegation to the General Assembly), Anthony Eden and Selwyn Lloyd decided, as Pearson put it in his diary, 'that if the worst came to the worst and the American amendments went too far to be acceptable to the Indians, we would vote for the Indian proposal as it stood, come what may'.[1] On that same day Nehru made an impassioned plea in the Indian parliament that the General Assembly accept the Indian resolution, which, he said, had been put forward with the full concurrence of the Indian Government.

> A moment comes in the life of a nation and sometimes of the world when the future hangs on a decision that might be taken. That moment is here, and on the United Nations has been cast the great responsibility at this critical juncture of seizing the moment with courage and determination.

I made my courtesy call on Nehru a few hours after he had made that speech. The conversation was stilted. He made no effort to be welcoming or to display his charm. His mind was somewhere else—probably on the crisis in the U.N. about which I, at the time, knew nothing. In my four and a half years in India, I paid many calls on Nehru and this happened only once again. It was unnerving to have it happen on my first call. I did not know that Chester Bowles, the American Ambassador, had had a similar experience on his first call on Nehru.

The next day I received an urgent secret message from Pearson:

> As you know, we have been working very closely with the Indians here on their Korean resolution and have reached a point of strong disagreement with the United States in respect of it. The Americans insist on certain amendments which it is doubtful if the Indians can accept. There is one point which has a bearing on this and where you may be able to help, namely, has the Indian Government received anything authoritative in regard to the Chinese reaction to their resolution? What are its chances of acceptance in Peking? The Indian delegation will, of course, let us know here what they get from New Delhi, but it is possible that by a direct intervention, which would have to be very tactfully done, you might be able to secure earlier and more complete information. I would not, however, wish the Indian delegation here to know that we had asked you to attempt to secure such information, so you will have to enquire without referring to the source of this message.

This is the kind of message which one does not mind receiving after some months at a post. It was somewhat daunting to receive it five days after my arrival, and before I had even presented my credentials to the President of India. I decided that the best thing to do was for me to call on R. K. Nehru, the second-in-command of the External Affairs Ministry, whom I had already met informally at a lunch, and on the British High Commissioner, and for my second-in-command to talk to the American embassy and to a number of the leading foreign newspapermen in New Delhi. I reported to Pearson that R. K. Nehru had told me that the Indian Government had 'no idea of the reaction either of Peking or Russia' to their resolution and that our other talks in New Delhi confirmed this.

One of Pearson's subsequent telegrams to me, before Menon's resolution was adopted, was a message to Prime Minister Nehru which he instructed me to deliver to him immediately. This gave me an opportunity to make my first business call on Nehru. (My previous call had been a courtesy call.) Pearson was worried that the amendments which Menon had accepted to his resolution might be interpreted in New Delhi as a retreat by Menon under United States pressure and that Menon would not receive the backing from New Delhi which he needed, to get his resolution through the Assembly. (Later I learned that just before sending me his telegram of 27 November Pearson had been talking to Mrs Pandit and Menon, and that he had found them to be unhappy and worried about the present state of their resolution after the vicious attacks made on it by the Soviet representatives and the satisfaction of the United States and others over the amendments which the Indians had accepted.)

Because of this, Pearson started his message to Nehru as follows:

Your representative here [Krishna Menon] has, if I may say so, been handling with skill, integrity and patience what we now think of as the Indian peace initiative. I realize that he has been criticized from both extremes, but I feel certain myself that the resolution which, while it stands in the name of your delegation, expresses the feelings of nearly all delegations, does represent a real advance toward a peaceful solution of this problem. Even if the initial reaction in Peking is unsatisfactory, nevertheless, if this resolution, which does not involve a surrender of principle by any party, is approved by the Assembly, as I am sure it will be, it will provide a new and far better basis for armistice and peace talks in the future than any which has hitherto been attempted or contemplated.

When I called on Nehru with this message he was charming and forthcoming and immediately gave me the assurances Pearson wanted. It was, he said to me, most important to press ahead with Menon's resolution in the Assembly and afterwards in Peking where the Indian representative would do his best to explain the resolution to the Chinese: 'While you cannot force peace on people who do not want it you can create conditions making it easier for people to come to agreement and this the resolution does.' A few hours later I received a written message from Nehru for transmission to Pearson. Pearson showed this message to Menon. In Pearson's opinion, the message 'certainly removed any excuse for Menon withdrawing or even weakening'.

Five days later, on 3 December, the Indian resolution after further amendments was passed by the General Assembly unanimously except for the Soviet bloc of five states. Pearson had succeeded in getting through the Assembly a resolution satisfactory to India and the United States. He immediately cabled me a message for Nehru suggesting that the Indian Ambassador in Peking might deliver the resolution to the Chinese Government, on behalf of Pearson as President of the Assembly. The resolution would be accompanied by an explanatory and objective communication from him, pointing out its importance for peace in Korea and trying to remove misunderstandings about the proposals in the resolution. He went on to say:

It would be most helpful, for that purpose, if your government, through your embassy in Peking, could also urge its importance and acceptability on the Chinese Government. Indeed, if Mr Menon himself were in Peking, I know he would be in a very good position to remove many of the Chinese misapprehensions and misunderstandings which exist or have been created about it.

(Pearson presumably meant 'created about it' by the Soviet Government, which had viciously attacked the resolution.)

Nehru replied that he thought it would be wiser for Pearson to send the message direct to the Chinese Government. The next day Nehru was in Bombay and discussed the matter with Girja Bajpai, the former Secretary-General of the External Affairs Ministry. Bajpai phoned Pillai to suggest that Pearson be reminded that two years ago, Nasrollah Entezam, then the President of the General Assembly, had, as a member of the three-man cease-fire committee, sent a message direct to the Chinese and that if Pearson were not also to communicate the resolution direct to the Chinese, the Chinese might consider that he thought he was too big a man to communicate with them directly. I passed this message on to Pearson and followed it up the next day with a message from Nehru saying that he thought that the broadcast from Peking of the day before, with its unfriendly criticism of the part played by India in the passage of the resolution, made it even more desirable that Pearson communicate direct with the Chinese Government. Pearson forthwith cabled the messages direct to the Chinese Government and sent them simultaneously to me to deliver to Nehru. As soon as he received the messages, Nehru instructed the Indian Ambassador in Peking that in speaking to the Chinese Government he was not to be apologetic about the Indian role at the U.N. Assembly; he was to be firm but he was not to show resentment at the language used by Peking about India in its broadcast. On 15 December Peking rejected the Assembly resolution.

Nehru had expressed the hope in his message to Pearson on 4 December that even if the Assembly resolution was not immediately acceptable to the Chinese, the Chinese Government 'will appreciate that the resolution does not do any violence to their principles and can certainly lead to a satisfactory and honourable settlement. We shall instruct our embassy in Peking to work to this end.' The embassy was not, however, able to do much to this end. Up to the end of January, so Pillai told me, N. Raghavan, the Indian Ambassador in Peking, had not once been able to see Chou En-lai. He had been put off with one excuse after another. Chou En-lai had also shown his displeasure with India by not turning up at the Indian Republic Day celebrations on 26 January. Pillai said that in his opinion India had no special position in Peking which it could at present use. That was one reason the present Indian policy on the prisoners of war issue was to wait and see. The Indian resolution had, however, in his opinion served a useful purpose. It had helped to demonstrate to many people in India the real nature of the Chinese Communist Government. It had had a very considerable influence on Nehru's thinking about both Communist China and the Soviet Union. Nehru was now much more conscious than before of the nature of the Chinese and Soviet Governments.

The French Ambassador, Count Stanislas Ostrorog, also believed that the rebuff which India had received from China would have a considerable effect on Nehru's thinking on foreign policy. It was not so much the Chinese refusal to accept the Indian resolution as the insults which had accompanied the refusal. When the rest of us had been insulted by the Russians or the Chinese, the Indians had tended to think that it was because we did not know how to treat them.

Both Pillai and the French Ambassador were scathing in their remarks about Sardar K. M. Panikkar who had been India's ambassador to Peking until the previous June, when he had been appointed ambassador to Cairo. Pillai said that Panikkar, just before he left Peking, had misled the Indian Government about the willingness of the Chinese Government to be reasonable on the prisoners of war issue. Panikkar, Pillai said, had the reputation as an historian of mixing fiction with fact and in his reporting from Peking he had a tendency to believe what he wanted to believe. The French Ambassador was more forthright. He said to me that Pannikar had consistently and deliberately misled Nehru about China. Panikkar was highly intelligent, a man of very great culture and a complete cynic. He had no illusions about the policies of the Chinese Government and he had not been misled by it. He considered, however, that the future, at least in his lifetime, lay with the communists and he therefore did his best to get in well with them by misleading Nehru. This he found all the easier because, unlike most Indian ambassadors and most senior members of the External Affairs Ministry, he could talk to Nehru about things of interest to him such as history, art and philosophy, and Nehru would consider that Panikkar was the kind of man who understood him.

I found out that Mrs Pandit, far from sharing these low opinions of Panikkar, believed that one reason the Indians had failed to secure Chinese acceptance of their resolution was that

Panikkar had not been in Peking while the resolution was being drafted. She said to me that in various messages (she must have been referring to messages from the Indian embassy in Peking) there had been statements in the middle or end of the telegram along the lines of 'Panikkar knows all about this'. This was not, she said, very helpful, since Panikkar had by this time taken up his appointment as ambassador to Egypt.

In the post-mortem on the Indian resolution which I had with Mrs Pandit at the end of January she made clear her dislike of and lack of confidence in Krishna Menon. According to my notes on our talk,

Mrs Pandit said that at one time in New York she thought that the Russians might support the resolution. Looking back at it now, she wonders whether they ever intended to support it. She considers, however, that some psychological mistakes were made by Krishna Menon and indeed by all of them in New York. There was too much publicity given to the coming and going between the Indian, Canadian, United Kingdom, and United States delegations in order to try to get American support for the resolution. The result of all this probably was that the Russians might well have felt that the Indians were more interested in United States support than in carrying the Russians along. The Indian difficulties were of course multiplied first by the fact that the Americans for their own purposes played up the importance of the amendments that were made and secondly by many of the speeches that were given in the Assembly in support of the resolution.

In the middle of January I wrote Pearson a secret and personal letter on my introduction to diplomacy in New Delhi. I began by reminding him that he had, at the beginning of January, given me the assignment of making clear to Krishna Menon that he hoped that Menon would not give Nehru the impression that Pearson was advocating that he go to Peking to talk to the Chinese. (I did not add that it would not be surprising if Menon were to give this impression since Pearson in his message to Nehru at the beginning of December had suggested this.) Menon, I said to Pearson, was at the beginning of January in New Delhi staying with Nehru. Knowing that the relations between Menon and the senior External Affairs officials were bad I did not want them to feel that I was going behind their backs to see Menon, particularly before they themselves had had a chance to talk to him. Consequently I did not get in direct touch with Menon but sought an appointment with him through the External Affairs Ministry. To my surprise Menon offered to come and call on me that very day. This was the first time I had met him.

We had tea together in my office. I thought the best thing to do was to be frank. I therefore told him that you were afraid that you might not have made your position clear on one point—that while you hoped the Indian Government would keep exercising its influence in Peking in the direction of a more sympathetic approach to the United Nations resolution, you were not advocating that he go to Peking—a course which had its possibilities but also its dangers. Menon received this message very amicably and he stayed for about an hour, chatting about the Assembly and agreeing on what a nice person you were. Occasionally, however, he behaved like the dormouse in *Alice in Wonderland* and his head would nod with sleepiness for a few seconds. I didn't blame him because he had been travelling by air for the previous day or so.

The next day I decided that as part of an effort to establish my relations with Menon on friendly foundations my wife and I would invite him to a small dinner. An hour before the dinner he telephoned my wife. He said, 'That dinner you have invited me to. Do I have to dress for it?' My wife said, 'My husband is wearing a dinner jacket.' Menon banged the receiver down. When he arrived he was dressed elegantly in formal Indian clothes; he looked very handsome and was most charming and gracious to my wife, greeting her with 'This is the young lady who said I must dress for dinner.' It looked for a while at dinner as if he was going to eat nothing. Fortunately the Rajkumari Amrit Kaur, the Minister of Health who was a friend of his, and for whom we had provided a vegetarian meal, sent the waiter around with a vegetable dish for him, leaned across the dining room table and said in a firm voice, 'Krishna, you can eat that.'

Two days later my wife and I went to a cocktail party given by Tinoo Sen, the head of the publicity section in the External Affairs Ministry. Tinoo Sen met us at the door of his house and as soon as we entered the reception room he steered me over to Krishna Menon, 'your guest of the day before yesterday'. Krishna Menon immediately broke off his conversation with the Australian High Commissioner, Walter Crocker, and proceeded to give a public demonstration of how close and friendly our relations were by holding me in a prolonged and solemn conversation. In the course of our conversation he told me that I shouldn't bother discussing Korea with Pillai or R. K. Nehru, 'since they know nothing about the subject'. Instead he urged me to send that evening a letter direct and by hand to the Prime Minister, asking for an interview as soon as the Prime Minister returned from Hyderabad and before he, Krishna Menon, had left New Delhi. My wife, who was elsewhere in the room, noted that R. K. Nehru was regarding all this with the blackest of countenances and that Pillai did not look amused.

Later at the cocktail party I talked to Pillai and he gave me a friendly warning that I was in danger of burning my fingers because I was showing too much interest in Krishna Menon and not enough in Mrs Pandit, who, though she herself did not yet know it, would shortly be going back to New York for the U.N. Assembly. I then wrote to Mrs Pandit (whom I had not previously met) asking for permission to call on her to pay my respects, and adding that my wife and I hoped she would have dinner with us very soon. She telephoned within a few hours and could not have been more charming when she received me at her house. Her only catty remark was that so far she had had only a brief discussion with her brother about Korea and 'at that time Krishna Menon was still there and my brother's mind was confused'.

I concluded my letter to Pearson as follows:

So far as I can make out, the situation is simple. Krishna Menon has no use for Pillai and R. K. Nehru. Pillai has little use for Menon and considers that his anti-American speeches in the United States were stupid. Mrs Pandit has no use for Krishna Menon. The relations between Pillai and R. K. Nehru are strained. I am not certain what Pillai and R. K. Nehru think of Mrs Pandit and she of them, except that Pillai and R. K. Nehru undoubtedly consider that she is a lesser evil than Krishna Menon. Mrs Pandit and Krishna Menon compete for the Prime Minister's favour. According to Alec Clutterbuck [Sir Alexander Clutterbuck, the British High Commissioner to India], Mrs Pandit has tried to persuade her brother to make her foreign minister. This her brother has refused for two reasons: the Congress Party would object and she would argue with him on foreign affairs. In order to stop her from arguing with him face to face, he sends her off to international conferences. When I get an explanation of why he sends Krishna Menon to the same conferences, I'll let you know. Perhaps he doesn't want his sister to get a swollen head from too much limelight.

Pearson wrote back that my letter echoed some of the difficulties he had encountered at the General Assembly in steering a safe course between 'Mrs Pandit's vanity and Menon's sensitiveness. You have had the additional difficulty of the touchiness of Pillai and R. K. Nehru. You seem to have been very successful in what must have been a difficult introduction to Indian diplomacy.'

It was not until many years later that I came across an explanation of why Nehru sent both Vijayalakshmi Pandit and Krishna Menon to the General Assembly in 1952. Nehru had decided in 1951 to remove Menon from his post as High Commissioner in London because of the deterioration in his physical and psychological condition.

Nehru first considered the inclusion of Menon in the Cabinet but as Menon threatened to kill himself rather than return to his own country, Nehru offered him the Moscow embassy. This too Menon refused. 'All I now seek is to leave and fade out quietly and with dignity ... I am sorry you have come to rate my sense of values as that of a careerist!' Then Nehru suggested that Menon join the Indian delegation to the United Nations General Assembly. It would give him some work to do and get him out of London, where his presence was an embarrassment to his successor, B. G. Kher. Menon was willing to consider going to New York only if he were made leader and not sent as deputy to Vijayalakshmi. The compromise thought up by Nehru was to offer him the Korean question as a special assignment.[2]

My introduction to Indian diplomacy was followed immediately by an introduction to Indian villages. Even before we left for India my wife and I had decided that, instead of starting our discovery of India by visiting the big cities, as most if not all ambassadors did, we would start by visiting villages since it was in the villages that eighty to eighty-five per cent of the people of India lived, and it seemed obvious to us that, unless we saw something of what life was like in the villages, we would have no inkling of what life was like for the average Indian and we would have little chance of understanding India. The Indian authorities suggested that we start by visiting the village of Bichpuri, about half way between Agra and Fatehpur Sikri, and then go to villages in the Etawah project.

I had heard enough about visits by foreign visitors to villages in India to know that I would have to be firm if we were to succeed in visiting villages without a retinue of police and officials. I was right. When we arrived at the canal inspection bungalow at Bichpuri where we were going to stay for two days we found a welcoming party consisting of six policemen carrying rifles with fixed bayonets, a sub-inspector of police in plain clothes, five officials and twenty villagers. The officials wanted us to visit not the village but the local agricultural college. I insisted that it was the village we wanted to see, and that I did not wish to be accompanied by more than one or two officials. The next day I would be happy to visit the agricultural college. So we spent four hours walking through Bichpuri in the morning and a neighbouring village, Sadarban, in the afternoon.

My wife wrote that night in a letter to our two sons in Canada:

We started off our walk from the bungalow to Bichpuri on the sort of country lane you'd see in any country. On each side there were fields of mustard and pulse. We dodged water buffaloes and bullocks till we reached the village irrigation well. By this time we had collected about fifty villagers and we went on to the village itself. We saw terrific things which didn't depress us or sadden us as much as I'd expected because the people were glad to see us, eager to show us everything and proud of what they had, such as a new well and a few new brick houses. We were impressed by the cleanliness inside the houses, almost all of which were made of mud. How they keep their houses clean I don't know since there are no roads or sidewalks in the village, just mud paths full of water and cow dung. We saw the best houses in the village and the worst where the harijans live—the people who used to be called untouchables. The villagers uncovered the village chariot for us, a magnificent thing full of gold embroidery and tassels which is used only for weddings. They insisted on Daddy and me getting in and applauded and *salaamed* with glee. In the afternoon we went to another village on the canal near here. We were led by a grand old man in a turban and dhoti and, of course, bare feet; he is the richest man in the village and is the chairman of the village council. I wish you could see the old man—rarely does one meet such dignity and beauty.... So you see we've had our way and have seen something of the real India and are more content. Tomorrow we go on to see more villages.

We did. We went on to see fourteen more in the next ten days. They ranged in size from 130 people to 1500.

The next village we visited was Hazrahdpur. It was depressing. It was swarming with flies. Flies covered everything. We saw a sickly baby fifteen days old lying on a dirty bed covered with flies, and no one paying any attention. My wife was saddened and angered. She wrote that night in her letter to our sons:

As the people are so remarkably clever at making baskets and cloth, it would surely be simple to instruct the mothers to put their infants in baskets and cover them with cheesecloth. Nothing can be done about the flies so long as they have their cattle in their houses and have no sanitation but it would be so simple to protect babies. Another horror is the presence of eye disease among the children.

About half a mile from another village we passed small vegetable plots—potatoes, carrots, radishes. The executive engineer in the canal service who was with us said that he had been brought up in a village just like this and that five or six years before, vegetable plots like these were unknown in this area. It was a sign that the cultivators had got beyond the mere subsistence level. They grew these vegetables not to sell but to eat.

In Mahewa, a village near Etawah, the project officials told us that they had made an old masonry well sanitary by putting a concrete top on it and installing a pump. The Harijans had not formerly used the well. It had been reserved by custom for the highest caste, the Brahmins. The Harijans decided that since the well was now a 'project' well, they could use it. The Brahmins of the village made no open protest but every morning it would be discovered that something had gone wrong with the well. As a result of this incessant sabotage, the project officials had to have a completely new well built. Since this was a new well the Brahmins did not object to sharing it with the Harijans. I commented in my diary:

This story demonstrates that Indian experts who have worked for years in the villages can make mistakes in gauging how far the old prejudices have broken down. If foreigners had made this mistake they might have discredited themselves badly. It indicates the wisdom of leaving to Indians the management of this kind of project.

In addition to visiting villages and walking through the nearby fields, we spent a morning at an agricultural school farm; we visited a village night school for illiterate adults, two schools for training young officials to promote development in the villages (village-level workers), two agricultural high schools, a rural hospital for women, a dozen primary schools and three or four junior high schools. We attended the meeting of a village council. At the Etawah project we saw information centres and rural workshops, co-operative unions and a veterinary hospital. We drove through a part of the desert which was about two hundred miles long and eight miles wide between the Jamuna and Chambal rivers and saw in Fisher's forest how this eroded country could be reforested. Most of our travel was not on highways but along the banks of canals. I talked to about sixty officials—district magistrates, district medical officers, superintendents of police, civil surgeons, district planning officers, executive engineers of the Agra canal, deputy development officers, project executive officers, and secretaries of co-operative societies. We heard stories of successes and failures in efforts to help the villagers improve their conditions of life.

And we became conscious of the beauty of the countryside. During our visit to Mahewa in the Etawah district I wrote in my diary:

In the afternoon we drove along canal banks and country lanes, I in a jeep and Ruth and Morna in the front seat of a truck. We travelled, as it were, right through the fields. It was a perfect spring day; bright sun but a cool breeze. The fields were golden with mustard or bright with flowering peas. The canals were lined with trees two rows deep on each side and so we travelled through avenues of trees. The country lanes were full of life: bullock carts, tongas, camels, herds of goats and sheep, cattle being driven to market.

In an essay I wrote at the end of our village tour and sent to Ottawa, I said:

We fell in love with the Indian countryside we visited. It is flat country but it combines much of the loveliness of our prairies with the loveliness of the sleepy canals in rural England. My memories of it are full of colour, of fragrance and of music. The rose of sunrise turning to gold. The golden glow of late afternoon turning to the rose of sunset. The gold of the mustard fields. The fragrance of the flowering fields of peas and mustard. The sweet smell of boiling sugar cane that met us in a country lane. The long shadows of late afternoon and early morning. The bells of the bullock carts. And the gay singing of villagers heard across the fields or from the villages at night.

Shortly after we had returned to Delhi from our village tour a leading Indian newspaperman, Durga Das, used me as a stick with which to beat the group which surrounded Nehru, who, he said, were so westernized that they were aloof from the problems facing India. 'Even foreign diplomats are tired of the so-called social technique of New Delhi. The new High Commissioner of Canada recently undertook a strenuous, village-to-village tour to understand real India.' I certainly did not understand real India as the result of one village tour in one part of India. But I had had an introduction to life in some Indian villages.

CHAPTER FOUR

THE ARMISTICE IN KOREA

Ever since May 1952, the issue of Chinese prisoners of war had been the only obstacle in the way of an armistice in Korea. It was not until July 1953, fourteen months later, that agreement was reached on a formula on the prisoners of war issue and the armistice agreement was signed. The formula was essentially that set forth in the Indian resolution passed by the U.N. General Assembly on 3 December 1952, and rejected shortly thereafter by the Chinese Government. During the final ten months of the fourteen-month period Pearson was President of the General Assembly.

A good case can be made that Pearson's contribution during these ten months to securing the armistice in Korea was as important as, if not more important than, his contribution in 1956 to a resolution of the Suez crisis for which he received the Nobel peace prize. Chester Ronning, who worked closely with Pearson during the ten months of negotiations on Korea, believes that Canada's contribution to getting an armistice in Korea was 'fully as important as the Suez success to which greater importance was attached because Korea was away off in Asia' and because 'everything happened with lightning speed' during the Suez crisis, whereas 'the efforts by Canada to achieve a similar result in Korea took nearly a year'.[1]

Pearson had worked closely with Krishna Menon in the discussions which resulted in the General Assembly approving the Indian resolution on prisoners of war in December 1952. He continued to work closely with him in the discussions in the first half of 1953 which led to the signature of the armistice agreement in July, in the abortive efforts in the summer to have India invited as a member of the Korean peace conference, and in the discussions in the second half of 1953 and the first few months of 1954 on the final disposition of the prisoners of war. During this period Krishna Menon was the brilliant, constructive negotiator and draftsman. He went from delegation to delegation in New York, from capital to capital, and from ambassador to ambassador in New Delhi, working out his compromises, and drafting and redrafting formulas to embody the compromises. He drafted the Indian resolution adopted by the Assembly in December 1952, which led to the armistice, and the formula which led in January 1954 to the final disposition of the prisoners of war. His achievements were remarkable. He earned, however, at the time few plaudits and much abuse, especially from the Americans. This was in part his own fault. Most of the Americans he dealt with were suspicious of him and he of them; he magnified their suspicions by the language he used about the United States in public and in private.

I must have had in 1953 and the beginning of 1954 about ten talks with Krishna Menon on the various formulas relating to Korea which he was working on. He was always polite with me and patient in explaining his views when he called on me in my office. He never tried to mislead me about his views or the position he had reached in his negotiations. He would never, however, give me a piece of paper summarizing his views; and he was, I think, sometimes deliberately obscure. The probable reason was that he did not want to be tied to a precise formula until the last moment. I often felt that I should begin every telegram to Pearson reporting on a call which Menon had made on me with some such statement as, 'Krishna Menon called to see me today and we had an hour's talk. As usual he did not express his views clearly but I think that the following represents what he wanted me to report to you.'

Dean Acheson, whose judgement of Menon was distorted by his detestation of him, has written that Menon, in the negotiations which led to the passage of the resolution of December 1952, used his fuzziness of expression and unwillingness to furnish any written text as handmaidens of deception.[2] I never found in four years of dealing with Krishna Menon that he used his fuzziness of expression and unwillingness to furnish any written text to deceive me or my principals, St Laurent and Pearson, through me. Acheson's judgement of Pearson was also distorted at this time. He charged him in the discussions in the U.N. on Korea with conspiring with the Indians, with joining in a cabal with Krishna Menon, with intriguing with Menon,

Anthony Eden and Selwyn Lloyd, with indulging in sophistries with Menon and Lloyd, and with being the victim of illusions. My own belief is that the chief credit for bringing about the armistice in Korea should go to Krishna Menon and Pearson. Krishna Menon was backed by Nehru. Pearson was assisted by Paul Martin and backed by St Laurent.

A very different version of how the armistice was achieved was put forward, presumably by John Foster Dulles, in an authoritative article on his diplomacy of brinkmanship in *Life* magazine for 16 January 1956. The title of the article was, 'How Dulles averted war', and the sub-title, 'Three times, new disclosures show, he brought the U.S. back from the brink'. According to this article, Dulles, having confidence in Nehru's 'ability to communicate speedily with Peking', told him when he visited him in New Delhi from 20 to 22 May 1953, that, if the war in Korea continued, 'the U.S. would lift the self-imposed restrictions on its actions and hold back no effort or weapon to win'. The article explained that what was meant by this was that the United States would carry the war into China by attacking 'carefully selected . . . areas of clear military importance' in Manchuria and that the United States would use atomic weapons. The article went on to say that the North Koreans and the Chinese ultimately agreed to an armistice in Korea 'because they had had unmistakable warning that further delays would no longer be met with U.S. indecisiveness'. These statements were interpreted to mean that Dulles was affirming that Nehru had passed on to the Chinese a threat from Dulles that if China did not agree to an armistice the United States would drop atomic bombs on military targets in China.

Pillai told me a fortnight after this article had appeared that Nehru had instructed the Indian Ambassador in Washington to inform the State Department that he had made a note of his conversation with Dulles immediately after the conversation; in this note he had recorded that they had discussed the danger of the war being extended but that there was nothing in it about a threat to use atomic weapons; certainly he had not passed any such threat on to China. Pillai added that the Indian Government had informed the Chinese Government of what it had said to the State Department.

Eisenhower became President of the United States in January 1953, John Foster Dulles, Secretary of State, and Walter Robertson, Assistant Secretary of State and principal adviser on Far Eastern matters. Eisenhower told St Laurent in 1956, 'If Communist China is admitted to the United Nations, the United Nations will leave the United States and the United States will leave the United Nations.' Walter Robertson told me in September 1955 when I was visiting Washington, 'Mao Tse-tung is no more representative of China than William Z. Foster [the head of the Communist Party of the United States] and, I repeat, William Z. Foster is representative of the United States.' It is not therefore surprising that controversies over the armistice terms in the first half of 1953 and over the Korean peace conference in the second half strained relations between India and the new United States administration. They also strengthened the special relationship between India and Canada.

*   *   *

At the end of March 1953, Chou En-lai, on his return from Stalin's funeral in Moscow, issued a statement noting that the only issue standing in the way of an armistice agreement in Korea was the prisoners of war issue and that the Chinese and North Korean Governments were 'prepared to take steps to eliminate the differences over this question so as to bring about an armistice'. The armistice negotiations were resumed. The United States put forward proposals on prisoners of war which were more difficult for the Chinese to accept than those in the Indian resolution which had been passed by the General Assembly only four months before and for which the United States had voted. Canada and other countries which had sent forces to Korea to fight alongside the Americans objected. Canada's objections were conveyed privately to the United States. India's protest was made publicly by Nehru on 14 May.

The new United States ambassador in New Delhi, George Allen, called on me three days later to discuss the matter. I outlined to him the views which Pearson had expressed to the State Department. Allen said that it appeared that the Canadian views were almost the same as the Indian and that it would perhaps have been better if Pearson rather than Nehru had given public expression to them; India was already being criticized in the United States press for having come down on the Chinese side, thereby disqualifying itself as the neutral chairman of a commission on the repatriation of prisoners of war. I reported to Pearson that I had said to Allen,

that if the armistice negotiations succeeded, your hope clearly was that the differences of opinion between Canada and the United States would not have to be made public. I mentioned that you had been evading questions in the House of Commons on the subject. I added that, if the House of Commons, however, was about to recess as was the House of the People here, it might have been necessary for you to make some statement to the House.

As for the charge by the press in the United States that Nehru had come down on the Chinese side, I said to Allen that surely all that Nehru had said was that India continued to support the Indian resolution.

With reference to the departures in the United States proposals from that resolution, Allen said (presumably repeating the instructions he had received from Washington), it could be argued that since the Chinese Communists had turned down the General Assembly's resolution in December, the offer in it was no longer outstanding. It would, he said, be different if the Chinese were to confess that they had made a mistake in December and that they were now willing to accept the U.N. resolution. Instead of that they put up their own eight-point proposal with no reference to the United Nation's resolution. I reminded him of George Kennan's thesis that if you wanted a settlement with the Russians (and, I added, the Chinese), it was essential to give them some way of saving their faces. You could not reasonably expect the Chinese to say that they had made a mistake in December.

Within a month Eisenhower, under pressure from Britain, Canada, India and other countries, agreed to return to the principles of the U.N. resolution, and as a result the armistice agreement was signed on 27 July 1953. I wrote to my father that Eisenhower's willingness and ability to do this, and the general support he had received from his own country, were encouraging.

Once the fighting stops in Korea the political problems in the Far East become soluble. And if the atmosphere in Moscow continues to be more friendly there may be a solution of some of the outstanding problems between the Russians and ourselves. Certainly the world is a more hopeful place today than it has been for seven years.

I would not like to have been in George Allen's position when he arrived in New Delhi in May 1953. His predecessor, Chester Bowles, had been very popular with the Indians and had got on especially well with Nehru. It is always easier for an ambassador to follow a failure than a success. Immediately on Allen's arrival in New Delhi there was a public difference of opinion between India and the United States on the Korean negotiations, with the result that many hard things were said about the other country in the newspapers of each. I wrote to Pearson:

I did not fully realize until Mr Allen came here how difficult the position of a United States ambassador is in this country. I have the distinct impression from what newspapermen—both English and Indian—have said to me that every word and every action of Mr Allen is being scrutinized under a microscope and he is constantly being compared in private and in public with his predecessor. It is perhaps his realization of this, plus the fact that he looks younger than his years, which has led him to adopt an attitude which has been criticized as being too cocksure. The disadvantages of this are, however, to some extent, offset by his affability and his amazing facility for remembering names and faces.

Not having this facility myself I admired greatly those who had it.

Unfortunately Allen's affability and facility for remembering names and faces did not offset his cocksure attitude. I reported two months later to Ottawa that he seemed to have rubbed Pillai the wrong way and that he had given a number of Indians the impression that he was 'too sure of himself, too inclined to lay down the law, and to throw his weight around as the representative of the greatest power in the world . . . in private conversations whether in offices or at dinner parties'. I went on to say that I hoped he would be able to overcome the intial prejudices he had aroused but that this would take time 'and it would be unfortunate if a crisis in Indo-American relations were to arise before he has had sufficient time'. Not one but many crises arose before he had sufficient time—crises relating to Korea, Kashmir and United States arms aid to Pakistan.

The next crisis relating to Korea arose over whether India should be a member of the Korean peace conference. The majority of the members of the U.N. believed it should. The United States was opposed. On 19 June, a month before the General Assembly reconvened under Pearson's presidency to prepare the way for a peace conference on Korea, Pearson gave the State Department a paper setting forth some of his preliminary views on various points concerning the Korean peace conference which was at that time referred to as the post-armistice political conference. The paper contained a passage on Indian membership.

It is considered essential that India should be invited to be a member of the conference and should be given the opportunity of taking an important part in its deliberations. India has contributed very considerably towards the solution of the prisoners of war question, and will be playing an important role as a member of the Neutral Nations Repatriation Commission, in addition, of course, to being the largest and most important non-Communist state in Asia.

'Essential'; take an 'important part'; 'has contributed very considerably'; 'will be playing an important role'; the 'most important non-Communist state in Asia.' The language could scarcely have been stronger. I gave the paper to Pillai on 9 July.

A week later I had another talk with Pillai. Pillai had learned from the Indian High Commissioner in Ottawa, who had presumably got the news from the Department of External Affairs, that the United States was opposed to Indian membership. Pillai was most upset. He said that he attached the 'very greatest importance' to the question of Indian membership. If the United States were to oppose it, the United States would be making a 'terrible mistake', a 'frightful error'; the effect on Indo-American relations would be 'deplorable'. He was afraid that these relations might soon get so bad that India would tell the United States that it did not want any aid from it. The Americans seemed to think that because they were giving India $35 million a year in aid they could order India around on small points connected with its trade with Communist China. (He was referring to objections which the Americans had raised to the shipment of thorium nitrate from India to China.) Pillai said, 'When I know George Allen better I hope to be able to talk to him about these things.'

Pearson said in a letter to me that United States opposition to Indian membership was 'almost pathological . . . due in part to their feeling that India and Krishna Menon are the same thing at international conferences'. Henry Cabot Lodge, then the American representative at the U.N., went so far as to tell Mrs Pandit that America would oppose Indian membership in the Korean conference much less if the Indian representative were to be General G. S. Thimayya and not Krishna Menon. Mrs Pandit reported this to Nehru. His reaction was that he was not going to have the State Department appoint the Indian delegation. In my report to Pearson on this I said that I thought it had been unwise for Lodge to suggest a general.

The Indians have taken the view that there have been too many generals in the past concerned with Korean matters and too little political control, and even if Krishna Menon were not involved, I should think that it would be highly unlikely that India would want to send a general to a Korean *political* conference.

I told Pearson that my informant had also told me that the U.N. Secretary-General, Dag Hammarskjold, had been complaining to Mrs Pandit about the way in which Krishna Menon had been making his life miserable by bothering him frequently and at all times of the day and night, 'a penance which you yourself must often have endured'.

Perhaps Krishna Menon's increasing irritability in dealing with the United States was in part the result of his learning that the United States Government was at this time, through the U.S. Information Service, helping to finance a publication in India which attacked Menon with even greater vigour than that with which he attacked the United States. The British High Commissioner's office knew of this; I knew of it; presumably Menon knew of it. The publication was 'Freedom First', the organ of the Indian Committee for Cultural Freedom. The attack on Menon which it published was entitled, 'Is Krishna Menon pro-Communist?'

The end of the debate in the U.N. General Assembly in

August on whether India should be a member of the Korean peace conference served to widen the gap between India and the United States. It also provided another demonstration of the special relationship between India and Canada, for Canada was one of the leaders in the debates in the General Assembly of those countries which urged the United States to agree to Indian membership. The resolution providing for Indian membership was moved by Britain, Australia, New Zealand and Canada. (It required a two-thirds majority in the General Assembly.) Before the vote on it was taken the Canadian representative in the political committee, Paul Martin, appealed to the United States not to block the membership of India since its presence was essential to the holding of an effective conference. 'No one leader or nation', he said, 'today can, in this interdependent world, legitimately frustrate the will of most of its friends on an issue of not merely local but world-wide importance.'

On 27 August 1953, the political committee of the General Assembly voted on the resolution. The vote was 27 in favour, 21 against and 11 abstentions. Seventeen Latin American countries voted against the resolution; only two (Mexico and Guatemala) voted in favour; one (Argentina) abstained. The only countries outside Latin America which supported the United States in its opposition to the resolution were Pakistan, Greece and Taiwan. Pakistan was the only member of the Commonwealth to vote against the resolution; India and South Africa abstained; Britain, Australia, New Zealand and Canada voted in favour. Greece was the only member of NATO to vote against the resolution; four NATO members voted in favour; four abstained. Colombia and Greece were the only countries which had sent armed forces to Korea to fight alongside the United States forces to vote against the resolution; five of the other thirteen countries with forces in Korea voted in favour and eight abstained. In those days, when a country friendly to the United States abstained on a resolution on which the United States had taken a firm stand, this normally signified that it disagreed with the United States but did not wish to carry its disagreement to the point of voting against it. Thus it is reasonable to conclude that on this issue of Indian membership of the peace conference the United States did, in Paul Martin's words, frustrate the will of most of its friends on an issue of world-wide importance.

In the next few months there were many flurries over Korean questions; messages between Pearson and Nehru and between St Laurent and Nehru; talks by me with Nehru, Pillai, R. K. Nehru and Mrs Pandit and with the British and Australian High Commissioners and with the American Ambassador. At the end of 1953 the Indian custodial force under General Thimayya continued to hold 21,700 prisoners who had refused to be repatriated to North Korea or China. These prisoners were held by India on behalf of the Neutral Nations Repatriation Commission of which Thimayya was chairman. Krishna Menon worked out the formula which Thimayya put forward; this was that he would, on 20 January 1954, restore to the United Nations Command the prisoners formerly held by it. At one point when Menon was trying to explain his formula to me so that I could explain it to Ottawa I said of one of his points, 'That is a very subtle distinction' and he replied, 'A very subtle but a very necessary distinction'. On another occasion he said to me, 'If I have so much difficulty in explaining this solution to you, how much more difficulty will I have in explaining it to the U.N. committee in New York.' This was, I suppose, a back-handed compliment.

In our talk the day after Christmas in 1953 Menon was much more abusive of the Americans than he had ever before been in talking to me. He suggested that there was little difference between their expansionist policies and tactics and those of the Soviet government. He was only slightly less critical of Canadian policy.

CHAPTER FIVE
CHINA

Three months after my arrival in New Delhi I learned that Nehru was going to intervene in a debate in Parliament with a lengthy exposition of his views, and my wife and I decided to be present. When we took our seats in the diplomatic gallery we found that the House was crowded; about ninety per cent of the members of parliament were in their seats and the front benches on the government and the opposition sides were full. The press gallery was packed with about eighty correspondents. There was not a seat vacant in any of the galleries other than the diplomatic. In the diplomatic gallery there were only the ambassadors of Burma, Indonesia and Yugoslavia and ourselves. The contrast between the crowds in the other galleries and the almost empty diplomatic gallery was strikingly obvious to any observer—whether prime minister, member of parliament or newspaperman. I found out later that heads of diplomatic missions in New Delhi seldom, if ever, attended debates in Parliament, no matter how important the debates were, and that their absence was noted. Indians who noted it must have asked themselves, as I asked myself that afternoon of 18 February 1953, what engagements heads of mission had that afternoon between three and five when Nehru was speaking, which were so pressing as to preclude them from putting in an appearance in parliament. Even if they had had no interest in the proceedings it would, I thought, surely have been prudent to appear to be interested. I myself liked going to debates in parliament. It gave me some insight into Indian politics and politicians which I otherwise would not have got and it earned me merit among Indian cabinet ministers, officials and newspapermen.

At the beginning of his speech Nehru was somewhat schoolmasterish but as he went on he developed his usual first-rate parliamentary manner. I was surprised not only by the number of interruptions to which he was subjected, but by the way in which the Speaker allowed the House to remain in almost complete disorder for what seemed to me about five minutes after Nehru's statement that 'Here in the Delhi bazaars the cry has been raised "Hail to Godse".' (Godse was the assassin of Gandhi.) About twenty members of the House got up either to protest or to substantiate what Nehru had said. Just before this, Nehru had referred to the 'occurrences in August, September and October, 1947' and to the 30th of January 1948 'when the greatest man among us was shot down by a foolish youth'. A hush fell over the House when he said this.

The most striking statement in Nehru's speech was his assertion, as reported in the newspapers the following day, that he would like India to be compared with China in every way. He wanted to lay down that comparison for India for the future. He admitted that the Chinese were better than the Indians, and probably every other nation, in their capacity for hard work and co-operative endeavour. Moreover India had 'decided to build India according to democratic methods because, ultimately, we feel that democracy has something of the highest human value'. Nevertheless a democratic set-up sometimes made the pace of progress slow. Comparing India with China, Nehru said:

I am not saying that we are better or more virtuous than others. There is no question of virtue involved in this, ultimately. It is a question of which set-up and which structure of government, political or economic, pay higher dividends for the country or the world. When I say higher dividends, I do not mean merely material dividends, although they are important, but other dividends, cultural or spiritual, call it what you will. That is to say, it is important whether an individual or a group or a country grows in an atmosphere of intellectual and other freedom or not.

Thus Nehru publicly associated himself with the thesis which Barbara Ward had advanced two months before in an article in the London *Economist* on the first Indian five-year plan. She had said that the decision of the 'free nations of the world' on how much help they should give India

is, whether they like it or not, set in a framework of drama and destiny. Side by side in Asia the two most populous and ancient cultures the world has ever known are on the brink of an experiment of change and modernization. China's transformation will take place under the star of communism and totalitarian rule. If the Soviet analogy holds good, the people will be battered into economic growth. India, in choosing the way of liberal democracy, has renounced the weapons by which spectacular progress can be achieved.

The next time I heard Nehru talk about China was when I called on him on 10 December 1953, and he gave an hour-long *tour d'horizon*. He emphasized then, as he was accustomed to do when talking about China, that the Chinese were a very proud people; that they, even more than most nations, looked down on foreigners as inferiors; and that they took offence easily at what they assumed to be a slight. He then went on to say, and I can still hear him saying it, 'On the other hand the Chinese are a very cold-blooded, unemotional, rational people—a little too cold-blooded for my taste.' Because they were so rational they could be depended on to follow a rational policy in international affairs. A military attack by China on India was not rational. Moreover, India was defended not only by the barrier of the Himalayas but by the fact that in order to reach the border between Tibet and India, the Chinese had to pass over Tibet which was the most inhospitable country in the world. They had put 30,000 troops into Tibet but they had found they could not support them there and had already withdrawn some.

In June 1954 Chou En-lai visited New Delhi and he and Nehru talked in private for a total of thirteen hours. The External Affairs Ministry told me that Nehru had been convinced by his talks with Chou that China wanted peace in South-East Asia and elsewhere in order to get ahead with its internal development. In reporting this to Ottawa I said that 'convinced' might be too strong a word to describe Nehru's real feelings, but that he might become convinced if Chou, on the visit to Burma which he was just about to make, could persuade U Nu, the sceptical Prime Minister of Burma (for whom Nehru had great respect), of Chinese good faith and if, as a result of Chinese influence, military operations in northern Vietnam were stepped down. A fortnight later the Burmese chargé d'affaires in New Delhi told me that Chou had not, as a result of his visit to Burma, convinced U Nu of China's peaceful intentions. U Nu, he said, needed deeds to convince him. One such deed would be that the Chinese Government stopped putting pressure on the Chinese community in Burma. Another would be a change in the relationship between the Chinese Government and the Communist Party of Burma. If China, in its dealings with Burma, did not live up to the five principles (panchsheel), one of the first people U Nu would inform would be Nehru, and the Burmese chargé considered that this would have considerable influence on Nehru.

At the end of July, two weeks after my talk with the Burmese chargé, I called on Nehru to deliver a message from Pearson about the supervisory commissions in Indo-China. He was working on papers on his desk when I was shown into his office and did not notice that I had come in. He looked tired, rather ugly and rather old. When he smiled and started to talk, about ten years dropped from his face and he became handsome. I wondered at the time how far the mask he put on when he was welcoming visitors hid a deep fatigue. In reporting to Ottawa on our talk I said:

What surprised me in our conversation was the impression he gave me of being much more convinced than I had thought both of the peaceful intentions of China and of the possibility of China pursuing a policy independent of Russia. I think he was sincere in what he said on both points. If he had been saying what he thought the Canadian Government would like him to say, he would have expressed some scepticism about China's good faith until it had been demonstrated by more deeds.

Nehru was well before his time in not only hoping for, but foreseeing, a break between China and the Soviet Union and in the importance he attached to this break. Chester Bowles, then at the end of his first term as American Ambassador, told me early in 1953 that Nehru had said to him that the only way of avoiding a third world war was to split China from the Soviet Union, and that Stalin's death would make a split more likely because Mao Tse-tung would consider himself to be the leading communist in the world in the tradition of Marx, Engels, Lenin and Stalin and the Soviet successors to Stalin would reject this claim. Nehru's belief that India should do whatever it could to assist in the process of splitting China from Russia was, I said to Ottawa in October 1953, one of the reasons why he minimized in his public statements any disagreements India had with China. The other reasons were: first, that China was a near and powerful neighbour; second, that Nehru often went 'out of his way to emphasize in public ... that India is not a member of the western camp whatever may be the realities of the situation', and third, that if India could maintain a special position in Peking it could 'continue to play the role of honest broker in Peking between China and the West ... a role which the West has found very helpful in the past few years'. I do not recall Nehru being specific about what India might do to encourage a split between China and the Soviet Union but I do remember his contempt for the actions of western countries which in his opinion made a split less likely. Thus he said to me in December 1953 that he was sometimes asked by visitors from the United States what could be done to drive a wedge between China and the Soviet Union. He could not help but be amused since so much of what the western countries were doing was calculated to drive the two countries together. One example he gave was the refusal by western countries to export certain essential goods to China which meant that China had to depend on the Soviet Union for them.

When I reported to Ottawa on Chou En-lai's visit to New Delhi in June 1954, I said that Chou had in his talks with Nehru flattered Nehru by stressing his own limited knowledge of international affairs compared with Nehru's, and China's industrial and economic backwardness compared with India, and by suggesting that Nehru's 'peace area' should be extended to South-East Asia and that the South-East Asian countries should adopt Nehru's principles of non-alignment and no foreign bases. The meeting on Indian soil of the only two prime ministers in the world who together represented a billion people had, I said,

naturally been a source of exhilaration or even intoxication to many Indians. This and the flattery may encourage Nehru in his vice of allowing Indian diplomacy to outrun India's very limited resources instead of restricting India's interventions in foreign affairs to matters in which there is a direct and compelling Indian national interest. The most westernized prime minister India is likely to have has discussed international affairs at some length with the most westernized prime minister China is likely to have. The talks may well have helped to correct distortions in Peking's view of the world, resulting from inadequate or tainted sources of information.

The programme for Chou's visit to New Delhi included a reception given in his honour by the President and a dinner, given likewise in his honour, by the Prime Minister. To these, all the heads of mission in New Delhi were invited. This presented problems for those whose governments continued to recognize the government in Formosa as the Government of China since the invitation cards read that the functions were in honour of 'H.E. Mr Chou En-lai, Prime Minister of the People's Republic of China'. After consulting Ottawa I decided to accept the invitation to the President's reception since it came from the head of state to whom I was accredited but not to accept the invitation from the Prime Minister. The Australian High Commissioner, the French Ambassador and I were the only representatives of governments which continued to recognize the government in Formosa who attended the President's reception. Half the heads of mission in New Delhi refused to attend.

My wife and I were fortunate in not attending the Prime Minister's dinner. It was the end of June and the day was one of the hottest of the year; the temperature was 108. The drawing room and the dining room at Rashtrapati Bhavan where the dinner was held were not air-conditioned and the temperature in these rooms was over 90. Nevertheless the Indian protocol authorities insisted that the heads of mission wear full dress suits complete with white tie, stiff white shirt and decorations. The heads of mission asserted their independence by refusing to wear decorations. The discomfort of the heads of mission was not alleviated by alcohol. They stood around in the reception room before dinner from 8.30 to 9.45 sipping lemonade. Nehru's after-dinner speech was in Hindi and Chou En-lai's in Chinese. For almost all the diplomats the speeches might as well have been in Sanskrit. I said to Ottawa that now that the Indians had to wear Indian national costume at formal functions they apparently took delight in insisting that the diplomatic corps should wear the most formal clothes possible at these functions. The latter had not taken kindly to this. The Chief of Protocol had suggested to me that perhaps the way out of the difficulty was for heads of mission also to wear the Indian national costume. He said that if Indian diplomats in the West had in the past worn western formal clothes, there was no reason why western diplomats in India should not wear Indian formal clothes.

Four months after Chou visited New Delhi, Nehru made his return visit to China. Pillai accompanied him. On his return Pillai told me that he had the impression that Chou considered that India provided a useful bridge between China and the western world and that this bridge was useful to the West since the influence which India exerted on China was all in the direction of moderation. I said to Pillai that hostile critics might retort that the obverse of this was that China's influence on India was all in the direction of immoderation. Pillai denied this; India had not, for example, agreed as the result of Nehru's talks in Peking to take any specific course of action.

Mrs Pandit was in New Delhi in November 1954 in between travelling around the world and leaving for London to take up her post as High Commissioner. She said to me that since returning from his visit to China, Nehru had been very irritable and very worried. Usually, she said, when he returned from a trip abroad, whether to Ceylon or England for example, he was full of stories for days about his trip. This time he had nothing to say about the trip to China. Something probably rubbed him the wrong way in China but she did not know what it was. My guess at the time was that one thing which had depressed him was the drabness of dress in China. 'He likes good-looking women to wear colourful dresses at dinner, not sloppy blue uniforms. I think he also disliked the indications of lack of freedom of expression and the regimented crowds. He likes discipline but he dislikes regimentation.' Radhakrishnan, the Vice-President, said to me that Nehru had been impressed on his visit to China by the discipline and enthusiasm of the Chinese people and depressed by his inability to stir up enthusiasm in India for the economic reconstruction of the country.

According to the Indians I talked to, the question of precisely where the border lay between India and China never came up in discussions between India and China during my first tour of duty in India from the autumn of 1952 to the spring of 1955.

In parliament in the spring of 1954 Nehru asserted that the McMahon line was the border between India and Tibet but the agreement between India and China about Tibet which was signed in April 1954 was silent on this question. Nor was it discussed when Chou visited New Delhi two months later or when Nehru later visited Peking. When I spoke to Pillai about this in November 1954 after Nehru's visit to Peking he said that Nehru considered that the time was not ripe to raise this question with the Chinese. The Indian position was clear and the longer it was not challenged by the Chinese, the stronger it became. I suggested that the Indian position was also becoming stronger because India was increasing the effectiveness of its occupation of the territory up to the border it claimed and Pillai agreed. He also agreed that at some point India would seek the formal concurrence of China in India's boundary claims.

In January 1955 the Chinese embassy in New Delhi circulated an official magazine which contained a map of China showing the border with north-east India about 200 miles south of that claimed by India. R. K. Nehru told me that India had not made representations to the Chinese about this 'irritating' act but that India had informally told the Chinese embassy that this sort of action was calculated to cause difficulties between the two countries. He went on to echo Pillai's remarks, which obviously was the official line. He said that whereas the British had left much of the North East Frontier Agency unadministered, the Indian Government was extending effective administration as rapidly as possible. They had, for example, established last year the North East Frontier Service. At some time India would seek formal Chinese concurrence in its boundary claims. I gathered that India would do this when it had succeeded in extending its effective administration as far as possible. R. K. Nehru had the habit common to many Indians at the time of giving the most unfavourable interpretation possible of United States policy and the most favourable interpretation possible of Chinese policy. Thus in this interview he went on to say that one could understand why the Chinese had published this map. This was a map which showed the claims of the previous Kuomintang government. If they published a map with the boundary moved north they would be giving up land claimed by that government and could be criticized for giving up traditional Chinese claims. I suggested that in those circumstances it would have been better for the Chinese not to have published any map.

In December 1954 I gave Nehru a message from St Laurent and Pearson asking him if he could use his good offices in Peking to secure the release of eleven American airmen who had been serving in Korea and who had been taken prisoner by the Chinese, accused of espionage and imprisoned. We told him that if anyone could make a helpful move it would be he and that we would deeply appreciate any action he might be able to take to alleviate the situation. We suggested that he inform the Chinese that the imprisonment of the airmen had so aroused feelings in the United States that a dangerous situation had developed which could have serious consequences. Nehru did as we asked and when the Chinese reply came in he transmitted it to me. My telegram to Ottawa summarizing the message from the Indian Ambassador in Peking on his conversation with Chou En-lai began, 'Chou En-lai appreciated the action of Prime Minister Nehru in conveying to him information about the strong reactions in the United States to the imprisonment of the United States airmen.' I gave the United States embassy in New Delhi a copy of my telegram to Ottawa. The State Department, instead of being grateful to Nehru for his intervention in Peking, was 'astonished' that the Indians had not brought directly to the attention of the United States the Chinese rebuttal of the American case on the imprisoned airmen. I said to Ottawa:

It seems clear that Mr Chou En-lai's conversation with the Indian Ambassador in Peking arose out of the message which the Indian Ambassador had given him based on the message of 5 December from Mr St Laurent and yourself to Mr Nehru, the gist of which had been transmitted by Mr Nehru to Mr Chou En-lai through the Indian Ambassador in Peking. Was it not, therefore, natural that India would transmit the reply of Mr Chou En-lai to me for transmission to you, presumably assuming that you would transmit it to the State Department. I do not know why Mr Robert Murphy of the State Department should be astonished by this, more particularly since the American Embassy here had, since Mr George Allen's departure at the end of

November, deliberately refrained from discussing with the Indian Ministry of External Affairs any issue connected with the imprisonment of the United States airmen.

The Indians were also criticized in the American press for maintaining a position of neutrality on the merits of the dispute over the American airmen when, as I said to Ottawa, 'it should have been clear even to someone who is suspicious of Mr Nehru that once India had been asked by us, and later by the Secretary-General of the United Nations, to use its good offices in Peking, it was essential that India should maintain a rigorously neutral position on the merits of the case'. My conclusion on this episode was:

The Indians may feel that on this, as on other occasions when they have tried to be helpful, their efforts have served to deepen rather than lessen the suspicions which so many people in the United States appear to have of them.

Perhaps this episode helped to explain Nehru's lack of enthusiasm a month later when Pearson made another request to him to use his good offices in Peking, this time in relation to Formosa and the off-shore coastal islands of Quemoy and the Matsus. This problem, as the Chatham House *Survey of International Affairs* for 1955–6 said, was of the international problems remaining unresolved at the beginning of 1955 probably the most likely to lead to war.[1] In the instructions which Pearson sent me on 19 February 1955 to see Nehru about this problem, Pearson said he was mindful of the kind of complications involved in an operation of this kind which I had pointed out following our intervention on the American prisoners; that he did not wish to appear as an intermediary passing messages from Washington to Peking via India, but that nevertheless I was to give Nehru the account he had sent me of his talk with Dulles in New York on February 16 on Formosa and the coastal islands. In this talk Dulles had said that he could give a ninety-nine per cent guarantee that the United States would prevent Chiang Kai-shek from using the islands for offensive action against the mainland; that he hoped to persuade the Chinese Nationalist Government in Formosa in due course to withdraw from the islands by convincing them that they had no future except on Formosa; but that meanwhile if the Chinese Communists attacked the islands and the government in Formosa needed help, the American Government would give it.

Pearson said that I was to tell Nehru that he thought it important that there be no misunderstanding in Peking either of American long-range intentions or of the consequences of an attack on Quemoy or the Matsus. I was also to tell Nehru that Pearson realized the danger that 'anything in the nature of a message to that effect passed from us to the Chinese Communists might well be interpreted by them as an attempt on our part to blackmail them on behalf of the Americans' but that if Nehru thought that it would do any good for him on his own initiative to report to Chou En-lai what Pearson had told him of his talk with Dulles, he would not be betraying any confidence.

When I gave Nehru this message, he did not commit himself to doing anything. Indeed he said that he thought that the Chinese were already well aware of Dulles' views. One main difficulty in finding a way out of the present situation was that there were no signs of any progress being made towards a more permanent settlement. India had suggested that the Security Council might ask the Soviet Union, the United Kingdom and India to explore what might be done to reach a more permanent settlement, possibly by holding a conference. No one had turned this suggestion down but it had not yet been picked up. Pillai, whom I saw just before I called on Nehru, said that it was not enough for the United States to dissuade the Chinese in Formosa from using the coastal islands for offensive action against the mainland. The government in Peking could not distinguish between attacks originating in the coastal islands and attacks originating in Formosa. The United States should therefore prevent Chiang Kai-shek from using Formosa as well as the coastal islands for offensive action against the mainland.

There was no response from Ottawa to Nehru's suggestion that the Security Council ask the Soviet Union, the United Kingdom and India to explore what might be done to reach a more permanent settlement, nor to Pillai's assertion that the United States must persuade the Chinese Nationalist Government not to use either Formosa or the coastal islands for offensive operations against the mainland. Pearson's failure to respond to these Indian suggestions was parallelled by Nehru's failure to let Pearson know if he had passed on to Peking Pearson's account of his talk with Dulles. Ottawa waited for ten days to learn whether Nehru had passed the message on and then told Washington that my impression was that the Indians had not done so. I had not in fact said this—I had said that I did not know whether they had transmitted the message—but I was content to let the matter rest.

If the Indians had transmitted the message to Peking, Canada's reputation in Peking as an authoritative interpreter of United States policy would have been damaged. Pearson reported Dulles as saying that he hoped to persuade the Nationalist Government in Formosa in due course to withdraw from the coastal islands by convincing them that 'they had no future except on Formosa. The implication was that Peking would not have to make any concessions in return for this withdrawal. Yet within a week or so of Pearson's talk with Dulles the United States Government was publicly demanding that as a precondition to the evacuation of the islands the Peking Government should promise not to resort to force in an effort to secure Formosa. The account of Dulles' views which Pearson wanted transmitted to Peking was thus misleading. Perhaps Pearson's realization of this was one reason why two months later he stated in public that Canada could not subscribe to all aspects of American policy in respect of Formosa and that it was Canadian 'policy to stay out of this struggle for these off-shore islands, and I think that other governments would be well-advised to adopt the same policy'.

Pearson had been much impressed at the Colombo meeting of Commonwealth foreign ministers in January 1950 by the number and force of the arguments marshalled by Britain and the three Asian members of the Commonwealth (India, Pakistan and Ceylon) in support of the decisions their governments had taken just before the meeting to recognize the newly-established Communist Government of China. Pearson gave special weight to one of the arguments which Ernest Bevin, the British foreign minister, had advanced: that if Mao Tse-tung wanted to follow a policy independent of the Soviet Union his bargaining power in discussions with the Soviet Government would be enhanced if his government had been recognized rather than kept at bay by the West. Bevin also pointed to the failure of the policy of non-recognition of the Soviet Government after the First World War and said that some of the misunderstanding and suspicion between the Soviet Union and the West could be traced back to the western policy at that time of non-recognition and isolation. This time the British wanted to act differently towards the Chinese. While the failure of United States policies in China made it difficult for the United States to assume any leadership, Bevin said that he thought that the action of the four Commonwealth governments in recognizing the government in Peking would make it easier for the United States Government to follow along in due course as they must inevitably do. In his report to Ottawa on the discussions Pearson said:

In summary I might say that the reasons favouring China developing a policy increasingly independent of the Soviet Union were so compelling that the United Kingdom and the three Asian Commonwealth governments consider it worthwhile to take the chance of trying cautious co-operation with the new government [of China] in the hope of drawing them away from the Soviet camp. All the other Commonwealth governments [Australia, New Zealand and South Africa] agree to the principle of recognition. For them it is just a matter of timing. If we are to get any advantage out of recognition I think we should avoid being the last to do so.

If it had not been for the outbreak of the Korean War in June 1950, five months after the Colombo meeting, Canada would in the summer or autumn of 1950 have recognized the Chinese Communist Government in Peking.

I did not during my first year in India try to persuade Pearson to recommend to Cabinet that the Government recognize the Peking government. Instead in July 1953 I urged him to support the seating of representatives of that government in the General Assembly of the U.N. before the end of 1953. Then, when the Security Council met with its new members at the beginning of January 1954, the Americans would realize that it would be ridiculous for them, once the Assembly had seated the representatives of Peking, to use their veto to prevent the Security Council from following the Assembly's example. (A year later I worked out for Pearson a procedure under which the United States would not be able to use its veto in the Security Council on this issue.)

Pearson decided not to push for the General Assembly seating the Peking representatives in 1953 but suggested I might take the matter up with him again. This I did in July 1954. Then I used our appointment to the supervisory commissions in Indo-China as a peg on which to hang my argument. I said in a letter to him at the end of July 1954:

It seems to me that our appointment to the supervisory commissions on Indo-China strengthens the argument for Canadian recognition of the Peking regime and that it may also provide an occasion for that recognition. When our representatives on the commissions have to take a line which the Chinese will not like, it might sometimes be useful if we had a representative in Peking who could explain frankly to the Peking Government the reasons for our decision. Similarly, when the Vietminh regime is being, in our opinion, unreasonable on some issue, it might be that we would want to suggest to the Peking regime that they use their influence on the Vietminh regime to be more conciliatory. If we do not have an embassy in Peking this sort of message will have to be sent either through the Indians or the British and that would not be as satisfactory. I would think that this sort of practical argument might be seen to be reasonable not only by many people in Canada but by many people in the United States.

As for the seating of the representatives of Peking in the General Assembly, I said:

I am in no position from here to judge how seriously one should take the American threats of withdrawal from the U.N. if the representatives of the Peking regime were seated. The Americans have been making threats of that kind for the last three and a half years. . . . I have myself too much respect for the intelligence of the American people to believe that they would be prepared to start in motion a series of events which might end by the Soviet bloc and the 'peace area' powers getting control of the name, the goodwill and the assets of the United Nations. What must worry you about the way in which Americans have used the threat of withdrawal from the U.N. is the damage which this does to the self-respect of the United Nations. It is humiliating for the U.N. to give the appearance of being blackmailed or bludgeoned into following a course of action which a great majority of its members disapprove of.

Americans and others at that time and for years later kept confusing the issue, whether deliberately or not, by referring to it not as one of who should represent China in the U.N. but as the admission of Communist China to the U.N. In order to make the real issue clear I suggested to Pearson that the Peking Government should send to New York a delegation to the General Assembly and that this delegation should present its credentials to the Secretary-General. The Secretary-General would then have to submit to the credentials committee of the Assembly the credentials of two rival Chinese delegations, one from Formosa and one from Peking. Care should be taken to have a credentials committee elected which would recommend acceptance of the credentials issued by Peking; the General Assembly would adopt the report of the credentials committee by a simple majority vote. The American public, I said, was familiar with the problem of credentials committees of their party conventions having to decide between rival State delegations. They knew that when this happened it was not a question of admitting, say, Texas to the convention, but of deciding which of two rival Texan delegations to seat. Was there not some hope that if care was taken to have the problem before the United Nations Assembly presented to the American public in these terms, an increasing number would comprehend that the question under consideration was not the admission of Communist China to the United Nations but which Chinese delegation to seat. I went on to say that the seating of Peking representatives in the General Assembly should be followed as quickly as possible by seating their representatives in all the other agencies of the U.N. of which China was a member before the question of the representation of China was raised in the Security Council. The American position would then be weakened by the absurdity of having Formosa represent China in the Security Council when in every other agency of the U.N. it was represented by Peking.

Nothing came of this and the perpetuation under pressure from the United States of the absurdity of the government in Formosa representing China in the U.N. continued to weaken the U.N., exacerbate relations between the United States and most of its friends and allies, increase doubts about the wisdom of the foreign policies of successive American administrations and increase greatly the difficulties of maintaining world peace. Nehru's belief in the mid-fifties that there was no more vital or urgent issue in international affairs than the seating of Peking in the United Nations made him increasingly impatient if not contemptuous of what he called in 1956 the 'persistent obstinacy' of the United States in refusing to accept the realities of the situation in China. It must also have made him increasingly disappointed with the behaviour of countries such as Canada which tagged along behind American policy.

CHAPTER SIX
INDO-CHINA

On 18 February 1954, the foreign ministers of the United States, Britain, France and the Soviet Union agreed that an international conference should be held at Geneva in April to discuss Indo-China and Korea. Four days later, Nehru, in a speech in parliament, appealed for an immediate cease-fire in Indo-China. Canada supported Nehru's appeal. At the Geneva Conference Krishna Menon and Lester Pearson worked closely together on all aspects of the discussions on Indo-China. At the conclusion of the conference in July both countries accepted membership in the international control commissions for Vietnam, Laos and Cambodia which the conference set up. During this period from February to July 1954 Indo-China was an example of co-operation between India and Canada on foreign policy. Within six months the Geneva settlement on Indo-China was collapsing and as it collapsed Indian and Canadian policy on Indo-China began to diverge. Within a few years Indo-China became a major irritant in Indo-Canadian relations and one of the principal causes of the erosion of the special relationship between India and Canada.

The initial Canadian support for Nehru's views on Indo-China was accidental. It would not have been forthcoming if Louis St Laurent, then Prime Minister of Canada, had not been in New Delhi when Nehru publicly appealed for a cease-fire. St Laurent was present in parliament when Nehru made this appeal. When two days later he held a press conference in New Delhi, he was asked a series of probing questions about Nehru's appeal. He replied that he was in favour of it; it was practicable; it was apt to have considerable influence since it would be 'listened to very attentively and with very respectful consideration by the heads of all the governments with whom' he had had any contacts. The Canadian Government endorsed the appeal 'without any reservation or hesitation whatsoever'.

We wouldn't have ventured to make it ourselves because we wouldn't have felt that our importance in world affairs was sufficient to justify us in making it, but we would have no hesitation whatsoever in rejoicing at the fact that Prime Minister Nehru was able to make that appeal.

Eden in his memoirs states that he 'was not very happy' about Nehru's proposal for a cease-fire before the Geneva Conference.[1] Presumably he was not very happy about St Laurent's support of it. If Eden was not very happy, Dulles was probably angry. As for the French, they were 'furious'. This was the term the French Ambassador in New Delhi used to describe to me the tone of the telegram on St Laurent's statement which the French foreign office had sent to the French Ambassador in Ottawa.

The three principal western powers were opposed to an armistice in Indo-China before the Geneva Conference because they believed or hoped that something would happen before or during the conference to improve their bargaining position. Their bargaining position had been weak for at least two years and it had recently worsened. According to Eden, by the early months of 1952, two years before the Geneva Conference was convened, senior officers of the French General Staff were already admitting privately that evacuation of the 175,000 members of the French armed forces in Indo-China would be inevitable in the end; the problem was to compel Ho Chi Minh to negotiate terms which would enable the French to make a respectable withdrawal.[2] (Twenty years later the problem was to compel or persuade Ho Chi Minh's successors to negotiate terms which would enable the Americans to make a respectable withdrawal of their armed forces from Indo-China.)

In the first half of April 1954 the position of the besieged French garrison at Dien Bien Phu worsened and John Foster Dulles began issuing public threats against continued Chinese assistance to Ho Chi Minh. He also tried to persuade the British and the French Governments that before the Geneva Conference met an *ad hoc* coalition should be formed of the United States, Britain, France, Australia, New Zealand, Thailand, the Philippines, Vietnam, Laos and Cambodia, and that this group of countries should issue a public warning that, if China continued to interfere in the Indo-China war, the coalition (meaning the United States and Britain) would blockade China, embark on naval and air action against the coast of China, bomb China's internal and external communications and intervene actively in Indo-China itself. The *ad hoc* coalition would also, before the Geneva Conference met, set about organizing the collective defence of South-East Asia by taking steps to establish a South-East Asia defence organization.

Eden says that he welcomed the idea of a South-East Asia defence organization but opposed taking steps to establish it before the opening of the Geneva Conference and that he also emphasized to Dulles that 'although India and other Asian countries might well choose to remain outside such an arrangement, they should nevertheless be given every opportunity to participate and should be kept fully informed'. Dulles warned him that any attempt to include India would be countered by the inclusion of Formosa. Eden also opposed Dulles' proposal of a warning to China before the Geneva Conference met. He believed that it would have no effect and that the *ad hoc* coalition would have to withdraw ignominiously or embark on warlike action against China. This would 'give China every excuse for invoking the Sino-Soviet Treaty and might lead to a world war'. Eden was also exasperated by Dulles' habit of disregarding British views and of presenting the British Government with *faits accomplis*. He told the British Ambassador in Washington:

Americans may think the time past when they need consider the feelings or difficulties of their allies. It is the conviction that this tendency becomes more pronounced every week that is creating mounting difficulties for anyone in this country who wants to maintain close Anglo-American relations. We, at least, have constantly to bear in mind all our Commonwealth partners, even if the United States does not like some of them.[3]

If Britain was so worried about United States policies in South-East Asia and so exasperated by Dulles' tactics, it is not surprising that India was even more worried and exasperated. This became clear from a talk I had with Krishna Menon in the middle of April 1954. He said that Nehru had asked him to talk to me about the discussions on Indo-China at Geneva which were to start in twelve days' time. He had earlier that day had similar talks with the French Ambassador and with the British and Australian High Commissioners. He had been bitter about the United States and critical of Canada when we had had a long talk three and a half months before about the problem of the prisoners of war in Korea. Then there was little difference between the expansionist policies and the tactics of the United States and of the Soviet Union, and Canada was little more than a satellite of the United States. This time Krishna Menon was studiously moderate in his language. He did not go in for tirades against the United States or for criticism of Canada for being a satellite of the United States. Nor did he take the line that there was nothing much to choose between the two sides in the cold war. He said indeed that India's policy was not one of 'a plague on both your houses'. The existence of parliamentary democracy in India and the way in which the Indian Government treated the Communists in its country showed where India stood. He said that he did not question United States motives but he questioned the wisdom of their policy. He made flattering remarks about Canadian foreign policy and about St Laurent and Pearson, and the moderating influence which Canada and the United Kingdom had exerted in the past and could exert in the future on United States policy. Krishna Menon could be flattering when he was trying to persuade Canada to support India; he could be caustic when he became disappointed with Canada's failure to give what he considered to be sufficient support.

Krishna Menon began his talk with me by explaining the main reasons for India's special interest in the discussions on Indo-China. India did not presume to be a spokesman for Asia, but India was an Asian power and it was Asia which would be most affected if the war spread. The intensification or extension of the war would create special problems for India as a country in the area. Already, for example, India had had to refuse requests by France to ferry reinforcements across India by air. When I tried to sound him out on what kind of final solution he thought was possible, he said that if he were to suggest a unified Vietnam under a coalition government including Communists, he would be accused by the West of proposing Communist domination. I said that my recollection was that this was the proposal that Nehru had made at the Colombo

Indo-China

meeting of Commonwealth foreign ministers four years before. Menon said that if that suggestion had been adopted at that time the result by now would have been that a unified Vietnam would be controlled by mild Communists, like the Communists in India, and that there would have been no trouble in Laos and Cambodia. When I asked him what he thought about the other possible solution of a division of Vietnam into two states, he suggested that the Vietminh might not be willing to accept this.

After comparing notes with the French Ambassador and the British High Commissioner, I wired to Ottawa:

It seems clear that India is deeply disturbed by recent developments. The bomb explosions [the first explosions of the hydrogen bomb on 1 March] and Dulles's threats are interpreted here as indicating that the United States is not willing at this time to seek a peaceful solution of the Indo-Chinese problem. The Indians think the Chinese will not be overawed by the threats but will match increased western assistance to Vietnam with increased Chinese assistance to Vietminh, with consequent risks of an intensification and extension of the fighting. Many of the arguments the Indians used against United States military assistance to Pakistan apply in their minds with even greater force to the proposed Pacific Security Organization: the return of western domination to Asia thinly disguised as an alliance between western countries and two or three Asian satellites; the shrinkage of the peace area; the risk of provoking dangerous Soviet and Chinese counter measures. The Indians have never denied that their national security would be endangered by Chinese domination of South-East Asia but they consider that the Chinese do not wish to go in for military adventures in that area and that the way to prevent Chinese domination is to give independence and economic assistance [to the Indo-Chinese states].

A Locarno Pact for South-East Asia

Throughout the period of the Geneva Conference India remained strongly opposed to the formation of the kind of South-East Asia treaty organization (SEATO) proposed by Dulles, but it showed an increasingly favourable attitude to the kind of Locarno pact for South-East Asia proposed by Eden. The difference was that a SEATO would be an alliance against Ho Chi Minh, China and the Soviet Union whereas a Locarno-type pact would be an agreement of all the countries concerned to oppose aggression by any country. Dulles succeeded in establishing SEATO. Eden failed to establish a Locarno-type pact. This failure, I told Ottawa, was 'one of the tragic lost opportunities of the middle fifties'.

The first indication that Nehru might be prepared to consider Indian participation in a Locarno-type agreement came on 24 April, two days before the Geneva Conference opened. He then advocated in a speech in parliament that the conference should bring about 'a solemn agreement on non-intervention denying aid, direct or indirect, with troops or war material to the combatants [in Indo-China] or for the purposes of war, to which the U.S., the U.S.S.R., the U.K. and China should be primary parties' and that the U.N. should 'formulate a convention of non-intervention in Indo-China embodying [this] ... agreement and including provisions for its enforcement under U.N. auspices'. Then came the significant sentence: 'Other states should be invited by the U.N. to adhere to this convention on non-intervention.' A week later in a confidential message to Eden, Nehru went further. He indicated that India might be prepared to join in a guarantee of an Indo-China settlement though it would, of course, have to see the pattern that emerged from the Geneva Conference, know to what extent and to whom the guarantees would extend, and who the parties would be. The parties would, in Nehru's opinion, have to include both sides. In my report to Ottawa on this I said:

It would be more difficult for India to become a co-guarantor of a sort of Locarno pact for Indo-China if the conclusion of this pact were accompanied by the establishment of an anti-Communist SEATO which, inter alia, would guarantee Indo-China. The advantages of having a SEATO extending to Indo-China would therefore have to be balanced against this fact. Indeed one of Nehru's objectives in his message to Eden might well be to try to head off the establishment of SEATO. His argument might be that a Locarno Pact on Indo-China would make SEATO superfluous. The advantages to the western world of having India become a co-guarantor of the Indo-China settlement are substantial. It would lessen the chances that the other side would commit aggression in Indo-China; it would mean that if they did commit a flagrant act of aggression which resulted in war, India would be on our side from the outset. Our own experience and that of the United States in the past six years indicates that it is the first step in the acceptance of guarantees outside of one's borders which is the most difficult. The taking by India of this first step might, if the western world is patient and imaginative, result in the next few years in an increasingly closer association between India and the West.

From then on I did my best from New Delhi to promote the idea of Indian participation in a Locarno-type agreement on Indo-China both by my discussions in New Delhi and by my reports to Ottawa.

Thus I tried to allay what I gathered were Nehru's apprehensions that under a Locarno-type agreement India might have to participate in a debate in some international body on whether China had committed aggression, and that the United States might dragoon a majority of the members into declaring that some minor incident constituted an act of aggression. When Pillai raised this issue with me in the middle of May I said that the guarantee articles in the security pacts I was familiar with left the decision to each individual member state. It had to decide whether in its opinion a breach of the agreement had taken place. There might be a reference to some body like the United Nations Security Council but the failure of that body to reach agreement would not release the guarantors from their obligation. I suggested that experience showed that it was not usually very difficult to determine who was responsible for a major breach of such an agreement. I was not, of course, referring to petty frontier incidents.

I was at the same time trying to impress on Ottawa the importance of an Indian guarantee of an agreed settlement on Indo-China accompanied by independence for the Indo-Chinese states. Independence would, I said, mean that a clear line would be drawn in Asia between the two sides (somewhat similar to that in Europe in 1947) and there would be no colonial areas on our side of the line which, in the opinion of India and countries like it, were struggling against western imperialists for freedom. A Communist act of aggression might then have in Asia the catalytic effect that the seizure of Czechoslovakia in 1948 had had in the western world. In such circumstances it would be extremely difficult—if not impossible—for the Indians not to desert their policy of non-alignment, particularly if they were guarantors of an agreed Indo-Chinese settlement.

I had hoped that Eden would, during the month of June, make clear to Nehru precisely what he meant by a Locarno-type agreement. For some reason he did not. Possibly he did not want to be too precise in his discussions with Nehru until he had sold his idea to Washington which he visited at the end of June. I told Ottawa at this time that if the confusion in New Delhi about what Eden meant persisted there was danger that Britain and India might be talking at cross purposes. I then made five suggestions on how a Locarno-type treaty might be made palatable to the Indians. A month later, after the Geneva Conference had reached agreement on Indo-China, I embodied these suggestions in a draft of the precise text of a treaty. I sent this draft to Ottawa.

Meanwhile Chou En-lai had visited New Delhi and had had long talks with Nehru. In these talks Nehru suggested, and Chou En-lai agreed, that a proposal from Eden for a Locarno-type treaty deserved careful consideration though no commitments could be made at the moment. (Shortly before Chou's visit to New Delhi a spokesman for the Chinese had told the Canadian delegation at Geneva that after a peaceful settlement had been reached in Indo-China, China would be prepared to join the four great powers—the United States, Britain, France and the Soviet Union—and the four states in Indo-China—Vietnam, the Vietminh, Laos and Cambodia—in a guarantee of the territorial integrity and independence of the Indo-Chinese states.) Nehru in his talks with Chou said that before there could be a guarantee there would have to be not only an agreed political settlement but also regimes in Indo-China based on popular support. In reporting this to Ottawa I said that Nehru could contend that regimes based on popular support would not exist until, in accordance with the Geneva agreements and related documents, elections had been held in Laos and Cambodia in 1955 and in Vietnam in July 1956. Consequently Nehru might propose that the Locarno-type treaty should not come into force until it had been ratified by the new government of Vietnam, which would, in accordance with the Geneva settlement, be constituted in a united Vietnam following the elections of July 1956.

The Geneva settlement was concluded on 21 July 1954. A week later I sent Ottawa my draft of a Locarno-type agreement.

In the first article the parties to the treaty undertook to base their mutual relations on the five principles (panchsheel) which had been set forth in the preamble to the Indo-Chinese agreement of April 1954 on Tibet: mutual respect for each other's territorial integrity and sovereignty; non-aggression; non-interference in each other's internal affairs; equality and mutual benefit; and peaceful coexistence. In the second article the parties undertook to respect and support the settlement on Indo-China of 21 July 1954. The third article affirmed that, in support of this settlement, the parties to the treaty undertook, as set forth in the Charter of the United Nations, to settle their disputes by peaceful means and to refrain from the threat or use of force. The fourth article provided that the parties would contribute towards the further development of peaceful and friendly international relations by promoting conditions of stability and well-being in South-East Asia. The consultation article followed: 'The parties will consult together whenever, in the opinion of any of them, any of the principles set forth in Article 1 has been violated or the settlement of 21 July 1954 is threatened.'

Then came the core of my draft treaty, the guarantee article. I said that this article should make clear that it did not apply to the coming into power of Communist governments as the result of internal movements; it should therefore refer to 'an overt unprovoked act of external aggression'. Secondly, it should establish that each party had the right to decide for itself whether such an act of aggression had taken place. Thirdly, the promise to take action against the aggressor should be no stronger than that which Tom Connally, then Chairman of the Foreign Relations Committee of the United States Senate, had proposed for the North Atlantic treaty on 15 February 1949. Consequently the guarantee article which I proposed read as follows:

If a Party is satisfied that an overt unprovoked act of external aggression has taken place in the area covered by the settlement of 21 July 1954, it will individually or in concert with the other Parties take, in accordance with its constitutional processes, such measures as it may deem necessary to restore and maintain the security of the area.

At the end of June, Eden discovered to his surprise that in the

United States Locarno was a dirty word since it was, as he later wrote, entirely wrongly associated with appeasement and 'the bad old days'. Dulles told him that the United States could not guarantee an Indo-China settlement since this would mean guaranteeing 'the subjection of millions of Vietnamese to communist rule'; the most the United States could do would be to take note of the settlement and undertake not to disturb it.[4] It was clear that the United States preferred a SEATO treaty *without* India and China to a Locarno-type treaty *with* India and China.

While I considered that this decision of the United States was deplorable I hoped that Britain and France might be prepared to press for a Locarno-type treaty even if the United States would not be a party. I therefore suggested to Ottawa that the absence of the United States could be balanced by the omission of the Soviet Union. The signatories of the treaty would be confined to the governments of Indo-China (Vietnam, Vietminh, Laos and Cambodia), the five Colombo powers (India, Pakistan, Ceylon, Burma and Indonesia), other neighbouring states (China, Thailand and the Philippines), France because of its association with the states of Indo-China, and Britain because it was in charge of the foreign affairs of Malaya.

Nothing came of this. The United States and Britain went ahead with forming SEATO. They invited the Colombo powers to be members. All refused except Pakistan. On 8 September 1954, the South-East Asia defence treaty was signed in Manila. The only Asian members were Pakistan, Thailand and the Philippines. The other members were the United States, Britain, France, Australia and New Zealand. This was just the kind of treaty which I had warned Ottawa in mid-April would be considered by India to denote 'the return of western domination to Asia thinly disguised as an alliance between western countries and two or three Asian satellites'. Pillai indeed told me a few days after the treaty was signed that Nehru considered that the treaty was worse than he thought it would be; he had not expected that Laos, Cambodia and South Vietnam would be included in the area guaranteed by the treaty; he felt that this was contrary to the Geneva agreements and that it was unwise because it was provocative to China; what was wrong was that the guarantee was given by one side against the other side; it would have been entirely different if both sides had, under a Locarno-type treaty, guaranteed the Indo-Chinese states against attack.

The International Control Commissions

The Geneva Conference established international commissions for each of the three Indo-Chinese states to supervise the ceasefire agreements. India was chairman of the commissions. Canada and Poland were the other members. Nehru immediately suggested that a preliminary meeting be held in New Delhi at the beginning of August of representatives of India, Canada and Poland and, if possible, of France, the Vietminh, and of Laos, Cambodia and Vietnam. The meeting was held on 4 August. It was confined to India, Canada and Poland. R. M. Macdonnell of the Department of External Affairs and I represented Canada. Macdonnell was on his way from Ottawa to Indo-China. Poland was represented at the first few meetings by the Polish Ambassador and India was represented by Krishna Menon.

Before Nehru had made his suggestion for a meeting in New Delhi my wife and our two sons and our daughter had left for Ranikhet in the Himalayas. I was to join them during the last week of July and we were going to trek through the mountains on the way to the Pindari glacier. Our cook left for a holiday in East Pakistan. Our principal servant went to hospital for an operation. A few days before the meeting was to take place I had an acute attack of dysentery. My doctor was on holiday. I went to his substitute, an Austrian. I said, 'I have to attend an international conference tomorrow. I can't be constantly leaving the meeting to go to the lavatory. What shall I do?' He said, 'The best solution is the old-fashioned one of opium pills. They will tie you up.' The weather was the worst early August weather in fifteen years—hot, sticky and no rains to bring relief. The central air-conditioning plant in my house broke down on 31 July and could not be repaired until a new part came from Chicago. The house was stifling hot and it took three days to have ceiling fans installed. I borrowed a portable air-conditioning unit for my bedroom which I then used as bedroom and office. One evening during the conference I had a meeting there with Krishna Menon, the French and others.

The official Canadian residence in New Delhi was noted at this time for possessing what was then rare, an efficient air-conditioning system. I gave a lunch for the twenty Indian, Polish and Canadian members of the conference, having borrowed a cook and a butler from my second-in-command. My Indian friends and colleagues arrived expecting to be bathed in coolness and were instead overwhelmed by heat. The next day I gave a reception for two hundred people in honour of the delegations to the conference. It was to be held in the garden. I decided that if it rained I would receive my guests at the front door and suggest to each that he get a drink in the next room and leave immediately from the side door in that room. Fortunately it did not rain.

The heat, the dysentery and the opium made me somewhat light-headed, with the result that I delivered a burst of oratory at the opening meeting on 4 August when the spokesmen for the three delegations were called upon to make statements. Nehru spoke first. I followed. I paid a tribute to Krishna Menon:

> His Holiness the Pope referred some years ago to the virtue of holy obstinacy in a good cause. We have with us today one of the most eminent practitioners of that virtue, Mr Krishna Menon. He has been holily obstinate in the assistance which he has given to the statesmen at Geneva who were seeking for a peaceful settlement in Indo-China.

I went on to say:

> It was forty years ago today that the First World War broke out. Since then it has only been rarely that fighting has not been taking place somewhere in the world. Ten days from now the guns will all be silent in Indo-China and nowhere in the world will there be war. Forty years is a period of special significance. The children of Israel wandered forty years in the wilderness before they entered the Promised Land. Since 1914 our generation has wandered in the wilderness for forty years. We cannot hope that the activities of our commissions will lead us to the Promised Land. Let us, however, resolve that we shall each of us do our best to ensure that they lead us a step closer to the Promised Land.

When Nehru spoke in parliament three weeks later he was more cautious than I. He said that as a result of the Geneva settlement, there was no war anywhere in the world for the first time since the Second World War.

The conference ended on Friday, 6 August. The next morning I got up at four and went to the airport to say good-bye to Macdonnell and the Canadian army officers who were members of the advance mission. I saw them off and was about to return home when I was told that a group of half a dozen Canadian army officers had just arrived at the airport and would be leaving in a few minutes. They had been flown in from Korea where they had been serving in the United Nations forces and were being transferred to Indo-China to serve on the inspection teams of the international supervisory commissions. I had a pleasant time talking to them and waved them good-bye when their plane left. This time I got as far as the waiting room in the lounge of the airport. Here I found the British High Commissioner's office assembled in full force. It was still only seven in the morning. They told me that their High Commissioner was on the plane from London which was due in twenty minutes. He had been away from Delhi for a month on holiday. To his surprise he found me waiting at the bottom of the runway of his plane to welcome him back to Delhi. But the morning's ceremonial duties were not yet done. Entering into the spirit of the game, my British colleague said to me, 'There's a Canadian colonel on the plane you might like to greet.' I introduced myself to the colonel. He was on his way to Kashmir to serve as a United Nations observer. At the New Delhi airport on that early morning in August 1954 was demonstrated the extent of the participation of the Canadian armed forces at that time in U.N. peace-keeping activities. Here were army officers who had just served or were just about to serve in U.N. activities in Korea, Kashmir and Indo-China.

The following day after finishing a telegram to Ottawa on the conference, I had lunch with the British High Commissioner and told him some of the things that had been happening in India during his absence. Krishna Menon called on me at 5.30 in the afternoon to talk about Goa. At 6.30 I called on the American Ambassador who was leaving the next day for two months' holiday at home. At 7.00 I called on Pillai and at 7.30 on the Australian High Commissioner to tell him what had happened at the conference. The next morning I was called at 3.45 and left an hour later for Ranikhet which I reached in twelve hours. I slept for most of the next few days.

The Collapse of the Geneva Settlement

Within six months the Geneva settlement on Indo-China was collapsing. I wired to Ottawa at the end of January 1955:

The Indians, as you know, suspect that the United States intends to torpedo the settlement in Vietnam and that in particular the United States will use its best efforts to see that a free election does not take place. The Indians also believe, on the basis of reports from their own people in Vietnam, that in a free election the Democratic Republic [Vietminh] would receive up to three-quarters of the vote in the south. They are confirmed in this view by reports of independent observers. ... My impression also is that the Indians consider the Geneva settlement as a package deal under which the North gave up the possibility, or indeed the probability, of a complete military victory in the South in return for a promise of free elections. They consider Ho Chi Minh an intelligent statesman and they would find it hard to believe that he will not be willing to agree to any reasonable requirements for free elections, since in their opinion he is certain to win them. Because of these Indian beliefs they have for some time assumed that Vietnam would be unified under Ho Chi Minh and that the problem which they and their friends face is to prevent an extension of his influence into Laos and Cambodia which they would consider disastrous. I had hoped that if the western world played its cards well we could get substantial co-operation from India in this task [by, for example, Indian membership in a Locarno-type security pact on Indo-China]. If, however, the Indians come to believe that the prospect of free elections in Vietnam has been frustrated by the United States and its friends, their inevitable tendency will be to wash their hands of the results. Among the results might be a collapse of the regime in South Vietnam and a renewal of hostilities.

As the Geneva settlement on Indo-China began to collapse, the Indian and Canadian views on Indo-China began to diverge more and more. I had had a talk with Nehru at the end of July 1954, a few days before the preliminary meeting in New Delhi of the supervisory commissions on Indo-China. At the end of our talk I said to Nehru that I hoped that our joint membership in the commissions would not result in our ruffling each other's feathers too much. He said he was sure it would have the opposite effect. I was not myself so optimistic at the time and my lack of optimism was soon to be justified.

In my telegram at the end of January 1955 from which I have

just quoted, I dealt with one of the first examples of the growing divergence between India and Canada. I had been instructed by Ottawa to put to the Indians our views on the electoral commission for Vietnam provided for in the Geneva agreements. I replied to Ottawa saying that these views were very different from our preliminary views, which I had, under instructions from Ottawa, given to the Indians only three months before; that I had recently reported that the Indian views were substantially in accord with these preliminary views of ours; and that it would be likely that the kind of marked change in our views which Ottawa proposed that I should inform the Indians of would be interpreted by them to mean that we were giving in to United States pressure to sabotage the arrangements for elections in Vietnam.

I had not, however, realized how far the views of the Canadian and Indian Governments were diverging until I was in Ottawa on home leave six months later and was asked to give a report about India at a meeting of the senior officers of the Department of External Affairs. In this report I spoke of the intent which I understood lay behind the acceptance by France and Britain of the Geneva settlement—that it was not possible to hold a line against communist expansion in Vietnam, but that it was possible to hold a line at the border between Laos and Cambodia on one side and Vietnam on the other, and that France and Britain had implicitly acquiesced at Geneva in Ho Chi Minh taking over the whole of Vietnam as the result of elections. This, I said, was the Indian view and I agreed with it.

The roof fell in on top of me. Officer after officer at the meeting attacked me for my callous, immoral proposal which would betray millions of anti-communist people in South Vietnam into the clutches of the communists of North Vietnam. (Twenty years and millions of deaths later not only they but also the Laotians and Cambodians would be 'betrayed' into the hands of the communists.)

In February 1956, a few months after I had returned to India from home leave, Krishna Menon was appointed to the Cabinet as minister without portfolio. Though he was not made foreign minister he was given a large office in the External Affairs Ministry and he immediately began to act on issues in which he was especially interested, such as Indo-China, Korea and

Kashmir, as if he were the foreign minister. The day his appointment was announced I saw him at a dinner in honour of Hammarskjold. He brushed off my congratulations on his appointment and immediately began talking to me in an arrogant way about Laos and Vietnam and how he had 'told' M. J. Desai of the External Affairs Ministry to talk to me and the Polish Ambassador about our commissioners in Vietnam not behaving like advocates of opposing sides. I told Ottawa that Menon was probably putting on an act for the benefit of the Secretary-General of the U.N. of a foreign minister speaking in forceful terms to a foreign envoy.

Two months after his appointment to Cabinet I warned Ottawa:

Negotiations here on the work of the supervisory commissions in Indo-China, or any other matter in which Menon takes an interest, are going to become increasingly difficult during the periods when Menon is in New Delhi. He is becoming increasingly arrogant and whereas he used to be careful about his facts, if not about his interpretation of facts, he is now asserting mis-statements of facts as self-evident truths.

My apprehensions about a growing divergence between India and Canada on Indo-China were confirmed by a talk about the commission in Vietnam which I had with Menon at the end of May 1956. He said that Diem, the President of South Vietnam, was like the kind of Indians the British used to put into high positions in India before Independence, people who, they used to say, would 'rally the moderates'; these people had had no strength whatever in the country. Diem would do whatever the United States wanted him to do since he knew that if the United States withdrew its support he would collapse. Diem also knew that he would collapse if the supervisory commission pulled out of Vietnam. The United States must force Diem to agree that South Vietnam accept its responsibilities under the Geneva agreements as the successor state to France. The only reason Diem did not agree was that the United States was not putting enough pressure on him. Why did Canada not realize it was inevitable that Vietnam should be united under the Communists? It was not sensible to try to hold the line at the border between North and South Vietnam.

Though I agreed with most of what Menon said, it was essential that he understand that Ottawa did not. I, therefore, as I reported to Ottawa, refused to accept his analysis of either the legal or the political positions of South Vietnam. I reminded him of the opinion of the legal adviser of the Canadian Department of External Affairs that South Vietnam did not inherit the obligations France had undertaken under the Geneva agreements. He contemptuously dismissed this opinion as valueless. I retorted that the opinion of the legal adviser of the British Foreign Office was substantially the same. I said we also differed on the extent to which Diem was susceptible to pressure from the Americans or anyone else. I understood that many people in South Vietnam, including, I thought, some of the Indian officials there, now credited Diem with much more popular strength than they had previously thought he had, and certainly did not consider him a mere puppet of the Americans. Menon concluded our talk with what I said to Ottawa were 'his usual remarks about Canada, on a matter like the supervisory commission in Vietnam, having no independent views or judgement of its own, but instead carrying out faithfully the United States line, whatever it might be'.

The special relationship between Canada and India was being subjected to severe strains.

CHAPTER SEVEN

LESTER PEARSON'S VISIT

Lester Pearson spent twelve days in India at the end of October and the beginning of November 1955. This was his second visit to India as foreign minister of Canada. The first had taken place after the meeting of Commonwealth foreign ministers in Colombo in January 1950 and had lasted only a few days. In October 1955, just before he was to arrive in India, he wired me that he was very tired as the result of an exhausting visit to the Soviet Union followed by a Colombo Plan conference in Singapore. Could I arrange for him to have four days' holiday with no official business? I remembered that Nehru had once said to me that the loveliest spot in the world in which there was an official Indian residence was Gangtok, the capital of Sikkim, and that when he retired from the prime ministership the job he would like would be that of Indian political officer in Gangtok. My wife and I were friends of the Indian political officer, Apa Pant, and of his wife, and they had invited us to stay with them. I appealed to them. Could they put up Mr and Mrs Pearson, Mr Pearson's secretary and my wife and myself for four days, immediately after Pearson's arrival in Calcutta from Singapore and find accommodation elsewhere in Gangtok for the Canadian foreign service officer who was accompanying Pearson? They generously agreed.

My wife and I knew that we were taking a chance when we arranged this visit. We liked this sort of thing. We were not certain whether the Pearsons did. We soon found out that they were not as accustomed as we to being driven up and down mountains on steep, narrow roads with hairpin bends, with a wall of rock on one side and a precipice on the other. Driving up to Gangtok from the airport in the foothills Pearson urged my wife to maintain a continuous flow of interesting conversation to keep Maryon Pearson's mind off what seemed to her the perils of the drive. This was not an auspicious beginning to the holiday we had arranged but when we arrived at the Indian residence in Gangtok we found that fortune had smiled on us, for there we saw one of the most spectacular mountain views of the world available to people who are not mountaineers. Spread out in front of us was a quarter circle of high Himalayan mountains with bright sunlight on their snow-clad peaks. Apa Pant told us that this was the first time in two weeks that the mountains had not been hidden by clouds. The next day the Maharaja of Sikkim's eldest son drove us in a jeep ten miles along what Pearson called in his journal 'a rocky, turning, terrifying track' to a point about ten miles from the Tibetan border. I told Pearson that he had almost got within sight of recognizing China.

Pearson wrote in his journal:

This is the immemorial trade route from Tibet into India, and it is used the same way by mules and by men and women, carrying incredible loads, as it was a thousand years ago, with the same customs, same clothes, same greetings. It is certainly a page out of history and at times we have to pinch ourselves to make sure we are not dreaming it.

Our gamble in taking the Pearsons to Gangtok was successful. Pearson noted in his journal that at Gangtok, 'no cares of the international world' bothered him and that he had been 'enchanted by this remote corner of Asia'.

About a year before the Pearson visit to India I had visited the Mayurakshi dam on the border of West Bengal and Bihar which was being financed by Canada under the Colombo Plan. There I saw thousands of Santal villagers, men and women, moving in single file up and down ramps carrying building material to the dam, and rubble out. It was my first sight of the Indian method of construction which Le Corbusier had described as using men and women like innumerable ants. The site of the dam was beautiful. According to Indian studies the economic benefits from the dam would be impressive. It would, therefore, I thought, be an excellent place for Pearson to visit. To my surprise I found that the Indian External Affairs Ministry did not agree. They said there was nothing at Mayurakshi for Pearson to open; the dam was in operation and the hydro-electric development was not ready. The real problem, I suspected, was that the Chief Minister of West Bengal, B. C. Roy, could see no reason why he should put on a show at Mayurakshi for the Canadian minister for external affairs; as far as West Bengal was concerned there was no element of Canadian gift in the dam; Canada gave the money to the Indian Government; the Indian Government did not transfer it as a gift to West Bengal but as a loan. I had to intervene with Nehru. Nehru immediately got in touch with the Chief Minister and the whole situation changed. The Chief Minister agreed that the dam should be called the Canada Dam and that he would attend a ceremony at the dam with a distinguished party of Indian politicians, officials, newspapermen and photographers. The usual arrangements were also made for the attendance of thousands of peasants, for a visit to a nearby community project and an exhibition of dancing by the local Santal villagers.

At the ceremony at the dam Pearson pulled a lever and the water cascaded through the spillway into the irrigation canal. Pearson wrote in his journal:

A moving and dramatic moment, signalized by a great cheering shout by the thousands of peasants who had come from far and near, on foot, on mule, and the plutocrats, on bicycle. This water means something to them, and the Colombo Plan, after this morning, will mean more to me.

Pearson was delighted by the pride of the Indian engineers and workmen in the dam and impressed by the community project; and he enjoyed the superb beauty and rhythm of the dancing of the Santal villagers. He wrote:

A full and exciting day—much more rewarding and illuminating than many of the visits to officials in the great cities. It emphasized to me the staggering nature of the problems facing this country, and the courage and determination of those, like Dr Roy, who are trying to solve them and give these people a better life. I wonder if they will be successful or if the centrifugal forces, the divisive forces, will prove too strong. With communists exploiting the awful living conditions, especially in the great cities, and widening the rifts which already exist between classes and sects and races, it is going to be a touch-and-go struggle for India.

The visit to Banaras was fun. We stayed at the Maharaja's city palace. At sunrise we went up the Ganges in his boat to his

Escott Reid presenting his credentials to Rajendra Prasad, President of India. Looking on is R. K. Nehru.

S. Radhakrishnan,
Vice-President of India,
Escott Reid and
Ruth Reid.

Escott Reid and Krishna Menon at New Delhi Airport. ('If the Canadian government want to protest, let them protest.')

Escott Reid and Mrs Pandit.

They spoke to each other of their common exasperation and each spoke to her father, with the result that Nehru asked me one evening to arrange that we cut short our visit to Agra the next day so that he could have another talk with St Laurent. In this talk they did have a useful discussion.

When Dulles visited New Delhi in March 1956 Nehru gave a dinner for him. Dulles sat on Indira Gandhi's right, I on her left. She turned to me half-way through dinner and whispered to me: 'You know my father and Mr Dulles talked together for three and a half hours this afternoon. I saw my father immediately after he came out of the meeting and can you imagine what he told me. He said that for the first three hours and a quarter they chatted about nothing important. Finally fifteen minutes before the interview was to end Dulles asked a question about Indian policy and there was fifteen minutes of useful discussion.' Indira Gandhi added that the same sort of thing had happened on Nehru's visit to the Soviet Union some months before, but that after the chit-chat had gone on for a few minutes she would insist that the conversation get down to business. When I saw Dulles the next morning his account of the talk was different. He said that Nehru and he had covered a lot of ground in a general discussion 'which is the only kind of discussion one can have with Mr Nehru'.

In my report to Pearson on this incident I said:

The way in which Mrs Gandhi made the remark to me about the three and a half hour talk which her father and Mr Dulles had just had seemed to me to make clear that her father was disappointed in the talk. This confirms my belief that, while Mr Nehru will himself take no initiative when a visiting statesman calls on him, he expects the visiting statesman to bring up important questions. If the visiting statesman does not bring them up Mr Nehru will continue to talk about lions and bears and birds and flowers. It may also be that the pattern of Mr Nehru's behaviour which emerges is that during the first long talk with a visiting statesman Mr Nehru will not himself make many comments on issues brought up by the visiting statesman. In this case it is up to the visitor to do what you did during your talk with Mr Nehru here when you brought up one question after another, elucidating your own view, and when it became clear that Mr Nehru was not prepared to comment, you passed on to another question.

Pearson, on his visit to New Delhi, had interviews with the

President (Rajendra Prasad), the Vice-President (Radhakrishnan), the Minister of Finance (Deshmukh), and the Minister of Commerce (T. T. Krishnamachari). He found the President to be 'a sturdy, rather quiet veteran Indian nationalist', the Vice-President to be 'a witty and wise but a somewhat garrulous philosopher', and Deshmukh to be 'a man of great ability and integrity but not physically strong and with no great political following'. The Vice-President told Pearson of the definition of logic by Jowett of Balliol College, a definition which he said also applied to diplomacy, 'Logic is not an art. It is not a science. It is a dodge.'

Pearson in his journal summed up his impressions of India:

I was received with the greatest friendliness—as a Canadian. Our position is very high in India. The Indians appreciate our sympathy as much as our support. Indeed, I think they give us credit for virtues which we may not possess, by contrasting our attitudes and policies with the Americans. We are strong enough to help them, but not powerful enough to be considered 'imperialist'. Our High Commissioner, Escott Reid, has increased our reputation in India, where he is very highly regarded for his friendliness and imaginative understanding of India's problems. I was impressed by the apparent ability and devotion of Indian ministers and officials I met, but worried about their ability to solve the terrific problems—economic, social and political—that face them. They are certainly making progress, but lifting these people into the second half of the twentieth century by democratic processes and in a short time is a terrific task. People here are morbidly sensitive about their independent position, and satisfied with, even proud about their 'neutralist' stand. Indian press conferences—and I had a few—reflect both this sensitiveness and this pride. At times, this makes them unreasonable and self-righteous, as does their occasional assumption of superior virtue vis-à-vis the West. Nehru is still the one dominant figure. He plays an indispensable part in holding the country together. No one remotely challenges his pre-eminence. This, of course, has its own dangers, as no one seems to be growing under his shadow.

I, in a letter to my children, summed up my impressions of Pearson.

Mr Pearson did a superb job in India. He arrived feeling exhausted. The seven days in Russia had put him through the wringer. The conference in Singapore had been no holiday. Then the last straw was his R.C.A.F. plane breaking down in Malaya. But the four days' holiday in Sikkim was just what he needed. And he went through the rest of the Indian tour with his colours flying. I was exhausted merely following him around but he had to give speeches and a press conference. My admiration for him has always been great. It is now profound. He has had a very difficult time in the past three years. He has had to be a sort of leader of the opposition to Dulles in the North Atlantic Community. His great responsibilities have matured him. He's still gay but he's at bottom more serious and solid.

Pearson flew from Delhi to Lahore. The Government House he stayed at there was 'not only spacious, with magnificent grounds, but warm and "homely" '. He had not found Rashtrapati Bhavan, the President's residence which he had stayed at in New Delhi, either warm or homely. He described his suite there as grandiose and uncomfortable with 'many flunkeys dancing attendance which at times was more intrusive than effective'. But it was not only the official residences in Lahore and New Delhi which he contrasted to the disadvantage of India. He wrote in his journal:

It is surprising, the difference in the atmosphere between India and Pakistan. The people of the latter country—or at least West Pakistan —seem much easier to talk to, more like ourselves, than the Indians. They seem franker and more straightforward, more vigorous. Of course, this apparent difference may be partly the result of 'suggestion'. The British, with few exceptions, will tell you that the 'Paks' are a better people, more 'our type', you know; so when you arrive here you subconsciously look for and find this difference. Another factor is that the people from this part of the sub-continent have provided such a large part of the old Indian army and are maintaining many of the old military traditions. Then, finally, the Pakistanis seek, and very often secure, your sympathy as the smaller state, divided into two far-separated parts, pressed hard by India and attempting, against terrific disadvantages, to build up a stable and united society. Anyway, we seem to like the Pakistanis. Lahore was a happy but short visit, with the only sight-seeing a visit to the 'Old Fort' and Mosque.

Pearson's preference for the West Pakistanis over the Indians was shared, I think, by most western politicians who visited South Asia at that time. This preference was, indeed, one of the obstacles India confronted in trying to obtain support or sympathy in the West for its views and problems, particularly problems arising out of its relations with Pakistan.

About twenty members of the National Defence College of Canada came to New Delhi in the mid-fifties. I took them to see Nehru. We had agreed that the visitors would ask Nehru questions. One of them said, 'Prime Minister, we have just been visiting West Pakistan. Could you tell us something about the differences between India and Pakistan?' By differences he meant disagreements, but Nehru, deliberately I think, interpreted it to mean dissimilarities. His answer went something like this. 'The difference between the members of the government of Pakistan and the members of the government of India is that we were leaders in the struggle against the British for independence and they were not. Because we were leaders in the struggle for independence we have mass support in the country. If I ceased to be Prime Minister I would still have influence. The leaders of West Pakistan are admirable men but they did not participate in the struggle for independence and they do not have mass support. They were officials or officers in India.' Then he named four or five of the leading figures of the Pakistan Government. One of them, he said, had been a middle-ranking officer in 'our' audit service. One had been an official in 'our' political service, another a colonel in 'our' army, another a judge. ('Our' was an assertion that the Republic of India was the successor state to undivided India as, indeed, in international law, it was.)

People who had been officials or officers in undivided India were more likely to be highly anglicized than people who had been politicians. Most of them bore little or no resentment to the British; indeed they usually had respect and even affection for the British whom they had served under and who had trained them. Unlike the political leaders of undivided India they had not been beaten up by British-officered police who were putting down demonstrations or been jailed under British rule. It is not, therefore, surprising that western politicans found the leaders of Pakistan easier to get on with than the leaders of India.

And, because the leaders of Pakistan were Muslims, western politicians like Pearson found them 'more like ourselves' than the Hindus they met in New Delhi. They found them more like themselves because the culture of Islam is much closer to that of the West than is the culture of Hinduism. Hinduism is indeed farther removed from the culture of the West than any other of the great contemporary cultures of mankind. I put this once in a despatch to Ottawa from New Delhi, a despatch written by a brilliant member of my staff, Klaus Goldschlag.

With the Arab world the West shares a common heritage of Aristotelianism and of Hellenistic thought; with Russia there is the common bond of the Byzantine tradition and, more recently, of the mainstream of nineteenth century European philosophy; with China we share an essentially practical if not pragmatic outlook; Japan has by its own efforts embraced much that is basic to western civilization. India, on the other hand, has almost no common intellectual or religious roots with the West and the mind of the Indian people has remained essentially speculative and slow to adapt itself to the demands of material progress.

PART THREE

THE EROSION OF THE SPECIAL RELATIONSHIP

CHAPTER EIGHT

AMERICAN ARMS FOR PAKISTAN

In the autumn of 1953 I contended in a despatch to Ottawa that Nehru's foreign policy was not 'neutralist' but that Nehru was on 'our side'. (I was encouraged a few weeks after I had written this despatch by the discovery that the French Ambassador, Ostrorog, in whose judgement on such matters I had confidence, agreed with me. He told me that he believed that Nehru was a liberal democrat and that he was not in any real sense of the term neutral in the struggle between the democratic world and the totalitarian world but was on the side of the democratic world.) In support of my views I cited in my despatch statements by Nehru at a recent Commonwealth meeting. In a discussion of the possibility of the United States having to resort to more widespread military operations if the Korean truce broke down, Nehru had said that this would have the effect of 'seriously increasing *our* subsequent difficulties'. Later he had referred to the necessity of keeping the peoples of South-East Asia 'on *our* side' and to avoid mistakes which '*our* opponents' took advantage of. I went on to say:

These are not the remarks of a neutralist. Mr Nehru is, I submit, not neutral between our side and the U.S.S.R. He is a member of our side.... Some of the other members of our side may consider that he should give our side a little more active support than he usually does, but that's a different thing from saying that he's not a member of our side.... This does not mean that Mr Nehru and the Government of India have not an ambivalent attitude towards the West. They have, and this attitude derives from the attitude of India as a whole toward the West which it learned to know under the tutelage of the British: half reluctant admiration, half volatile resentment. But this attitude is certainly not 'neutralist'. Canadians should find it easier than many other people to understand this Indian ambivalence. It is not unlike the ambivalent attitude of Canadians to the United States.

Looking back now at my four and a half years in India it seems to me probable that the high point in the special relationship between India and Canada and, indeed, in India's relations with the West was reached at just about the time I wrote this despatch and that it continued from the autumn of 1953 throughout 1954. After that a process of erosion set in. Some of the causes of the erosion were: the resentment aroused in India by the United States military aid agreement with Pakistan concluded early in 1954; the differences of opinion between the West and India over Kashmir; the resentment aroused in the West by the treatment accorded by India to Krushchev and Bulganin on their visit to India in the autumn of 1955; the attitude of the Indian Government to the Hungarian Revolution of 1956 and the Soviet-imposed counter-revolution; and the activities of Krishna Menon. This and succeeding chapters tell the story of this erosion.

On 8 March 1957, two months before I left India, Pearson wrote me a personal letter which sounded the death-knell of the special relationship. The letter was written on the day the U.N. General Assembly adjourned. The Assembly had been in session since 1 November 1956. It had dealt with the crises over Hungary and Suez. In the early months of 1957, while it was in session the Security Council had been debating the Kashmir issue. Pearson had been involved in all these issues. He had also been involved in efforts to work with Krishna Menon. He may have been tired and dispirited when he wrote this letter and it is possible that he put his views more bluntly than he normally would have done. This is what he wrote:

I think it would be fair to say that in the last year or so . . . Asian membership [in the Commonwealth] and Asian policies inside the Commonwealth have given us some ground for increased concern; a concern as to whether in the long run the Commonwealth can exist in its present form and spirit when there are such growing divergencies of policy and approach and feeling between the Asian and the other members. My concern in this matter has been increased by my experiences at the recent U.N. Assembly. India has, I think, played an ambiguous part there and one which has at times caused both irritation and impatience, even in friendly delegations like the Canadian. The tendency to indulge in moralizing at Western expense when we seem to be doing something wrong stood out in sharp contrast with the obstinate determination to protect national interests and to belittle U.N. principles and majority views when questions like Kashmir were under consideration.

*   *   *

Chester Bowles, who was the American Ambassador during my first few months in New Delhi, told me in my first talks with him in December 1952 and January 1953 that some time before there had been a proposal that Pakistan should join a projected Middle East defence organization but that Archibald Nye, then British High Commissioner to India, had killed it in London and he thought that he had killed it in Washington. It had, however, he said, recently been resurrected and he had told the new Republican administration in Washington that he considered the proposal unwise. I gathered that the new British High Commissioner, Alexander Clutterbuck, and the French Ambassador, Stanislas Ostrorog, had likewise told their governments that they too thought the proposal unwise. In any event the issue did not arise since plans for establishing a Middle East defence organization miscarried.

In October 1953 I learned from the British High Commissioner that the United States was proposing to announce, probably before the end of December, that it was giving Pakistan military aid worth $25 million. When I reported this to Ottawa I said that the United States embassy and the United Kingdom mission had both put in strongest terms to their governments the deplorable effect this would have on Indo-Pakistan relations and that the United Kingdom mission was particularly concerned that this announcement should not be made while India and Pakistan were discussing the appointment of a plebiscite administrator for Kashmir the following April. I said that I concurred in these views. 'There is now some hope of a settlement of the Kashmir problem but this hope would, I am afraid, vanish if the United States persists in its proposed policy.'

It must have been at about this time that the Indian Government learned of the possibility of the United States giving military aid to Pakistan. Pillai first raised the subject with me a fortnight after I had sent this telegram. He gave me what turned out to be two of the principal arguments which Nehru was to advance against the proposed military understanding: it would bring the cold war to India's borders; and any strengthening of the armed forces of Pakistan would encourage the hotheads in Pakistan who might believe that a change in the military balance between India and Pakistan in Pakistan's favour would make it possible for Pakistan to succeed in an armed struggle with India over Kashmir. He did not rule out the possibility mentioned in some Indian newspapers that the United States might be seeking air and naval bases in Pakistan, perhaps naval bases in Karachi and Dacca and air bases in Baluchistan.

The next day Nehru gave a press conference in order to make clear how disturbed he was by the implications of the proposed agreement. A press campaign against the agreement had already been launched, organized by the Indian Government, and this campaign was then intensified. When Richard Nixon, Vice-President of the United States, visited New Delhi at the beginning of December, Nehru and he had a two-hour talk with no one else present. The American embassy told me that Nehru had devoted ninety per cent of his time to putting persuasively and frankly to Nixon the Indian arguments against the proposed agreement and that Nixon had been impressed by the weight of these arguments.

If Nixon told the American Ambassador that he had been impressed by the weight of Nehru's arguments, he had presumably left Nehru with a feeling that he was going to give these points sympathetic consideration. The reverse was the truth. Nixon went on from New Delhi to a three-day visit to Karachi. While he was there, Robert Trumbull, the correspondent of the *New York Times* in India, sent out from Karachi on 8 and 9 December two despatches which, though they did not name Nixon as the source, were clearly reporting Nixon's views. Nixon was not simply saying that on balance, in spite of India's objections, he favoured a military agreement with Pakistan; he was making a bitter personal attack on Nehru. Nehru must have read Trumbull's despatches with surprise, chagrin and mounting anger, for Trumbull reported that 'informed sources' in Karachi had told him that the time had come to put 'an end to Washington's patience with Asian neutralism' as exemplified in Nehru's policies. The United States should take a 'position of greater independence in relation to Mr Nehru, a firmer course with him'. Nehru 'will be affected in his purposes by strength, decisive action and people who can say

"No" with power to back it up'. Nehru's 'neutralist influence' has often embarrassed the United States and its allies. It is the United States which is 'his major rival for influence in South Asia'. Nehru wants Indian dominance in Asia, the Near East and Africa. In order to secure this dominance India has been intriguing with two aims in view: to keep its neighbours individually weak and divided among themselves; and to sabotage a Washington–Karachi entente. The basic reason for Nehru's opposition to United States military aid to Pakistan is that a stronger Pakistan, with all that that implies in the Muslim world, would threaten the dominance of India in Asia, the Near East and Africa. Nehru's neutralist influence would receive a setback if Pakistan, which is an Asian power openly opposed to communism, were to gain a position of greater prominence. Therefore the decision on United States military aid to Pakistan 'may ultimately determine whether India, a country often opposed to the United States in vital international dealings, is to obtain unquestioned dominance over [Asia, the Near East and Africa] or is to remain merely the strongest individual power in an Asia–Arab–Africa bloc'.

Pillai told me that Nehru had said to him that Trumbull's despatches had made United States policies clear. This was an over-simplification. Trumbull's despatches had made clear the views of Nixon and those in the United States administration who agreed with him. It was not yet certain that these were the views of the administration as a whole.

Similarly a puzzling call on me by a senior officer of the American Embassy, who may have been the principal C.I.A. representative in India, further clarified the views of those who agreed with Nixon. We had known each other at Oxford in the late twenties. When we were both at the airport to say goodbye to Nixon he told me he very much wanted to have a very private talk with me. We talked for an hour and a half on 11 December 1953. His conversation was oblique, but I gathered from what he said that his argument ran somewhat as follows. India had been the source of mass armies for the western powers in both world wars. In the First World War undivided India had raised an army of one and a half million, in the Second an army of two and a half million. India was the only possible source of a mass army for the West in a third world war.

A military agreement between the United States and Pakistan would isolate India. India would find that it would not be able to build up its armaments to match the increase in Pakistan's because the United States would put pressure on Britain not to provide arms, and would also see to it that India did not receive other essential imports from western countries. The United States had been turning a blind eye to the shipments of thorium nitrate from India to China, as otherwise it would be compelled by statute to cut off all economic aid to India. The United States would cease to turn a blind eye to these shipments. These developments would weaken Nehru and the Congress Party and strengthen the right-wing Hindu group, the Jana Sangh, some of whose members were prepared to support a military agreement with the United States. The objective of the United States in making a military agreement with Pakistan was thus to put India in a position where it had no recourse but to make a military agreement with the United States which would ultimately lead to India becoming an ally of the United States, and the source of a mass army for the West in a third world war. (During the Second World War the Soviet Union with a population of about 200 million maintained about 12 million men in its armed forces. Using the Soviet Union by way of analogy and ignoring the demographic, social and economic factors which might make a difference in one direction or the other, the comparable figure for India in the mid-fifties with a population of 375 million would be over 20 million.)

The threat which was conveyed to me in this conversation that the United States might cut off essential supplies to India if India refused to enter into a military aid agreement was taken seriously by the business community in India. In mid-January 1954 the managing director of Ford of India, which was controlled by Ford of Canada, told me that the Indian authorities feared that the United States might, in these circumstances, interfere with the export of trucks from the United States to India. Could I tell the minister of commerce and industry of India that Ford of Canada was independent of the parent firm in Detroit and could therefore pursue a different policy on the provision of trucks to India than Ford in the United States? I referred this to Ottawa and, as I expected, was not given the authority to say this.

A month after the senior officer of the American Embassy had called on me, I was invited to a lunch organized by the American Embassy to discuss with Maurice Zinkin the question of American military aid to Pakistan. Zinkin was a former member of the I.C.S. and was then with Lever Brothers in Bombay. He kept in close touch with his friends in the I.C.S. who now held high positions in the administration. The American Ambassador and three of his most senior associates at the embassy were present at the lunch. The Ambassador and his second-in-command pressed Zinkin to answer the question whether the effect of large American military aid to Pakistan would not be that India would itself request military aid from the United States. Their tenacity in pressing this question confirmed my feeling that this was indeed the hope held by important groups in the American administration. (Zinkin's answer was that the chances of India asking the United States for military aid were one in ten or one in twenty.)

On 10 December when the controversy over the rumoured American military aid agreement with Pakistan was at its height, I called on Nehru with L.-P. Picard, who was then Chairman of the External Affairs Committee of the House of Commons of Canada. Nehru could have met the requirements of courtesy by a fifteen-minute interview. Instead he gave us an hour-long exposition of his views. I was surprised at the time. A few days afterwards the Nepalese Ambassador told me that he had called on Nehru shortly after Picard and I had left him. The purpose of his call was to discuss with Nehru the possibility of the United States entering into a military agreement with Pakistan. Nehru told him that he had just had an hour's talk with me in which he had expounded the views of the Indian Government on this question. Nehru must have decided that he would take advantage of my call on him with Picard to give me a statement on Indian foreign policy in which he would put his arguments against the proposed U.S.–Pakistan agreement in the perspective of an exposition of his views on the world situation. He knew that I would send Ottawa a full report of the conversation and he presumably hoped that this would make the Canadian Government more sympathetic to his views. It was easy for him to give a considered exposition because he had, though I did not know it at the time of the interview, written only two weeks before a memorandum giving a general view of the world situation as he saw it. This memorandum had been sent to a number of Indian heads of mission along with a despatch setting forth the Indian arguments against the proposed military aid agreement. Nehru knew that Picard would ask him the kind of questions which would facilitate his giving us the arguments he wanted to put forward because I had warned him in advance through Pillai that Picard would raise the question of the military aid agreement.

Nehru began his exposition of his views by emphasizing the truism that the essential thing was to do everything possible to avoid another world war since it would be disastrous for everyone concerned. He could not say how such a war would end. The western powers would not have enough men on the ground to occupy such territories as Russia and China. The mere fact that China was an under-developed country and Russia so to a lesser degree meant that blows against their industrial and administrative centres would not have the same paralysing effect as blows against similar centres of the western powers. To put it in an extreme fashion, Mao Tse-tung could once more retire to the caves. Later in the conversation Nehru said that what the United States lacked was manpower. The population of the western world was small compared with the populations of the Russian and Chinese bloc. 'That is why the western powers are so anxious to get the support of Germany, Japan and [pause] Pakistan.' When Nehru said Pakistan he clearly meant India because Pakistan with a population of only 80 million could not be a source of mass armies while India with a population of 375 million could.

Nehru went on to say that, of course, if countries were attacked they would have to resist and countries had to build up their defensive forces. There was, however, 'a fine line' to be drawn between taking adequate measures of defence and taking steps which would inspire fear in the other side that they were going to be attacked. Nehru was clearly referring to what he would consider the unwise move of bringing Pakistan into a military agreement with the United States. It was also necessary, Nehru said, to balance purely military considerations against other very important considerations. It might, for example, be that the setting up of one base might alienate the sympathies of a million people. Nehru meant by this that the benefits to the United States and the western world generally of the establishment of United States bases in Pakistan might be more than offset by the loss of strength to the West which would result from alienating India.

Nehru went on to argue that the West would not be serving its own interests if it tried to bring India into a military alliance with it. If a third world war should break out, he did not believe that India would be attacked by Russia or China. The war, so far as Russia was concerned, would be fought in Europe and to a lesser degree in the Middle East. So far as China was concerned the war would be fought along its eastern borders. Why should either of them want to add to their difficulties by opening up another front against India? He then asked whether, if a third world war should break out, it was in the interests of the western powers that countries such as Pakistan and India should enter the war on their side. If they did enter, their resources were such that they could do nothing except try to defend themselves. Moreover, the fact that they were allies would mean that there was at least a moral obligation on the other allies to send them supplies and give them support. If India were to go in at the beginning of a war, it would be faced with serious internal difficulties. There would be millions of people in India who would not understand at all why it had been necessary for India to do such a thing. Certainly, in so far as India was concerned, his view was that a 'benevolent' Indian neutrality would serve the western powers better than Indian participation. A benevolently neutral India might be able to play some constructive role. (He used the word 'benevolent' at least three times.) He indicated clearly that he did not rule out the possibility that events, as the war proceeded, might make it necessary and useful for India to intervene as a belligerent on the western side.

In an effort to explain to Ottawa Nehru's suspicions of American motives in pressing for a military aid agreement with Pakistan I said that the Indians were a history-minded people and, according to their version of history, the British conquered and ruled India by playing on divisions within the country and especially by playing Muslims off against Hindus. Some Indians now suspected the Americans of a similar policy of dividing and controlling the whole subcontinent. Others believed that once a great power like the United States started on a policy of military aid to Pakistan it would willy-nilly find itself pulled more and more into the affairs of the whole subcontinent just as London had found itself drawn by its representatives in India into the conquest of India.

Since I knew that Ottawa would find it difficult to understand why the Indians were getting so excited about military aid to Pakistan of only $25 million a year I said that the Indians believed that once a programme of aid was started the United States would find itself involved in a large and continuing programme.

Dulles in his discussion with the Indian Ambassador in Washington on 17 November spoke in large terms of the importance of closing the gap in the Middle East and of the necessity of the United States helping countries such as Turkey and Pakistan which are willing to help close the gap. The Indians argue that the 35 million people of West Pakistan are not going to be able to do much to close the gap unless the United States spends hundreds of millions of dollars to help them. The Indians know that the United States has been warned by its Ambassador here of the serious effects of the agreement in India and they believe that the United States would not run these risks merely to strengthen Pakistan's armed forces by a few tens of millions of dollars.

Krishna Menon, a year or so after his resignation as minister of defence in 1962, asserted that between 1954 and 1960 the United States had 'given the Pakistanis as much as a billion dollars' worth of [military] equipment which in real as distinct from money book-value terms is probably about two and a half billion dollars' worth of equipment'.[1] Another estimate is that 'between 1955 and 1965, $1.5 billion worth of tanks, planes and a submarine were delivered to Pakistan by the United States'.[2]

On 30 November, a few days before Nixon's arrival in New Delhi, the Indian Government sent a circular despatch on the rumoured United States military agreement with Pakistan to about fifteen Indian ambassadors and high commissioners. The despatch was about twelve hundred words long and was drafted and signed by R. K. Nehru. Attached to the despatch was a memorandum by Prime Minister Nehru giving a general view of the world situation as background to the despatch. The heads of mission were instructed to speak to the government to which they were accredited on the basis of these documents. The

Indian High Commissioner in Ottawa, R. R. Saksena, not only spoke to the Acting Under-Secretary for External Affairs but followed up his talk with a letter summarizing the Indian Government's views.

The Department of External Affairs in Ottawa told me that they were surprised by the 'extravagance' of these views. I told Pillai this and showed him Saksena's letter. He said he was shocked by it. He interrupted his reading of it to protest violently against one statement in it that India's 'only offence, if it can be called an offence, has been to refuse steadfastly to subordinate her conscience to the will of the United States' and another that the arming of Pakistan by the United States would

in all probability [force India] to seek such outside assistance from other quarters as she is able to get. The cold war would thus be brought to India and it would be difficult to prevent the outbreak of actual hostilities. Because of international repercussions, hostilities in India could scarcely be localized and the probability is that these developments would lead to a world war.

When Pillai came to the last paragraph which stated that the Indian Government felt 'that the consequences of such a Pact will be serious, far-reaching and unpredictable', he said if they were unpredictable, why did Saksena try to predict them? Pillai said that he was convinced that Saksena had used stronger language than that warranted by his instructions—which he had not, however, seen—an extraordinary confession of the independent position which the author of the instructions, his second-in-command, R. K. Nehru, had established within the External Affairs Ministry.

Before I had heard from Ottawa about Saksena's letter, R. K. Nehru had read to me from his circular despatch. The despatch went into the question of the internal effects on India of the proposed agreement; it would, the despatch claimed, strengthen the extreme right, the extreme left and the communalists. The despatch also spoke of the necessity of India increasing its expenditure on defence if Pakistan received military aid from the United States. There was great emphasis on the brittle and unstable quality of the regime in Pakistan. R. K. Nehru agreed when I said to him that presumably the inference to be drawn was that if Pakistan had a strong stable government there would, in India's view, be less danger of an increase in its armed forces leading Pakistan to run risks of war with India. I told R. K. Nehru that one difficulty which India had in getting its case accepted by the mass of the people in North America was that they found it incredible that Pakistan, a country of only 80 million people, would think of attacking India, a country of 375 million. R. K. Nehru said that they should remember that Pakistan had already done this in Kashmir immediately after the partition of India, and that there were people in Pakistan who preached a holy war against India and talked of raising the crescent over the Red Fort in Delhi. I replied that it was one thing for Pakistan to send its armed forces into Kashmir to take part in a localized war, but it would be quite another for Pakistan to provoke hostilities with India which they must know would be likely to lead to a general war with India with all that that meant for the 40 million Muslim minority in India.

When this crisis broke in December 1953 I had been in India for only thirteen months. I was conscious of how slight my knowledge was of what moved the government and people of India and of how to distinguish between the propaganda of the government in the press campaigns which it inspired and its real views. I went around therefore to friends and colleagues in other diplomatic missions to share information and perceptions. In the month of December I must have had several hour-long talks with each of the top two members of the American and British missions, with the French Ambassador and with the Australian High Commissioner. I also talked to the ambassadors of Afghanistan and Nepal and with the High Commissioner of Pakistan. I found that the American, British, Australian and French envoys and I were all using much the same arguments in trying to persuade our governments of the folly of the United States in making a military aid agreement with Pakistan. The American Ambassador had little hope that his arguments would tip the balance in the administration in Washington. The rest of us had little hope that our governments would try to dissuade the United States from making the agreement.

India's position in Washington was weak. It was also weak in London. George Middleton, the second-in-command of the British mission, told me that one reason for this was that there was a pro-Pakistan lobby in London but no pro-India lobby. Most of the British army officers who had served in undivided India were pro-Muslim. Philip Noel-Baker and others like him believed that India had behaved extremely badly with Pakistan over Kashmir. Another group resented India's criticism of British colonial policy. Finally there was the Prime Minister, Winston Churchill, who was certainly not very sympathetic to India. The French Ambassador told me that when he had been in Paris on home leave a few months before he had found boredom and resentment about India among officials in his foreign office. He also found that many of them stubbornly believed that Nehru was pro-communist. When he spoke to them of his admiration for Nehru, and his conviction that Nehru was a great man, a liberal and as pro-western a prime minister as India could have, he found that his remarks were met with a feeling of impatience. He said to me in December that he had put in the strongest possible terms to the French Government his belief that the proposed agreement between Pakistan and the United States was most dangerous but he was afraid that the French Government could exert little influence in Washington on this issue. There were so many other questions of more direct concern to France on which it had to deal with the Americans—Germany, North Africa and Indo-China, for example.

In the second half of December, I tried to persuade Ottawa that the proposed military aid agreement was unwise. I began with a statement in which, I said, I thought that the American Ambassador and the High Commissioners of Britain and Australia would concur.

The short-run consequences in India of the conclusion of the agreement would be deplorable. Indo-Pakistan relations would be seriously strained and any hope which may now exist for the settlement of the Kashmir dispute would be dissipated for at least some time to come. Indo-United States relations which have been deteriorating steadily for a year would reach a new low. The relations of India with the western world and in particular the United Kingdom would be seriously affected. Many Indians now friendly to the west might become neutral or unfriendly. India would feel compelled to try to increase the strength of its armed forces *pari passu* with Pakistan's, and if it were successful in obtaining military supplies presumably from sources such as the United Kingdom and Canada, it would have to divert scarce resources from its economic development programme on the success of which the future of democratic institutions in India so largely depends.

I went on to say that the Indians might wonder whether failure by the allies of the United States, especially the United Kingdom, Canada and Australia, to dissuade the United States from making a military agreement with Pakistan at this time did not suggest that they had little influence over the policy of the leader of their coalition. The Indians might also wonder where the United Kingdom, Canada and Australia were likely to be able to exert influence on the United States if they could not do so in a matter directly affecting two other members of the Commonwealth (India and Pakistan) in an area in which, until recently, the United Kingdom had been the dominant power. If the Indians should think this way, India's ties with the Commonwealth and the value of the Commonwealth as a bridge between the Asian democracies and the west would be weakened. Other longer-run consequences of an agreement might include the strengthening of right-wing Hinduism within and outside the Congress Party. 'This group is inclined to xenophobia, is suspicious of western civilization, and has even now an equivocal attitude to the Muslim minority in India of forty millions.' Only two months before I had been fairly certain that, though there were cross-currents, in general the stream of events in India was moving in what we in the West would consider the right direction both in foreign policy and in internal development.

Even then, however, the balance was nicely poised between centrifugal and centripetal forces, between xenophobia and western influence, between frustration at the slow pace of economic advance and pride in the advance achieved. But, if the depths are stirred in India, as they probably will be if the United States gives substantial military aid to Pakistan, I do not know what the longer-run results will be. In the short run of six months or a year the Congress Party may gain strength by clasping the nationalist banner. But my guess is that in the longer run the probable result will be a strengthening of the forces in India which are inimical to the best traditions of the West and whose interests are opposed to the interests of the West.

I reported to Pearson that the American Ambassador felt that he had done all he could to dissuade his government from making a military aid agreement with Pakistan and that he had virtually requested me to urge Pearson to make clear to Washington that he considered that the disadvantages of the agreement outweighed the advantages. He had himself stressed in his communications to his government the bad effect on Commonwealth relations that such a step would have, and he thought that Pearson could use this as his point of departure.

My impression of the attitude of the United States administration to India gave me, I said, 'the uneasy feeling' that it was not 'based on a cool calculation of the long-run national interests of the United States', or on 'a careful weighing of military, political, economic and "moral" considerations, and of long-run against short-run factors' but rather that it was greatly influenced by wholly understandable but nevertheless irrational factors—in particular a resentment against Nehru for his moral lectures to mankind, his general attitude of moral superiority, his criticisms of United States policy, his organization of an opposition to the United States in the United Nations, and his failure to show gratitude to the United States for the economic aid it had given India. I concluded my appeal to Ottawa by referring to my conversation with Nehru on 10 December in which he had contended that the 'benevolent neutrality' of India and Pakistan in the event of a global war would serve the interests of the West better than belligerency, and in which he had gone on to make clear that he, himself, did not rule out the possibility that events might make it necessary and useful for India to intervene as a belligerent on the western side as the war proceeded.

My attempt to persuade Pearson that the proposed American military aid agreement with Pakistan was unwise was unsuccessful. He wrote me at the beginning of February 1954:

I agree that the United States initiative over Pakistan, if pressed relentlessly, might have a serious effect in India; certainly it has already made matters more complicated, and it does seem to reveal an inadequate appreciation by the United States of the complexities of the situation in South-East Asia. But in itself and within its limits it is not altogether a bad thing, especially when viewed in relation to forces at work elsewhere.

On 1 March 1954, four days after Eisenhower had announced

that the United States had accepted the Pakistani request for military assistance, Nehru made the kind of extreme statement in the Indian parliament which I had feared he would make. No exception could reasonably be taken to the first part of the statement in which he said:

This grant of military aid by the United States to Pakistan creates a grave situation for us in India and for Asia. It adds to our tensions. It makes it much more difficult to solve the problems which have confronted India and Pakistan.

He then, however, unwisely went on to say:

The military aid being given by the United States to Pakistan is a form of intervention in these problems.... At the present moment there are a considerable number of American observers attached to the United Nations team on either side of the 'cease-fire' line in the Jammu and Kashmir state. These American observers can no longer be treated by us as neutrals in this dispute and hence their presence there appears to us to be improper.

Louis St Laurent had been on an official visit to India when the controversy over the military aid agreement was at its height. He left India the day before this statement was made. When he read it he told one of his advisers that he strongly disapproved of it; Nehru's attitude, he said, was unworthy of a statesman. Before learning of this I had reported to Pearson that St Laurent's visit to India had deepened the understanding and friendship between St Laurent and Nehru. Clearly this judgement needed to be qualified. St Laurent's speeches in India and his press conference had increased knowledge of and respect for Canada in India. St Laurent, himself, as a result of his visit, had more sympathy and respect for the people of India; he had more understanding of their problems; but he may have had less respect for Nehru as a statesman, and this, I think, not just because of Nehru's rash statement about American U.N. observers in Kashmir but also because of Nehru's use of the military aid agreement as a reason or excuse for not going ahead with arrangements for a plebiscite in Kashmir. St Laurent's views were shared by Pearson.

It is possible that Nehru at this time was beginning to realize that he had in the past, as Pearson had suggested to me in September 1952, tended to exaggerate Canada's influence and freedom of action in international affairs. Nehru himself gave me no indication of this, but Krishna Menon, who sometimes reflected his views, was by January 1954, as I reported to Ottawa, becoming more and more pessimistic about the possibilities of the allies of the United States, such as the United Kingdom and Canada, exercising their independent judgement on matters in which the United States took a firm line. He instanced as an example of this what he understood had been the inactivity of the United Kingdom, Australia, New Zealand and Canada on the question of United States military aid to Pakistan.

American military aid to Pakistan continued, for the rest of my stay in India, to bedevil relations between India and the West. In a despatch on Indian foreign policy which I sent to Ottawa just before I left India in May 1957 I said that this aid indeed constituted the most important single issue dividing India from the West and that it coloured Indian attitudes to many other—perhaps most other—international questions. The reason was that Pakistan played much the same role in the formation and carrying out of Indian foreign policy as Russia did in the formation and carrying out of United States foreign policy. Indian foreign policy was dominated by a fear of Pakistan just as United States foreign policy was dominated by a fear of Russia. In order to contain Russia the Americans were willing to make friends and allies with any country that would stand up and be counted on their side, no matter what the motives of that country or the nature of its internal regime. Similarly India was prepared to make friends with countries such as Saudi Arabia, Egypt and Yugoslavia, in its efforts to contain Pakistan. The United States had on many occasions had to sacrifice a lesser good to gain a greater good. Similarly India had to fall in with Arab views on Israel even to the extent of having to repudiate in public the suggestion that it might be contemplating establishing diplomatic relations with Israel. The Indian attitude to military pacts had been entirely determined by its feelings towards Pakistan. India had voiced no objection to military pacts and to the provision of arms by the United States and Britain to allied and friendly countries until the United States began to contemplate giving arms to Pakistan and bringing Pakistan into its military pacts. My conclusion was that unless the United States ceased to build up Pakistan's armed forces India would have to increase its expenditure on defence.

This will mean greater imports of expensive armaments at the expense of supplies for the second five-year plan which is already being set back by India's shortage both of foreign exchange and of domestic resources. In order to diminish the drain on its scarce foreign exchange India may feel itself driven to accept Russian offers to deliver arms quickly at relatively low prices and on easy credit. The effect of this on the direction of Indian foreign policy could be enormous.

At the end of the seventies the State Department in Washington admitted that some of the criticisms made in the fifties of American policies in the Middle East and South Asia such as American arms aid to Pakistan were justified. A spokesman said in October 1978:

In our preoccupation with the outside threats to the area we were, no doubt, not sufficiently conscious of the conflicting motives of the nations of the area in joining with us [in defence arrangements]. They had their local objectives, their local rivalries which often transcended their concern over external forces. . . . The one-dimensional strategic view of the 1950s and early 1960s has been replaced by a more diverse, and more complex outlook. . . . We no longer look at the region exclusively through the prism of East–West rivalry. . . . We have no desire to return to the rhetoric and political environment of the fifties and sixties.[3]

CHAPTER NINE

KASHMIR

When Louis St Laurent was in New Delhi at the end of February 1954 he said to Nehru in a private conversation that outside India Nehru's policy on Kashmir was quite widely regarded as incompatible with the idealistic and pacific principles of which he was the spokesman. (St Laurent also put this point to the Vice-President, Radhakrishnan.) Nehru's reply to this was that he knew that he was accused of being intransigent on Kashmir because his family was of Kashmiri origin. This was not true. The idea that the Vale of Kashmir should go to Pakistan merely because it was Muslim was contrary to his whole concept of India. He did not believe, as the theorists of Pakistan did, that before partition there had been two nations in India, one Hindu and one Muslim, that the partition of India was based on this two-nation theory, and that India was a Hindu state. India was not a Hindu state; it was a secular state.

I believed then and I believe now that Nehru was right in stating that the Vale of Kashmir should not go to Pakistan merely because it was Muslim and contiguous to Pakistan. If the majority of the people in the Vale wanted to be part of India their wishes should prevail. But equally, if the majority wanted to be part of Pakistan, whether because they were Muslims or for any other reason, their wishes should prevail, and almost every impartial observer agreed that if the people of the Vale were given a choice between India and Pakistan the great majority would choose Pakistan. Whether they would do so if they were given the alternative of independence was another matter. The more I studied the Kashmir dispute the more I regretted two errors which it seemed to me Mountbatten had made at the time of partition. The first was that before partition took place he did not press the Maharaja of the state of Jammu and Kashmir to arrange for the accession of Kashmir, which was predominantly Muslim, to Pakistan, and of Jammu, which was predominantly Hindu, to India. (I did not know until years later when I read B. N. Pandey's *Nehru* that Mountbatten would not have had to press the Maharaja to do this since this was in substance what the Maharaja wanted to do. He wanted to accede to India in respect of Jammu and leave Kashmir to its fate, which presumably meant that it would become part of Pakistan. It was Nehru who insisted that the whole of Jammu and Kashmir should accede to India.[1]) The second error which it seemed to me Mountbatten had made was that he advised the Indian Government that before it sent help to Kashmir to repel the invasion of tribesmen from Pakistan the state of Jammu and Kashmir should accede to India. There had been no necessity for this. An independent state has the right to ask a friendly country to send it help to repel an invader; a friendly country has the right to accede to the request; Kashmir, at the time, had in this context the status of an independent country. During the whole of the discussion of the Kashmir issue by the United Nations the waters were muddied by India's constantly repeated assertion that, because Kashmir was legally a part of India, it was wrong for the United Nations to treat Pakistan as having equal status with India in the dispute.

*   *   *

In March 1953, three months after my arrival in India, Pillai brought up the subject of Kashmir when I was making one of my periodic calls on him. He made it clear to me that he had set his heart, in what he said was going to be a brief tenure as Secretary-General of the External Affairs Ministry, on getting a settlement on Kashmir and that he had always had reservations about the wisdom of what Nehru's critics called his intransigent position on Kashmir. His idea was that, before the next talks between India and Pakistan on Kashmir, he would suggest to Nehru that the time had come for India to make a new approach to the Kashmir question in an effort to get a settlement, even though this would involve departures from principles which the Indian Government had considered important. My impression is that Pillai did speak to Nehru and with some success, for when the next conversations between India and Pakistan on Kashmir took place four months after my talk with Pillai, Nehru was prepared to make more concessions than in previous discussions.

Kashmir

These talks began with a visit by Nehru to Karachi in July 1953 to talk to the new Prime Minister of Pakistan, Mohammad Ali. The new High Commissioner of Pakistan to India, Raja Ghazanfar Ali Khan, told me on 7 August that he was greatly encouraged by the good results of the visit. The spontaneous popular demonstration of welcome to Nehru in Karachi must have convinced him that the people of Pakistan had no feelings of enmity or bitterness towards him or India and that they wanted to get relations between the two countries established on friendly foundations. The talks had strengthened Mohammad Ali's hands. When he first took office, he had given speeches about going more than half-way to meet India and he had made very friendly references to Nehru. When he gave the speeches he could not know whether or not he had the people behind him, but the demonstrations on Nehru's visit and the fact that, during his visit, there was no criticism of Mohammad Ali's position in any Pakistan newspaper, were indications that he did have the people behind him. Finally, Mohammad Ali and Nehru had got to know each other. The Pakistan High Commissioner added that, if the Kashmir dispute was not settled in a matter of weeks, it would never be settled or at least not settled for years. It must, he said, be settled when Mohammad Ali paid his return visit to New Delhi.

Mohammad Ali arrived in New Delhi on 17 August. Two days before I had attended the Indian Independence Day celebrations at the Red Fort in Old Delhi. In his speech to the hundred thousand people gathered in front of the Red Fort, Nehru appealed to the people of Delhi to give the Prime Minister of Pakistan a warm welcome when he arrived at the airport. They responded with an excess of enthusiasm. The heads of mission went to the airport to join in the welcome. We were seated in front of a flimsy barrier separating us from thousands of people. Nehru walked up and down in front of the barrier, before Mohammad Ali's plane had arrived, lecturing the crowd on how they were to behave. Afterwards when they broke their ranks and chaos ensued, he tried to clear a way for the visitor by waving his baton at the crowd and shouting angrily at them. A day or so later I mentioned this incident to him. He said, 'You can do anything to an Indian crowd, even curse at them, and they won't mind, provided you do it in a friendly way.'

On the second day of Mohammad Ali's visit a state dinner was held in his honour at Rashtrapati Bhavan, the President's residence. Almost every prominent Indian Muslim was there. They met old colleagues, friends and relations who had accompanied Mohammad Ali to New Delhi. At the dinner some Muslim families were reunited for the first time since partition six years before. I had about half an hour's talk with Nehru after the dinner. He was very tired and I did not try to find out what had happened in his talks with Mohammad Ali. We talked about the reception which the city of Delhi had given to Mohammad Ali at the Red Fort that afternoon. Nehru said that it had been a very moving performance and that Mohammad Ali had been deeply touched by it; even some of the tough people who had come with him were touched. Nehru, himself, had obviously been greatly moved. He said to me that the people of Delhi were capable of great brutality, but they were also capable of great affection. What had happened as a result of Mohammad Ali's visit was that Delhi had once again realized that it was a city of two cultures. Poems had been recited in Urdu saying to the former Muslim citizens of Delhi who had migrated to Pakistan—'We wish you were back with us'. Four days later Nehru again spoke to me about the demonstrations. He said Mohammad Ali had not been known personally in Delhi. The only thing the people of Delhi knew about him was that he stood for friendship with India. That was why they had acclaimed him.

The day after the reception in the Red Fort the newspapers reported that Mohammad Ali had said at the reception that he was 'overwhelmed and deeply touched by the cordiality and exuberance of the reception' that had been given to him by the citizens of Delhi. 'I feel I am in no foreign country and I am no stranger among you. Delhi has given me a right royal reception and I shall cherish this memory for the whole of my life.' He referred to India and Pakistan as twin sister nations.

On 20 August, the day the talks between the prime ministers ended with the issuance of a joint communiqué, Pillai and his wife dined alone with us. He was so optimistic about the results of the talks as to be euphoric. The impression I gathered from him was that Nehru had told Mohammad Ali that it should be possible to hold the plebiscite in Kashmir in April 1955 or at least between April and October of 1955. The only qualification which Pillai put on his optimism was 'provided the atmosphere in Karachi remains good'. What he meant by that was, provided the Governor-General of Pakistan (Ghulam Mohammad) and Mohammad Ali could hold the line against extremists in the Pakistan cabinet.

My impression at the time, chiefly derived from talks with Pillai and with Badr-ud-din Tyabji, the senior Muslim officer in the External Affairs Ministry, was that the Indians considered that it should be clear to any well-disposed member of the Pakistan cabinet that India, for the first time in many years, was prepared to make substantial concessions in the Kashmir dispute. The principal concession, according to them, was implicit in India's agreement that the plebiscite administrator should be appointed by the end of April 1954 and that, before then, the two prime ministers would, on the advice of committees of military and other experts, consider the 'preliminary issues', arrive at agreements on them, and give effect to those agreements. They said that this agreement on a fixed date meant that India had decided to compromise on the preliminary issues: demilitarization of Kashmir, the nature of the administration in various parts of Kashmir at the time of the plebiscite, and the size of the areas which could opt out of the result of the voting in the state as a whole. In my report to Ottawa I said:

The communiqué rejects any decision on the future of Jammu and Kashmir other than by a plebiscite of the whole of Jammu and Kashmir, but this is qualified by the proviso that the settlement of the Kashmir dispute should cause 'the least disturbance to the life of the people of the State'. This phrase has been interpreted, in my opinion correctly, as meaning that the prime ministers agreed that, regardless of the total vote in Jammu and Kashmir, areas contiguous to India which vote overwhelmingly for India will go to India, and areas contiguous to Pakistan which vote overwhelmingly for Pakistan will go to Pakistan. The bad word 'partition' is carefully avoided but partition is what is meant. It is thus legitimate to assume that the prime ministers agreed that Jammu, which is overwhelmingly Hindu, and Ladakh, which is Buddhist, should go to India, and that the mountainous region now occupied by Pakistani troops should go to Pakistan. Thus, though the plebiscite would cover the whole of Jammu and Kashmir, its practical effect would be limited to the Vale of Kashmir.

In the two weeks following the talks between the prime ministers, the pendulum in government circles in New Delhi swung from somewhat incautious optimism about the future of Indo-Pakistan relations to restrained pessimism. The Indians I talked to said that instead of encouraging India in its new willingness to make concessions to Pakistan over Kashmir, the Pakistan Government had administered a series of rebuffs to India. All but one of these were directly connected with the talks on Kashmir. The unconnected rebuff was that Pakistan was the only member of the Commonwealth to vote on 27 August in the U.N. General Assembly against Indian membership of the Korean peace conference. From New Delhi this vote looked like a childish exhibition of spite. The other rebuffs or attempts to sabotage the efforts of the prime ministers to reach agreement were the violent press campaign against India which had been directed by some of the cabinet ministers and senior officials in Karachi, and the Pakistani insistence on taking the most difficult of the 'preliminary questions' first, the appointment of a plebiscite administrator, instead of taking the easiest first and so creating an atmosphere which would facilitate the solution of the more difficult.

I reported to Ottawa on 5 September, two weeks after the conclusion of the talks between the prime ministers, that the Indian officials I had talked to had not given up hope but that they were pessimistic. In their opinion, everything now depended on the stability of Mohammad Ali's regime. There were bound to be ups and downs in the relations between the two countries until a plebiscite was held, there were bound to be setbacks, there was bound to be friction since both governments would be bidding against each other for votes in Kashmir. But if Mohammad Ali could assert his position and get his government behind him, the Indians believed there could be a satisfactory settlement of the Kashmir problem. My own opinion was that if the forces of moderation could secure control of the situation in Pakistan, there was a good possibility that within two years a settlement of the Kashmir question could be reached, with all that that implied for the future of the relations between what Mohammad Ali had called the twin sister nations of India and Pakistan.

No settlement was reached. Most of the heads of mission in

New Delhi whom I talked to at the time, including the American Ambassador, believed that Nehru had never intended to make a settlement. This also appears to have been the dominant view in the State Department in Washington. Donald Kennedy was then concerned with Kashmir affairs in the State Department. Later he became United States Chargé d'Affaires in New Delhi. He said flatly to me (in January 1955) when he was chargé that he 'knew' that Nehru was never prepared to run the risk of losing the Vale of Kashmir. A small minority of heads of mission in New Delhi, including the Australian High Commissioner, Walter Crocker, and I, believed that in August 1953 Nehru was for the first time prepared, in the interests of improving relations with Pakistan, to run the risk of losing the Vale but that his willingness to make concessions to Pakistan which would have made possible the holding of a plebiscite had ceased to exist in or around December 1953 because of the negotiations between the United States and Pakistan for a military aid agreement. I was supported in my view by conversations with the Vice-President of India, the Pakistan High Commissioner to India, and three senior officials of the Indian Government with special responsibilities for Kashmir matters.

The Vice-President, Radhakrishnan, told me (in March 1954) that he had pleaded with the American Ambassador, George Allen, to urge his government to announce that, in the light of the very strong reaction in India to the proposed military aid to Pakistan and particularly of the danger that this aid might interfere with the peaceful settlement of the Kashmir question, the United States was postponing for a year the actual granting of military aid to Pakistan in order to give India and Pakistan an opportunity to reach a peaceful settlement of the Kashmir question. The Pakistan High Commissioner told me (in April 1954) that before the issue of American military aid to Pakistan had been raised he had been extremely hopeful of a peaceful settlement of the Kashmir question but that he was now most pessimistic. He said that, if it had not been for American military aid to Pakistan, he thought that a plebiscite administrator would have been appointed by then. Radhakrishnan confirmed this. He told me that, just at the time the controversy broke out over American military aid to Pakistan, India was about to agree with Pakistan on a Swiss or a Swede as the plebiscite administrator in Kashmir. Pillai said to me (in March 1954) that before the military agreement was made there had been a good possiblity of India and Pakistan reaching agreement on Kashmir and that, even granting the American case that the arming of Pakistan strengthened the free world, a delay of six months or so, to give India and Pakistan time to settle their differences, would not have been serious. Vishnu Sahay was at the time Secretary of Labour (that is, the senior civil servant in the Department of Labour) and also Secretary of Kashmir Affairs. He told me (in March 1954), in commenting on the American military aid agreement, that if the United States had only let things alone for another six months, India and Pakistan would have come to a peaceful agreement on Kashmir. M. J. Desai, a senior member of the External Affairs Ministry, had been in charge of the Indian group of officials who conducted the negotiations with Pakistan officials which resulted from the agreement reached by the two prime ministers in August 1953. He told me (in April 1956) that there had then been a good chance of agreement being reached between the two governments on Kashmir if the Pakistanis had been acting in good faith, but while they were pretending to be trying to reach agreement with India they were at the same time negotiating without India's knowledge with the United States in order to secure arms.

When I read in 1979 the authoritative biography of Nehru by Sarvepalli Gopal which is based on access to Nehru's private papers I found to my delight that Gopal believes from his study of these papers that Nehru was prepared in August 1953 to agree to a plebiscite in Kashmir even though this might well result in India losing the Vale of Kashmir. 'The evidence', he writes, 'suggests that [Nehru's] offer [of a plebiscite] had been genuine and would have held if the prospect of a military alliance between Pakistan and the United States had not impinged on it.'[2]

Whether the United States ever considered postponing their military aid agreement with Pakistan for six months or a year in order to give India and Pakistan a chance to settle their dispute over Kashmir without this extraneous disturbance, I do not know. If George Allen, the American Ambassador, believed, as I am pretty certain he did, that Nehru had never intended to make a settlement on Kashmir, it is unlikely that he would have recommended this. I was myself, as I put it in a telegram to Ottawa in mid-December 1953, 'inclined to believe' that the indefinite deferring of the military aid agreement 'would restore an atmosphere in which a settlement of the Kashmir dispute might again become possible'. When I asked George Allen at the end of March whether Washington had considered this possibility he said that if at any time from December to February the United States Government had received an authoritative indication from the Indian Government that their objection to the aid had not been based on wide considerations about military aid to countries in this part of the world generally, but on the effect on the Kashmir dispute, they might have been prepared to speak along these lines to the Indians. The danger, however, was that the Indians would consider that they were being blackmailed into coming to an agreement on Kashmir.

My belief that Nehru in August and September 1953 was prepared to make a settlement with Pakistan over Kashmir even though this involved the possible loss of the Vale to Pakistan and that the settlement was frustrated by American military aid to Pakistan, did not mean that I believed that it was right or prudent of Nehru to allow the issue of American military aid to Pakistan to frustrate the possibility of a settlement of the Kashmir question. I did not believe this. I said to Ottawa, 'I cannot see any logical connection between United States military aid to Pakistan and a denial by India of the right of self-determination for the people of Kashmir.'

In the year 1954 Nehru did not, so far as I was aware, rule out an eventual plebiscite in Kashmir, but from some time in 1955 on he did and he began saying in private that he saw no solution to the Kashmir problem except the acceptance by India and Pakistan of the existing situation: the ceasefire line would be made permanent with minor adjustments, with the result that Pakistan would get one-third of the State of Jammu and Kashmir and India, two-thirds. The first time I had firm confirmation that this was Nehru's position was at the beginning of March 1956 when Selwyn Lloyd, the British Foreign Minister, visited India. Selwyn Lloyd then told me that Nehru had said this to him. A few days later Pillai confirmed to me that this was indeed Nehru's view.

It seemed to me at the time that the unconvincing, legalistic, often irrelevant and sometimes internally inconsistent arguments which India advanced in public against a plebiscite in Kashmir were not the arguments which Nehru would advance in private in a frank off-the-record discussion with St Laurent or Pearson. I therefore reported to Pearson in a despatch in April 1956 that I thought that in such a discussion Nehru might speak along the following lines:

It would be possible for the pro-Pakistan elements in Kashmir to fight the plebiscite campaign on the orthodox Muslim League theory that there are two nations on the sub-continent, one Hindu and one Muslim, and that the Vale of Kashmir, being a predominantly Muslim area contiguous to Pakistan, should become part of Pakistan. The campaign might begin this way, but it is almost inevitable that as it developed the pro-Pakistan elements in Kashmir would make an emotional and communal appeal to the Muslims of Kashmir, urging them that it was their duty to their religion to vote for Pakistan since their traditions and their religion would not be safe if Kashmir were part of Hindu-dominated India. This argument, if valid in Kashmir, would be equally valid in India. This means that the pro-Pakistan elements in Kashmir would be telling the 45 million Muslims in India that their traditions and their religion are not safe in India with its 300 million Hindus. This in itself would increase tension in India between Muslims and Hindus. The increase in tension within India would add fuel to the flames of communal controversy in Kashmir. If the plebiscite resulted in a vote in favour of Pakistan, Hindu extremists in India would say that the Muslims in Kashmir had demonstrated by their vote for Pakistan that if their 45 million co-religionists in India also had a similar chance to express a preference between India and Pakistan, they too would express a preference for Pakistan. The Hindu extremists would go on to say that here was clear proof of what they had always asserted—that the loyalty of the Muslims in India is to Pakistan and not to India. The Muslim minority in India should, therefore, be forced to get out of India or be relegated to the role of second-class citizens.

The increase of tension in India between Muslims and Hindus would be accompanied by an even greater increase of tension in East Pakistan between the Hindu minority of eight million and the Muslim majority of 35 million. Already the Hindus in East Pakistan are finding life so intolerable there that they are streaming out of Pakistan into India at a rate of 30 to 50 thousand a month. As tension between Hindu and Muslim grew in the sub-continent, the fears of the Hindu minority in East Pakistan would increase. Their persecution would increase and the flow of Hindus from East Pakistan to India might become a mass exodus accompanied by the usual stories of looting, rape, murder and forcible conversions to Islam. Already the flow of Hindu refugees out of East Pakistan into India is arousing bitterness and communal passions in India. If this flow becomes a mass exodus it is likely to lead to increasingly strong demands in India, either to seize land from Pakistan on which to settle the refugees or at least to eject a corresponding number of Muslims from India to make room for the Hindu refugees from East Pakistan. No one who was present in India or Pakistan in the tragic days of 1947 would be prepared to rule out the possibility of much worse than this happening. There might once again be mass communal disturbances in both India and East Pakistan and mass slaughter and this could lead to armed conflict between the two countries. The catastrophic effects of such a development would extend far beyond the borders of this sub-continent. Even if armed conflict did not break out, certainly relations between the minorities and the majorities in both India and Pakistan would have become much more tense, as would have relations between India and Pakistan. Mounting defence expenditures would interfere—perhaps fatally—with programmes for economic development. The forces of Hindu xenophobia in India and of Islamic theocracy in Pakistan would be strengthened. The possibility of success in establishing secular states in India and Pakistan would become remote.

I said to Pearson that I considered that Nehru's argument against a plebiscite in Kashmir was strong but that it was not, as Nehru appeared to suggest, an argument in favour of the partition of Kashmir on the basis of the ceasefire line. Rather it was an argument for Azad Kashmir (the part of Kashmir occupied by Pakistan) remaining with Pakistan; Jammu and Ladakh remaining with India; and the Vale of Kashmir becoming an independent state of which both India and Pakistan would be guardians. India would have a right of passage through the Vale to Ladakh. The area of the Vale was only about one-eighth of the area of the state of Jammu and Kashmir. It had a population in 1956 of about a million and a quarter of whom ninety per cent were Muslims. An independent Vale of Kashmir would be separated from China by a belt of Pakistani or Indian territory at least a hundred miles wide.

In February 1957, ten months later, the Kashmir issue once again came to the boiling point. Pakistan submitted the question to the U.N. Security Council. Britain and the United States put forward a resolution which the Indian Government, according to Pillai, considered to be loaded against India. It was the kind of resolution, Pillai said, which made it much more difficult for Nehru, after the general election campaign which was then taking place was over, to come forward with some constructive suggestions for a solution as an alternative to a plebiscite. He did not add what I told Ottawa were two other relevant facts. The first was that many Indians suspected that the British Government's attitude on Kashmir was motivated mainly by its anger at the Indian attitude to its actions over Suez. The second was that to the Indians the present membership of the Security Council represented a low ebb. Not only was China not represented but Asia was represented by Iraq and the Philippines, and the Commonwealth seat was held by Australia.

Krishna Menon spoke in the Security Council at great length and with much passion against the Anglo-American resolution. Nehru declared in an interview with the press that in speaking with passion Menon had 'represented the passion of India'. Menon may have faithfully represented the passion of India but he did not present on behalf of India arguments which were convincing to most friends of India in the West.

In the middle of February 1957 I was, for the first and last time in my four and a half years in India, summoned to the External Affairs Ministry to be given an exposition of the views of the Indian Government on Kashmir. The Indians at this time believed that the Kashmir issue was about to be referred to the U.N. General Assembly and I later found out that almost all the heads of mission of members of the U.N. had received similar summons. This was also the first, and only, time in my stay in India that in a talk with a senior officer at the External Affairs Ministry I was constantly addressed, in order presumably to emphasize the formality and solemnity of the occasion, as 'Mr High Commissioner'. The officer I talked to was M. J. Desai who worked directly under Krishna Menon on the Kashmir question. Though he spoke without notes he was obviously speaking on the basis of a memorandum written or at least approved by Krishna Menon and Nehru. When I indicated to him that I thought that some of the language he was using was too strong he said, 'Mr High Commissioner, I do not, as you know, normally use strong language but in this case I am using strong language deliberately.'

Desai began our conversation by saying that until he had seen the text of the resolution submitted to the Security Council by the United States and Britain he had assumed that they had misunderstood the Indian position, but he now knew that the resolution was a deliberate and mischievous attempt to harass India. When the issue went before the General Assembly, what would be Canada's position? 'Do you want to split the Commonwealth?' Presumably he meant by this, 'Does Canada want to help drive India out of the Commonwealth?' He then put forward the Indian argument that India was no longer bound by its promise to hold a plebiscite in Kashmir because the U.N. resolutions had stipulated that the plebiscite was to be the last of five steps, and Pakistan had failed to carry out the preliminary step of withdrawing its forces from Kashmir. He followed this up by the argument against a plebiscite which I had put in my despatch to Pearson of April 1956.

After Desai had completed his exposition of the Indian case on Kashmir I told him that I had received no instructions from Ottawa on Canada's position and what I would say represented only my personal views. He had said that the essence of the Indian case was that a plebiscite was not in the interests of India or Pakistan because it would cause instability in the whole subcontinent and would especially endanger the position of the 45 million Muslims in India. In my attempt to put forward to Ottawa what I considered to be the Indian case I had developed this point at some length. I assumed, however, that it was difficult for the authorities in Ottawa to agree that this was the substantial Indian case when it formed a very small part of the arguments put forward by Krishna Menon in the Security Council and by Nehru in his speeches in India. Desai replied that the Security Council was a 'court of law' and Menon had to put forward India's full case for the record. I said the Security Council was not a court of law but a political body whose task was to find practical solutions in accordance with international justice. It seemed to me that people in the West regarded the issue as one of the right of the people of Kashmir to self-determination. The Indian reply to this presumably was that the people of Kashmir would have to be deprived of this right because the exercise of it would be bad for the peoples of the whole subcontinent. (An Indian official later put this argument succinctly to me: 'The Muslims of Kashmir must be sacrificed in the interests of the Muslims of India.') The Indian spokesmen had, however, never made this position clear. Moreover, he (M. J. Desai) must know that for one reason or another, be it the stupidity of people in the West or the inadequacy of the Indian Government's Information Service, almost all of India's best friends in the West had for long been convinced that India was in the wrong on Kashmir. So far as I knew Menon's speeches in New York had not served to convert one of India's friends to India's side. My guess, for example, was that if India made a list of those it considered its hundred best friends in Britain and polled them on the Kashmir issue, it would find that ninety thought India was in the wrong. My feeling was that India had a strong case on Kashmir which it had not put, but that the case which India had put had not impressed the West.

Desai had used particularly violent language about the proposal in the resolution before the Security Council that a U.N. force be sent to Kashmir. Because of the violence of his language I took him up on this. I said I could not believe it was right to assume that everyone who favoured a U.N. force did so out of malevolence to India. For the last three years the Indians had been trying to persuade everybody that they were frightened of a Pakistan, armed by the United States, attacking India. Surely some friends of India might say that interposing a U.N. force between the Indian and Pakistan forces in Kashmir might at least prevent an invasion of India from Pakistan on that part of the border. This angered Desai. He said, 'First of all the United States gives arms to Pakistan. This creates a danger of war. Then it is said that western troops have to move into Kashmir to protect India. The next point in the argument presumably would be that western troops should move into the whole of India to protect India against Pakistan.'

At the conclusion of our hour-long talk I promised Desai that I would, of course, report immediately to Pearson his exposition of the Indian case and India's appeal for Canadian support when the issue came before the General Assembly. I added that

I myself had been deeply disturbed by developments on the Kashmir issue during the previous few months, particularly since I knew that these developments had put a further strain on India's relations with Britain, already greatly strained because of the Suez affair: 'Since India still seems to think of the Commonwealth as a wheel with Britain at the centre and the rest of us on the rim, I realize that for India the strain in its relations with Britain means a strain on its relations with the whole Commonwealth.'

When I reported to Pearson on my talk with Desai I said:

It would be unwise to discount the depth of feeling aroused here by the recent British actions in relation to Kashmir. My impression is that India's connection with the Commonwealth may be more in danger now than it was even at the beginning of November in the worst days of the Suez crisis. India then felt the moral glow of being a self-righteous chastiser of Great Britain. Nehru was willing to stay in a Commonwealth in which Great Britain was the culprit. He may be less willing to stay in a Commonwealth in which Great Britain and Australia line up with Pakistan in accusing him of being the culprit. I do not need to emphasize to you the effect of Indian withdrawal from the Commonwealth. It would diminish, if not destroy, the possibility of the experiment in a multiracial Commonwealth succeeding. . . . It would destroy a bridge between India and the West at a time when the bridge between India and the United States lacks firm foundations.

The Kashmir question did not come before the General Assembly. Canada did not have to speak or vote on a resolution on the question. India did not leave the Commonwealth. But the re-emergence of the Kashmir question at the U.N. in the early months of 1957, following the rift between India and the West caused by Nehru's attitude to the Hungarian Revolution (dealt with in a succeeding chapter), widened the gap between India and the West and eroded the special relationship between India and Canada. And what was even more important, Kashmir stood in the way of the establishment of good relations between India and Pakistan. In April 1957, on the eve of my departure from India, I tried in a farewell despatch to assess the main successes and the main failures of Indian foreign policy. Weighing successes against failures I concluded that on balance Indian foreign policy had been a failure since India had failed to achieve the most important goal of any realistic Indian foreign policy, the establishment of good relations with Pakistan. As soon as it was clear that there was going to be partition, the national interests of India required that the primary objective of Indian foreign policy should be the healing of the wounds of partition and the beginning of a period of reconciliation which should eventually lead to even closer relations between India and Pakistan than those which existed between Canada and the United States. First, for example, a Permanent Joint Board on Defence, an International Joint Commission, special facilities for border-crossing, low trade barriers; then joint organs for consultation on all matters of common concern; ultimately a customs union and a defence alliance. I went on to say:

Indian foreign policy and diplomacy have not been able to make progress in this direction. The responsibility for failure must, of course, be shared by Pakistan, but it is reasonable to place the greater share of the responsibility for failure on India, since India is about five times as important as Pakistan, and it has had, unlike Pakistan, the advantages of a strong, stable, popular national administration under a leader of genius. The stumbling block to the achievement of good relations between India and Pakistan is Kashmir. In order to hold Kashmir, India has sacrificed an immensely greater national interest.

CHAPTER TEN

KRUSHCHEV–BULGANIN VISIT

Krushchev and Bulganin (then the Soviet Prime Minister) spent two weeks in India at the end of November and the beginning of December 1955. After three days in New Delhi they went on a ten-day tour of India. Then after a week in Burma they returned to Delhi for three days. Just before they arrived I reported to Ottawa:

India is the only country on this side of the curtain that the two top Soviet leaders have considered warranted a two weeks' visit. This is flattering to India's feeling of self-importance. It and the week's visit to Burma also indicate, I suggest, that the Soviet Union attaches very great importance to winning the friendship and support of India and Burma. India is preparing to welcome the Soviet leaders with demonstrations and festivities modelled after those put on for Nehru during his recent visit to the Soviet Union. There is an almost slavish copying of Soviet precedents, such as highly organized spontaneous mass demonstrations chanting government-selected slogans. Miles of the route are being lined with thousands of flags and with triumphal arches. The Soviet leaders are being welcomed in a way in which no outsider has been welcomed since Independence.

Preparations for the Soviet leaders' visit extended to changing the road signs on the road from the airport to the President's house. They had been in English; now they were made bilingual, Hindi and English. Some people even thought that the decision to change the names of two of the principal avenues in New Delhi was taken in anticipation of the visit. Queensway was changed to Jan Path (people's road) and Kingsway to Raj Path (state road). The Indians, however, with the usual Indian affection for paradox, did not change the name of the principal road from the airport, Kitchener Road, nor Roberts Road which led from Kitchener Road to the Prime Minister's residence.

With the other ambassadors and high commissioners I was at

the airport to greet the Soviet visitors on their arrival in New Delhi, and I went to the civic reception for them the next day. The size of the crowds and their discipline were impressive. About a million people lined the twelve-mile route from the airport to the President's residence. At the civic reception at least six hundred thousand people were present. I had never seen such a mass of people in one place. The platform was about twenty feet high and Nehru told me that from there the crowds stretched farther away than he could see. The crowd was so well-behaved at the civic reception that Nehru had to tell them good-humouredly to be a little more demonstrative and he became a sort of cheer-leader, leading the crowd in shouting the slogans of Indo-Soviet friendship, *Hindi-Rusi ek hai* (Indians and Russians are one) and *Hindi-Rusi bhai bhai* (Indians and Russians are brothers). (At the banquet the Soviet leaders gave just before leaving India, the speeches were full of references to Russia and India being brothers. One senior Indian civil servant whispered to me, 'Do you remember Talleyrand's remark, "Je préfère les cousins." He had experienced too much "fraternité" during the French Revolution.')

In my report to Ottawa I tried to answer the question why such large crowds turned out for the Soviet leaders.

Many people think that it probably had not very much to do with the fact that the visitors were Russian. The Prime Minister had asked them to turn out, jeeps had toured the city equipped with loudspeakers the day before they arrived urging the people to line the route, a half holiday had been proclaimed and the government provided buses and trucks to carry people to the route. Pandit Pant, the wise second-in-command in the cabinet, beside whom I sat at the Prime Minister's banquet for the Soviet leaders, said that he thought that in a couple of weeks from now all that the villagers who came to Delhi would remember was that they had been to a big reception in Delhi for some important people, and that they had seen the Prime Minister.

Nehru was clearly on edge the day the Soviet leaders arrived but by the time the vast civic reception took place twenty-four hours later he was jubilant, and the next day at the President's reception for the Soviet leaders Indira Gandhi and he were overflowing with good spirits. At that reception, Marquis Childs, the American columnist, who was staying with us, and my wife and I had a talk with Indira Gandhi. She said the visit of the Soviet leaders was important because it had given the Indian people more self-confidence. Marquis Childs said he supposed that she was referring to the fact that the Soviet leaders had shown the importance they attached to India by their decision to spend two weeks there. 'No,' she said, 'it is not that at all, it is that our people have proved to themselves that they could put on just as good a show in Delhi as the Russians put on for my father in Moscow.' She went on to say that many people in India had seen the films of Nehru's visit to Russia, which showed the tremendous and disciplined welcome which masses of the Russian people had given him. Many of them had felt that the Indians were not disciplined enough to give this kind of mass demonstration. When the Russian visitors came, she was in the seventh car in the procession from the airport and as she passed in her car people would call out, 'Haven't we done just as well as they did?' Indira Gandhi went on to say how much she liked the easy, friendly informality of the relations between Bulganin and Krushchev. Marquis Childs said that he thought Bulganin looked like a southern senator and Krushchev like a Brooklyn politician. Indira Gandhi replied that she had by now travelled to most countries in the world and never had she seen so many American types as on her visit to the Soviet Union.

Many people in the West were irritated by the tumultuous welcome which the Indians gave to Krushchev and Bulganin. They were even more irritated by the crude anti-western statements which the Soviet leaders made in India and by Nehru's failure to take public exception to them. Thus the Soviet leaders charged that the western powers had precipitated the Second World War in 1939 and Hitler's attack on the Soviet Union in 1941. They also revived in their speeches grudges going back to the western intervention in Russia after the revolution in 1917. After the Soviet leaders had completed the first part of their visit to India and had gone to Burma I sent Ottawa a provisional assessment of the results of the visit. I said that my guess was that Krushchev and Bulganin must now think that they had gone a good way towards accomplishing what could have been the four main objectives of their visit to India. By arousing irritation in the West they had helped to widen the gap between India and the West, especially the United States. They had driven India and Pakistan further apart. The mere fact of their visit to the countries bordering on Pakistan—Afghanistan, Burma and India—must have aroused apprehensions in Pakistan and there was little doubt that the purpose of their forthcoming visit to Kashmir was to make a public demonstration of Soviet support of India in the Kashmir dispute. They had gone a long way towards destroying in the minds of a large number of the Indian people the old picture of Russia as a barbarous, dangerous northern bear, and by their joviality and friendship and offers of aid they had substituted a picture of a great, friendly, progressive, peace-loving country which had no quarrel with either the internal or external policy of India. By emphasizing the necessity for countries such as India to become self-sufficient in both heavy and light industry, they might have helped to make India more dissatisfied with the nature and quantity of the aid it had been getting from the West, especially since the Indians believed that the West had refused to export certain types of 'know-how' to India.

I said that the Soviet leaders would not have been able to accomplish so much in so short a time if their visit to India had not been so well timed. The steady deterioration in the relations between India and the United States in 1953 and most of 1954 had been checked towards the end of 1954 by Nehru's conversion to a belief in the wisdom and influence of President Eisenhower. Thus in Parliament in November 1954 he had paid a tribute to Eisenhower for the part he had played that year in avoiding war with China. (The External Affairs Ministry told me at the time that Nehru was referring to the vetoing by Eisenhower in September of a proposal supported by Dulles and the Joint Chiefs of Staff other than General Ridgeway that the United States air force should bomb targets in mainland China if the Chinese Communist forces continued their attacks on the Formosa-held islands off the Chinese coast.) At this time Nehru began in private conversation to call Eisenhower a 'good man', his highest term of praise. But in 1955 Eisenhower's illness, which opened up the possibility of Nixon succeeding to the presidency, re-awakened some of Nehru's old apprehensions about United States foreign policy.

In my report to Ottawa I gave a number of other reasons for the bad relations between India and the United States at the time of the Krushchev–Bulganin visit. I said that after Stalin's death the West had reacted much more slowly than Nehru thought wise to what Nehru had consistently believed to be a change in Russian tactics and perhaps in Russian strategy and objectives. Nehru had attached more importance than the West to conciliatory gestures and actions by the Soviet Union and China. The Soviet Union had been able to become a sort of associate or out-of-town member of the Bandung Club by paying the cheap fee of subscribing to the panchsheel. India's informal soundings over the past year or two of the United States, the United Kingdom and Canada for a very substantial line of credit to cover requirements during the second five-year plan had so far failed to elicit any positive response. Steel was vital to the success of the second five-year plan. The Russians were going to put up a first-class plant in India quickly and cheaply. The British negotiations over their steel plant were dragging and every six months' delay cost the Indians at least $50 million in foreign exchange if they could buy the steel abroad, and much more in a slowdown of their economic expansion if they could not buy the steel abroad. Recent developments in the Baghdad pact had aroused all of India's old apprehensions about the United States arms agreement with Pakistan and virtually every eminent Indian had recently, in talking to foreign newspapermen, blamed the United States agreement with Pakistan for the bad relations between India and the United States.

I went on to say:

No striking of the balance sheet can be made from here. The main factor in the balance is the reaction in the West. If the Soviet challenge leads to a creative response in the West, the West as a whole will benefit from the visit. If the western response is one of irritation or panic the Soviet Union will gain. It seems to me that the main thing is for the West not to show any signs of irritation with India. It would be wise, for example, for all western governments to refrain from saying anything in any public statement at this time which could suggest to sensitive Indians that we believe they are so naïve or stupid as to swallow Soviet propaganda.

I did not know when I sent this telegram that Pearson had a few days before made a statement in New York which showed signs of irritation with India. I did not learn of this until two days later when I almost simultaneously received a telegram from Pearson about the statement and a request to call on Subimal Dutt, the Commonwealth Secretary in the External Affairs Ministry. Dutt said that Nehru had asked him to speak to me about some of the references which Pearson had made to India in the statement and he read to me passages from it. He said that what he was going to say on behalf of Nehru was certainly not in the nature of a protest; it was a clarification of the Indian position. India very much appreciated the economic assistance it had received from the United States and other western countries. If Pearson had drawn the conclusion that India was not appreciative because India was critical of some aspects of United States policy, then his conclusion was not justified. India did not feel that its criticism was any indication of any lack of appreciation of United States aid. No matter what country India took aid from, whether the West or the Soviet Union, India took aid without political strings. If India were to take economic assistance from the Soviet Union, it would not feel precluded in any way from criticizing Soviet policy.

I said that there appeared to be a misunderstanding of what Pearson had said. He had made two points. The first was that the United States had not received sufficient popular credit in India for the economic aid it had given India; he had been referring to popular credit, not to the appreciation of the Indian Government for the aid. As a recent example of the lack of popular credit I said that more publicity had been given in the Indian press to the arrival of seven Soviet experts to advise India on petroleum exploration than to probably a hundred United States experts of one kind or another. The second point which Pearson had made was that some comment in India about United States policy had not been quite fair. These two points were entirely separate. Pearson's belief that the United States had not received sufficient popular credit in India for its aid was in no way related to the fact that India was a critic of certain aspects of American foreign policy.

In order to develop the point which Pearson had made about wondering what would happen if two leading politicians from the United States had gone around India making the same kind of speeches as the Soviet leaders had made, I concluded by reading to Dutt part of a telegram I had sent to Ottawa three days before.

The Soviet leaders have done about six things in India which western diplomats here would have warned similar western leaders against doing. They have used the Indian parliament as a forum for attacking countries friendly to India. They have in public speeches called India an 'ally'. They have boasted of the aid they are going to give India where we would not think it wise to boast of the aid we have given India. They have criticized Indian projects they were visiting, whereas our advice would be that a westerner who is new to India should be chary of giving advice because there may be a good reason for the Indian practice being different from the western and even if his advice is correct it would be resented if given publicly. They have in a public speech given full support to India on a controversy with a foreign government (Portugal over Goa). They have twice—at Bakhra and at Calcutta—warned India about what a nuclear bomb might do to the dam or to the city. There has been some public criticism of the misuse of parliament and of Krushchev's efforts to make India's 'flesh creep' by his reference to the nuclear bombs. The private criticism in 'informed circles' has been stronger than the public. Already Nehru has in clear forceful language in his speech at Calcutta on 30 November said that India's friendship and co-operation with Russia is 'not aimed at any nation or people' and that India intends to keep itself 'free from military or like alliances'. Presumably this language was carefully chosen to counter the Soviet use of the word 'ally'. The significant thing, however, is that the commission by western statesmen in India of any one of the six gaffes would have precipitated considerable public criticism in India and the commission of all six would have raised a tempest. The Russians have not raised a tempest.

Subimal Dutt restricted himself to the comment that I had been entirely correct in my references to Nehru's speech in Calcutta as being a careful rebuttal of certain statements by Krushchev and Bulganin. Nehru had done what was most unusual for him. He had written his speech out in advance and had circulated it to the press in advance. The only part of the speech which was extempore was the reference to Goa.

I concluded my report to Pearson on this interview by saying that his speech had probably touched Nehru on a sensitive spot.

He has been boorish, as well as short-sighted, in his failure to express gratitude for American economic assistance. He has even refused to say a few appropriate words of gratitude to American congressmen who call on him. He is so afraid of giving the impression that the acceptance of aid limits India's freedom of action that he has given the impression that India is not grateful for the aid.

A month later Pearson wrote me a personal letter about the Krushchev–Bulganin visit. He said he took a somewhat more pessimistic view of the eventual results of the visit than I did. One of the most unhappy results of the visit and of the visits of Asian leaders to Moscow was, he said, 'the apparently successful effort made by the Soviet Union to associate Asian governments in condemning western collective security arrangements and getting a certificate of purity for their own', whereas in fact, as the *Economist* had recently pointed out, the western alliances which had been freely created and could be freely left, were 'diametrically opposed to the chain-gangs into which expansionist and totalitarian regimes marshal their often unenthusiastic satellites'. 'It is thus', the *Economist* article had added, 'as easy, and as meaningless, for the Communist powers to offer to wind up their formal alliances as it would have been for war-time Japan formally to liquidate its Co-Prosperity Sphere, or for Hitler to renounce his "New Order" in Europe.' Pearson enclosed extracts from the *Economist* article in his letter to me and said:

I wish some of our Indian friends would read this paragraph, which I am enclosing herewith, and, even more important, occasionally speak accordingly. They could certainly do so without lining up on our side, or weakening their 'neutralism'.

Pearson's complaint about India's failure to make adequate public acknowledgements of its gratitude to the United States for its economic assistance had touched Nehru on a sensitive spot. Nehru's apparent condemnation of western security arrangements such as the North Atlantic treaty, which was dear to Pearson's heart, had touched Pearson on a sensitive spot.

Pillai had told me just before I received Pearson's letter that I could assure Ottawa that what Nehru had had in mind when he inserted a reference to military pacts in the joint Indo-Soviet communiqué issued at the conclusion of the Krushchev–Bulganin visit, was not the North Atlantic treaty but the Baghdad pact. I told Pillai that while I was happy to have this assurance from him it would do more good if Nehru would make clear in a public speech that it was the Baghdad Pact he was objecting to and not NATO. Pillai said that this was the kind of thing Nehru would not 'shout from the housetops' and that was why he was now telling me informally.

I decided that Pearson's letter to me gave me an excuse for putting to the External Affairs Ministry my worries over the effect of the Krushchev–Bulganin visit on India's relations with the West. I decided to speak not to one of the senior officials in the ministry but to the politician in the ministry, Anil Chanda, the Deputy Minister of External Affairs. He was a distinguished scholar, a member of parliament from West Bengal and a friend. I began by quoting from Pearson's letter. I said that it was a personal letter and that I had not been instructed to pass Pearson's views on to the External Affairs Ministry. I went on to say that even before I had received this letter it had become increasingly clear to me from reports which I had received from Ottawa and from the Canadian embassy in Washington that the Bulganin–Krushchev visit had had a more serious effect on the West than I had expected. I was very worried about this. There had already been in the minds of so many people of the West a distorted picture of India, of Nehru and of Nehru's policies. The effect of the Bulganin–Krushchev visit had been to distort this picture even further. I myself was sure that it was a distorted picture and that it was not correct to believe that Nehru did not care which society did more to shape the future of the world—the totalitarian society of Russia and China or the society of western Europe and North America.

Chanda said that he was sure that the Bulganin–Krushchev visit had served the interests of India because it had weakened the Indian Communist Party. The Communist Party had for years been bitterly attacking Nehru and his domestic and foreign policies. Now the Soviet leaders by embracing Nehru and heaping praises on his policies had made the Communist Party look foolish. Just before I had come in to see him he had been reading the fortnightly confidential police report. The police reported that throughout the whole of India the collections of the Communist Party had been dropping since the visit and that they had been weakened in other ways throughout the whole country. He had just returned from a meeting in his own state, West Bengal, of the district leaders of the Congress Party. (This state along with the Telengana section of the state of

Hyderabad and Travancore–Cochin had been the chief centres of Communist strength.) The West Bengal Congress Party, Chanda said, ran an efficient Tammany machine and its district leaders were tough party organizers. They all reported, both from the villages and from Calcutta, that the visit had harmed the Communist Party. The Communists were so weakened that it looked as though they would, in the next elections, concentrate their efforts on a few seats in West Bengal where they could pose as defenders of the non-Bengali immigrants against the Bengalis.

I said it was not surprising that the Soviet leaders would be prepared to sacrifice, for the time being, the interests of the Indian Communist Party. The Soviet Union had, about thirty years ago, sacrificed, for the time being, the Chinese Communist Party. It seemed to me, however, beyond dispute that the visit had served the national interests of the Soviet Union and that was what Krushchev and Bulganin were interested in, not the success of local Communist parties. Soviet national interests had been served by the fact that the visit had widened the gulf between India and the United States and between India and Pakistan. It was clear that in the Indian subcontinent the Soviet Union was following a policy of divide and rule. The worsening of relations between India and the United States made it more difficult for India to ask for economic aid from the United States and more difficult for the United States to give it. The conclusion of the Indian economists who had prepared the second five-year plan was that India needed, in order to finance the plan, somewhere between $1 billion and $2.4 billion in foreign exchange over and above what it could get from its exports. If the Indian government economists were right in this, and India did not get the foreign exchange it needed, then I assumed that the second five-year plan would have to be cut back by thirty per cent or forty per cent and this would mean an increase in unemployment and possibly a lowering of the standards of living in the villages.

When Chanda countered this argument by saying that the Chinese were going ahead with their economic reconstruction without economic assistance from the West, implying that India could do the same, I replied that the Chinese had adopted totalitarian methods and that it was always possible for India to

adopt such measures. India could, for example, take such short
cuts as liquidating the fifty million useless cattle and the fifty
million destructive monkeys and it could solve the problem of
rural debt by liquidating all the village money-lenders. It could
squeeze out exports to the Soviet Union by reinstituting food
rationing and driving down the food consumption of the people.
Even then I did not think it could pay for a billion and a half
dollars worth of capital equipment and other essential imports.
Clearly what the Soviet leaders were hoping for was that India
would not be able to get its foreign exchange requirements from
the West and that it would have to turn to the Soviet Union.
The Soviet Union would not, however, be able to give India
very much and the second five-year plan would fail. I said that
I had written to Pearson recently making some suggestions on
what the West could do to improve its relations with India but
that it was also obviously a matter of India doing something to
improve its relations with the West. I hoped, for example, that
Nehru might, in his speech at the opening of the forthcoming
annual meeting of the Congress Party, make clear the principles
of Indian foreign policy and, in particular, that he did not
favour everything that had happened in the Soviet Union and
China. Perhaps, for example, he might make clear what I was
sure he felt—his feelings of sorrow for what had happened to
the peoples of Czechoslovakia under totalitarian rule. He might
mention the cost which the Soviet Union had had to pay for its
economic advance, not only the cost in misery but also the cost
in those things of the spirit which Nehru cared for.

CHAPTER ELEVEN

HUNGARY AND SUEZ

'1956, as everyone knows, was a climactic year, a water-shed, a turning point, a cross-roads. . . . 1956 was a five-star year, classed with 1942: Stalingrad; or 1949: the birth of Communist China. . . . 1956 was particularly easy to see and to remember as extraordinary because of that one week when coincidentally the Hungarians rose against their Russian masters (impossible) and in Britain thousands of people made their ideas known about a view of Britain's role referred to as 'Suez': unlikely, for no one had protested about anything for so long. "Hungary"; "Suez"; violently juxtaposed.' Thus Doris Lessing wrote in *The Four-Gated City*.

For me in New Delhi the three weeks between the high point of success of the Hungarian revolution on 30 October 1956, and 19 November when Nehru belatedly came down on the side of the revolution and denounced the Soviet-imposed counter-revolution were the most crowded and demanding period of my posting in India. The strain came at a bad time for me. I was recovering from a severe attack of jaundice which had left me tired and depressed. I had during the first two weeks of November only one foreign service officer at the high commission to help me and he had been in India for only a month. There were two other foreign service officers on the strength of the high commission at the time but one was travelling in South India on Colombo Plan business and the other was in hospital.

Once Britain and France had at the end of October embarked on the use of armed force against Egypt, and Australia had a few days later supported them in the voting at the United Nations, Nehru was not prepared to listen to urgings from their governments or their representatives in New Delhi that he denounce the use of force by the Soviet Union to suppress the Hungarian revolution; he suspected them of wanting to divert his attention from what he considered to be the dangerous, arrogant, imperialistic aggression of Britain and France against

Egypt. If the United States had had an ambassador in New Delhi of the stature of ambassadors it had had, or was about to have in New Delhi—Chester Bowles, Sherman Cooper, Ellsworth Bunker or Kenneth Galbraith—he would have been the advocate of the western world in talking to Nehru about Hungary and he would have had the weight of a great power behind him. But the United States had had no ambassador in New Delhi for seven months. Canada by not supporting Britain in the voting at the U.N. General Assembly on the first resolution on Suez passed on 2 November did not forfeit its special relationship with India, and Nehru continued to have confidence in and respect for St Laurent and Pearson. A special responsibility therefore descended on me during the crises over the revolution in Hungary.

The responsibility was the greater because Pearson was so deeply involved in his efforts at the U.N. General Assembly to resolve the Suez crisis—efforts which were successful and which won him the Nobel peace prize—that he had little time or inclination to reflect on what guidance or instructions he might give me about the crisis over Hungary. His advisers in Ottawa and New York had likewise little time or inclination to reflect on what action they could usefully recommend to St Laurent and Pearson might be taken in response to the many suggestions I made during the crisis on how to put before Nehru the facts of what was happening in Hungary and their implications. If I had realized this at the time I would have sent fewer, shorter and less excited telegrams to Ottawa. One effect of the great flow of telegrams to and from Ottawa at this time, especially from Washington, New York and London, was that my telegrams to Ottawa asking for instructions and Ottawa's to me giving instructions often took days to reach their destinations rather than hours. I was left very much on my own.

A modern translation of the petition in the Lord's Prayer, 'Lead us not into temptation' is 'Do not bring us to the test'. The Hungarian revolution brought many people and many governments to the test. In this chapter I recount how some people and some governments met the test.

*   *   *

I returned to New Delhi at the end of August 1956 after convalescing in Kashmir from my attack of jaundice. Within a day or so of my return Nehru sent me a message that he wanted me to know that he was concerned by the news in the papers for that day, 1 September, that French troops had landed at Cyprus, that further landings would take place soon and that the North Atlantic Council was about to discuss Suez. During the next two and a half weeks as a result of talks with Krishna Menon, Pillai and others, I reported to Ottawa that the Indian Government was certain that an armed conflict between Britain, France and Egypt could not be localized; the references by the Soviet Foreign Minister to 'volunteers' were ominous. But even a localized war would probably result in closing the Suez canal and the increased freight costs and the delays which would result from traffic to India having to go around the Cape would gravely endanger India's second five-year plan. The Indians might indeed argue that the closing of the canal would be an economic sanction directed more against India than against Egypt. On instructions from Nehru, Pillai had told the British Government when he was in London in August that if Britain went to war over Suez it might be impossible for the Indian Government to resist public pressure in India to get out of the Commonwealth. India could see no case for Britain threatening war with Egypt over Suez. India had received an assurance from Eisenhower that the United States ruled out the use of force against Egypt. India had received no similar formal assurance from Britain though the British Deputy High Commissioner to India had given a personal assurance that Britain contemplated the use of force in Egypt only in a situation comparable to that in 1952 (when anti-western riots broke out in Cairo) when it might be necessary to use force to protect British nationals from violence. I added that Krishna Menon had told me that if only Britain would trust India and give it enough rope India could persuade Nasser to agree to a reasonable and satisfactory settlement of the Suez canal issue.

At the same time as the Middle East was moving to a crisis so was Hungary. The Soviet Union had imposed a Stalinist Communist regime on Hungary in 1949 against the wishes of the people of Hungary: in the elections of 1947 and 1948 Communist candidates had received only 22 per cent of the popular vote and many of those who voted communist were followers of L. Rajka, the leader of the more liberal Communists, who, together with some of his associates, was executed in 1949 after Stalinist-style purge trials. Krushchev's denunciation of Stalin in February 1956 precipitated outbursts of dissent in both Hungary and Poland against their Stalinist governments. Rajka was posthumously rehabilitated and two hundred thousand people turned out in the streets of Budapest on 6 October for his state funeral. Two weeks later Gomulka, the anti-Stalinist Communist leader in Poland, successfully defied Krushchev. This caused increasing excitement and expectations in Hungary. On 23 October a mass demonstration took place in Budapest of high school and university students and factory workers. They demanded solidarity with the Poles, neutralism and free elections. The Hungarian Government under Gero ordered the Hungarian security police to crush the nascent revolt; their efforts were unsuccessful and Gero called on Soviet troops for help. Within a few hours they were in Budapest and the next day, 25 October, Soviet tanks opened fire on a crowd of demonstrators in Kossuth Square killing many. By the 26th there was heavy fighting all over Hungary between the Soviet forces and the Hungarian rebels in which the rebels fought against superior forces with incredible gallantry. On 27 October the governments of Britain, France and the United States requested that an urgent meeting of the U.N. Security Council be held to discuss the situation created by the action of Soviet forces in violently repressing the rights of the Hungarian people. Pearson in a public statement that day supported this move. He deplored the bloodshed in Hungary, denounced the intervention of the Soviet Union and demanded that Hungary be enabled to choose its own course. Discussion at the Security Council on 28 October clearly registered the opposition of all but the Soviet representative to the continued presence of Soviet military forces in Hungary.

The most hopeful day in the Hungarian revolution was 30 October. On that day Nagy, who had become Premier of Hungary, announced the formation of a coalition government containing representatives of the non-Communist parties and said that the new government was going to request the Soviet Government to withdraw all its armed forces from Hungary. Nagy's statement over the radio was followed by a statement from another cabinet minister that free elections would be held and by a statement by Kadar that he approved of this statement and of the statements by Nagy. The new minister of defence announced that the Soviet Command had agreed to withdraw all its forces from Budapest by dawn of 31 October. That same day, 30 October, the Soviet Government issued a declaration affirming that the Soviet Union and the other socialist countries could 'build their mutual relations only on the principles of complete equality . . . and non-interference in each other's internal affairs', that troops of one member of the Warsaw Pact should be stationed in the territory of another member only with the consent of the host state and that the Soviet Union would withdraw its troops from Budapest as soon as the Hungarian Government considered withdrawal necessary. The next day Eisenhower said that if the Soviet Union acted upon the intention expressed in that declaration 'the world will witness the greatest forward step toward justice, trust and understanding among nations in our generation'; developments in eastern Europe were 'the dawn of a new day'.

Nehru made his first public statement about the movement towards greater national freedom in Poland and Hungary on 25 October. He knew then of the agreement which Gomulka had extorted from Krushchev on 20 October; he knew of the mass demonstration in Budapest on 23 October demanding neutralism and free elections; and he knew that Soviet armed forces had entered Budapest. His statement was made at just about the time that Soviet tanks were firing on demonstrators in Kossuth Square. He said that it seemed clear to him that the developments in Poland and Hungary were a 'nationalist upsurge' which was affecting the internal independence of these countries, 'a feeling that they themselves are going to fashion their policies and not necessarily others. Anyhow, it is not for us to interfere in any way even by expressing an opinion on the internal affairs of these countries.' On 28 October, three days after the firings in Kossuth Square and when there had been heavy fighting all over Hungary for two days between the rebels and the Soviet army, Krishna Menon said that developments in Hungary were an internal matter for the Hungarian people and he compared the fighting in Hungary to recent riots in the Indian cities of Bombay and Ahmadabad over proposals to redraw the boundaries of the states; he asked how Indians would feel if these riots were described in the foreign press as rebellion against the Congress regime. (The day before Menon made this statement, Hugh Gaitskell, then leader of the Labour Party in Britain, had deplored 'the ruthless intervention of Soviet tanks and troops against the Hungarian workers—most of them unarmed—and the bloodshed thus caused'; he had saluted 'the heroism of those who have given their lives in the battle for freedom'; and he had declared that what the Hungarians desired was 'the democratic socialism for which the Labour Party stands'.)

On 24 October Israel, France and Britain had reached at Sèvres a secret understanding on the action they would take against Egypt. In accordance with this understanding Israel invaded the Sinai on 29 October, and Britain and France issued ultimata on 30 October. (The understanding further provided that on 31 October British and French air forces would begin bombing Egyptian airfields preparatory to the landing of troops a few days later.) On 31 October, the day after the British and French ultimata, the Indian External Affairs Ministry issued a statement in the name of 'an official spokesman' and told the American embassy that it was 'the Prime Minister's statement'. Nehru in this statement said that the Indian Government considered that the Israeli aggression on Egyptian territory and the subsequent Anglo-French ultimatum which was to be followed by an Anglo-French invasion of Egypt was a flagrant violation of the U.N. Charter. 'This aggression is bound to have far-reaching consequences in Asia and Africa and may even lead to war on an extended scale.' The Indian Government earnestly trusted 'that even at this late hour this aggression will be halted and foreign troops withdrawn from Egyptian territory'. They hoped 'that the world community as represented in the United Nations will take effective action to this end'.

As soon as Pearson heard of this statement he telegraphed me:

A press despatch just received carries the story of Indian condemnation of the Israeli attack on Egypt. I have no quarrel with the Indian Government's decision on this matter but the contrast between its quick and strong denunciation of Israeli action with its complete silence over events in Hungary, and Russian intervention in these events, will have a very bad effect in this country.

Pearson's reference to the Indian condemnation of Israel is puzzling because Nehru in his statement had also condemned Britain and France.

My spirits had soared when the success of Poland under Gomulka in securing greater freedom had been followed by the success of the Hungarian rebels. I was struck with admiration for the gallantry of the rebels in their struggle against the much greater forces of the Soviet Union. I saw new vistas of hope opening up for greater freedom in eastern Europe and within the Soviet Union and for better relations between the Soviet world and the western world. The British invasion of Egypt angered me because it seemed to me a reversion to days which I had thought were ended—the days when wealthy, white European countries rode roughshod over the poor countries of Asia and Africa. My anger was the greater because the invasion diverted attention from Hungary and I felt that if the world's attention could be concentrated on Hungary, the Soviet Union might decide not to crush the revolt. I did not quarrel with Nehru's attack on Britain and France for their aggression in Suez. Indeed I agreed with everything he said. I was, however, deeply apprehensive that his failure to denounce Soviet aggression in Hungary would make a Soviet withdrawal from Hungary less likely, would damage his reputation and India's, and would weaken the links between India and the West, links which I believed served the interests of the West and India. I had a profound respect, admiration and affection for Nehru and I did not want him to damage his reputation. Thus I did not need Pearson's telegram to awaken me to the necessity of doing what I could to persuade Nehru not to postpone any longer making a public denunciation of Soviet actions in Hungary. Indeed two days before I received Pearson's telegram I had spoken to Subimal Dutt about this when I had called on him at the External Affairs Ministry to discuss the new immigration agreement which we were negotiating. I had then said to Dutt that he had no doubt noted that there was already criticism in North America of Nehru's silence over Soviet armed intervention in Hungary. That morning the *Times of India* had summarized an article by the authoritative columnist, James T. Reston, which had appeared in the *New York Times* the preceding day, in which Reston had said that the United States administration was trying to make clear that the Hungarian revolt was

not merely anti-Soviet but a movement expressing profound desires for freedom. Washington would like to enlist in this exercise the aid of those in the neutral world who have talked so much about freedom whenever the Western Powers were under attack and who now seem remarkably quiet in the face of action by tanks of the Soviet Army to put down Hungarian patriots in the streets of Budapest. This applies particularly to Prime Minister Nehru of India who has been extremely active in publicizing his zeal for Egyptian nationalists but who has said nothing to date in support of the Hungarian people.

I received Pearson's telegram on the morning of 1 November. I called on Pillai at noon. I told him of what I had said to Dutt and added that not only had Nehru been silent but Krishna Menon had said that developments in Hungary were internal matters for the Hungarian people. My fear that Indian silence would cause criticism in North America had been confirmed by a message which I had just received from Pearson and I read him the message, making clear that I had not been instructed to give the message to him but that I felt he ought to know about it.

Pillai's reception of my remarks was frigid. There was no parallel between what was happening in Egypt and what was happening in Hungary. Because of the Warsaw Pact and the request by the Hungarian Government for Soviet assistance in quelling the revolution a cloak of legality had been cast over the Soviet action. I replied that the cloak had been cast aside when Nagy had denied that the Hungarian Government had requested Soviet intervention. Pillai retorted that if Canada criticized India for not having come out strongly against Soviet action in Hungary he might criticize Canada for not having yet issued a strong public denunciation of the aggression of Israel, France and Britain against Egypt. I did not try to defend this silence by Canada, which I myself deplored, but I said that I would not have spoken to him about Pearson's message if it was a matter of mutual recrimination. The question of Hungary was, however, still before the Security Council. Would it not be possible for Nehru in the course of the next few days to make his position clear? The people of Hungary had put on one of the most gallant demonstrations of courage which the world had seen in many years. They had been fighting for national freedom against foreign domination. I could quote statements made by Nehru in the course of the Indian struggle for freedom which could be applied unchanged to the Hungarian struggle. Pillai said that I was the only diplomatic representative in Delhi who had expressed to him criticism of Indian inaction in relation to Soviet aggression in Hungary. He was not going to report to Nehru what I had said. If he sent Nehru a memorandum on it it would have an unfortunate effect and Nehru was so busy that he would not be able to speak to him about it. He suggested that the next time a convenient opportunity arose when I was talking with Nehru I might raise the matter with him delicately, perhaps not in reference to Hungary but in reference to what might happen in another country such as Romania. I left the interview disheartened. I had never in my four years in India been so rebuffed.

Just before I left Pillai's office, he let me read Eden's message to Nehru of 31 October on the Suez crisis and he gave me for transmission to Ottawa the reply which Nehru had made to Eden and Nehru's messages to Eisenhower and Dulles. He told me that Nehru had told him 'to show Canada everything'.

Later that day Nehru made a speech at Hyderabad. Malcolm MacDonald, the British High Commissioner, who had been seeing a good deal of Nehru, told me that he considered that this speech faithfully represented Nehru's views. Nehru said that in all his experience of international affairs he had come across 'no grosser case of naked aggression' than the British and French aggression against Egypt. (He did not even make an exception for some of Hilter's most blatant aggressions.) Independent India's relations with Britain had been close and friendly. Britain had been a force for peace. Because of this his sorrow and distress were all the greater at this amazing adventure. He was bewildered and astounded. The Anglo-French action was a return to the predatory methods of the 18th and 19th centuries but there were now influential and self-respecting nations in Asia and Africa. These nations would not tolerate this new incursion by colonial powers. If by threats and military action an attempt was made to subdue a country (Egypt) which had recently obtained freedom and to set up a puppet government there, countries in Asia and elsewhere would never bow before such things. In reply to the contention by Britain and France that they were acting on behalf of the world community, he exclaimed bitterly, 'Who has assigned the role of policeman to England and France?' As for Hungary all he said in this speech was that during the previous year and a half the internal pressure in the Soviet Union had been relaxed; this had had repercussions in other countries such as Poland and Hungary; people in these countries demanded that the influence and pressure Russia had in their countries should be ended and they should have complete freedom; the matter had been settled peacefully in Poland; in Hungary there was a conflict; he hoped the issue in Hungary would be solved peacefully.

On 31 October when Nehru gave this speech the news from Hungary was that the Soviet forces were leaving Budapest and that the rebels were jubilant. The jubilation was short-lived. The next day Nagy, on learning that new Soviet military units were entering Hungary, protested about this to the Soviet Ambassador, demanded their withdrawal and informed the Ambassador that the Hungarian Government was repudiating the Warsaw Treaty, was declaring Hungary's neutrality, was turning to the United Nations and was requesting the help of the four great powers in defending Hungary's neutrality. These events took place after Pillai had told me on 1 November that he was not going to pass on to Nehru what I had said to him. When on 2 November he learned of these events he sent a memorandum to Nehru saying that for the first time in his dealings with me over a period of four years he had dismissed my remarks to him as raising an unimportant matter (the Indian silence over Hungary) when attention should be devoted to the important matter of the crisis in the Middle East; his reason for dismissing my remarks had been that he believed in the Russian assertions that they were withdrawing their forces from Hungary; this belief had been demonstrated to be false. In his biography of Nehru, S. Gopal quotes as follows from the memorandum and terms it a warning to Nehru 'against an application of double standards' to Hungary and Suez:

If it is true that Soviet troops are trying to occupy Budapest and other areas in Hungary, whatever the ostensible reason, and if it is true also that this is being opposed by the Hungarian Government and that they have appealed to the United Nations, we cannot afford to appear to be indifferent in regard to these developments. I am not suggesting that we should raise our voice in the same way as certain others are doing; but I think the time has come for us to give further thought to the Hungarian situation with a view to deciding our attitude in the light of the principles we have been advocating.[1]

Immediately after receiving this memorandum Nehru instructed K. P. S. Menon, the Indian Ambassador in Moscow, to express to the Soviet Government his concern and distress at the latest developments in Hungary, and on 4 November he sent instructions to the Indian delegation to the U.N. General Assembly. Pillai told me that the instructions were that India should support a resolution that foreign troops be withdrawn from Hungary and that the Hungarian people should be given the right to decide their own future in free elections.

During the first three days of November protests against Soviet aggression in Hungary mounted throughout the world. Nehru added nothing to what he had said in his Hyderabad speech of 1 November. In the western world and especially in the white Commonwealth countries he was bitterly attacked for his silence. Within India there was more and more talk of India leaving the Commonwealth because of the British aggression against Egypt. Nehru said nothing about this himself, but senior officers of the External Affairs Ministry, presumably acting under his instructions, uttered warnings to the Australian and Pakistan high commissioners and to me that the British aggression would make it difficult for India to remain in the Commonwealth. I reported these statements to Pearson on 2 November and reminded him of the warning Pillai had given the British Government in August that if Britain went to war over Suez it might be impossible for the Indian Government to resist public pressure in India to leave the Commonwealth. I said:

India's decision to remain in the Commonwealth [after it became independent] was, in a very marked degree, the decision of one man, Nehru. There is little public support in India for membership and such support has certainly contracted greatly as a result of recent events. Because of the value which you attach to Indian membership in the Commonwealth I know that you will be considering whether there is any action we can take to make Indian withdrawal less likely. This is not an easy question, but one thing I am sure of. If all the white members of the Commonwealth line up in the United Nations General Assembly with the United Kingdom or abstain [on the Suez issue] the chances of Indian withdrawal will be increased. The fewer non-Commonwealth votes which Great Britain gets, the more obvious will be the unity of the white Commonwealth. Within India those who have consistently opposed Indian membership in the Commonwealth will contend that this demonstrates the hollowness of the claim Nehru has repeatedly made that membership in the Commonwealth increases India's influence while not limiting India's independence. I hope, therefore, that it may be possible for Canada not to separate itself in the voting in the General Assembly of the United Nations from the vast majority of the members of that body.

Almost at the moment I was sending this telegram the voting in the General Assembly on its first resolution on Suez was taking place. I, of course, did not know this. The resolution was mild. It did not label Britain and France as aggressors or accuse them of violating any of their obligations under the U.N. Charter. It called for an immediate cease-fire and a halt to the movement of military forces and arms into the area and it urged Israel and Egypt to withdraw their armed forces behind the armistice lines agreed to in 1949. Only five countries voted against the resolution: the three aggressors—Britain, France and Israel—and Australia and New Zealand. Canada abstained along with South Africa and four other countries. Sixty-four countries voted for the resolution. Of the five members of the 'old' Commonwealth, three voted against the resolution and two abstained. The two new members of the Commonwealth which were members of the U.N. (India and Pakistan) voted for the resolution. (Ceylon was not then a member of the U.N.) Two days later one of the leading elder statesmen of India, Rajagopalachari, launched a public campaign for the withdrawal of India from the Commonwealth. Pillai told me on the day after Rajagopalachari's speech that Nehru had so far refused to be rushed and that before taking any final step he would consult the other Asian members of the Commonwealth —Pakistan and Ceylon—and would inform Britain. I urged that Nehru should consult Canada.

In my talk with Pillai on 3 November I asked him whether, in the light of the accounts of Soviet aggression against Hungary contained in that morning's newspapers, it might be helpful if

I were to ask to see Nehru in order to raise with him the desirability of India issuing a strong public protest against Soviet aggression. Pillai suggested that I should hold my hand for two or three days and he would speak to me again. His advice to me was so firm that in the absence of a reply from Ottawa to the query I had put on 1 November whether I should speak to Nehru I considered it would not be wise for me to ask for an interview. I was, however, apprehensive. On Monday, 5 November, an important international conference was to open in New Delhi, the conference of Unesco. Nehru was to address the conference. I feared that he might denounce the aggression against Egypt and be silent on the aggression against Hungary and I knew that the effect on the reputation and influence of Nehru and India and on the relations between India and the democratic world of such a speech given before so important an audience would be profound.

On the morning of Sunday, 4 November, it was still not clear in Delhi how far the Soviet Union would intervene in Hungary and how far Britain and France would intervene in Egypt. The news in the morning papers was that the new Hungarian minister of defence had opened negotiations with the general in command of the Soviet forces in Hungary on Soviet troop withdrawals. In Egypt the British and French air forces had been attacking Egyptian airfields but there had been no landing of British or French forces. After dinner that night I tuned in to the BBC short-wave news broadcast from London. I heard that at four o'clock that morning the Soviet armed forces had launched an attack on Budapest with tanks, infantry and aircraft, that the Hungarians had put up a stout defence but had been overwhelmed, and that the Soviet authorities had installed a puppet regime under Kadar. I was sick at heart. I felt I must try once more to persuade Pillai to urge Nehru at the opening of the Unesco conference the next morning to speak out against the Russian suppression of the Hungarian revolution. I knew that Pillai was dining at the German embassy. I telephoned him there and asked him if he could drop in to see me on his way home. He said he would. He came at 11.30. I told him of the BBC broadcast. I said that no doubt at that very moment the Soviet authorities in Hungary were committing mass murders, torturing prisoners and rounding up every leader of the revolt in every village. In what I was going to say I was speaking personally, without instructions and without knowledge of the views of the Canadian Government.

Last week vistas of hope were opening up. There was a possibility that truly independent governments would be set up in eastern Europe and that Russian troops might be withdrawn. I myself had thought that in return for this the West might agree to the withdrawal of western troops from Germany, thus creating a buffer zone in Europe. Now the hope of this had gone and the hope of increasing liberalization of the regime in Russia had gone. Nothing but despair faced us if the Russians succeeded in maintaining their hold on Hungary. The Russians must get out of Hungary. If Nehru led the way, might not the Indian people be led to realize that Soviet aggression against Hungary was at least as bad as Anglo-French aggression against Egypt? The United States and India were now the only great powers with clean hands. Only Eisenhower and Nehru could speak for the conscience of mankind. Could not Nehru at the opening of the Unesco conference tomorrow pay tribute to the gallantry of the Hungarian people, express sorrow at their suffering and demand that every Russian soldier get out of Hungary immediately? He could also demand that every Israeli, French and British soldier get out of Egypt.

Pillai said that it was impossible to persuade the mass of Indians that Soviet aggression in Hungary was as bad as British and French aggression in Egypt. I knew the reasons: race and colour and the history of colonialism in Asia. He thought that Nehru could not avoid mentioning both Hungary and Egypt in his speech to the Unesco conference but that he would put off a considered statement of the views of the Indian Government until Parliament met on 14 November. Pillai said that if he were in my position he would recommend to Ottawa that St Laurent send a message to Nehru in the course of the next day or so which I would deliver to Nehru. St Laurent's message might be based on the most recent developments at the U.N. General Assembly. It should deal with the aggression against both Hungary and Egypt. St Laurent should plead with Nehru to make a public statement on Hungary since no one else could speak for the whole of Asia. St Laurent's message might also urge Indian support for certain specific actions which might be taken within the U.N. on both Hungary and Egypt. Pillai added that the only thing that encouraged him in the present situation was that Krishna Menon was not in Delhi. It was only when Menon was not in Delhi that he (Pillai) had any influence on Nehru. I said I was glad Menon was not in Delhi but I wished he were not in New York; one advantage of Nehru committing himself publicly on the Hungarian issue at the Unesco conference was that this would cut the ground from under the feet of Menon in New York. My talk with Pillai which had begun at 11.30 had gone on for an hour. I apologized to him for keeping him from his bed when I knew he was very tired. He said, 'It's not much to give up an hour's sleep when people are being tortured and killed in Budapest.'

Twelve hours after my midnight talk with Pillai, Nehru in his speech of welcome to the Unesco conference said:

> The Unesco does not concern itself with political questions and it would not be right for us to raise them in this gathering. But the Unesco is intimately concerned with the dignity of man and the vital importance of freedom. We see today in Egypt as well as in Hungary both human dignity and freedom outraged and the force of modern arms used to suppress peoples and to gain political objectives. Old colonial methods, which we had thought in our ignorance belonged to a more unenlightened age, are revived and practised. In other parts of the world also, movements for freedom are crushed by superior might.

Nehru went on to refer to the panchsheel, the five principles which should govern the relations between states. One of the principles was non-interference in each other's internal affairs. The Soviet Union had subscribed to the panchsheel; Britain and France had not; therefore when Nehru went on to say that the panchsheel had become 'mere words without meaning to some countries who claim the right of deciding problems by superior might' he was rebuking the Soviet Union for its intervention in Hungary.

Pillai telephoned me immediately after Nehru had spoken to say that in the light of our conversation the previous night he trusted that I had taken due note of the speech. I said I was happy that Nehru had said what he had but that I wished he could have gone further. Pillai replied that Nehru could not say more on this occasion.

My feeling of encouragement that Nehru had gone as far as he had in his Unesco speech was short-lived. The next morning I was able to draw Nehru aside for a couple of minutes at the airport where he was welcoming the Emperor of Ethiopia. I said, 'I am very glad you were able to speak as you did at the conference yesterday and to bracket the aggression in Hungary with that in Egypt.' For some time he remained silent with no expression on his face. He then said:

> One difficulty about the Hungarian situation is that there are disputes about the facts. Apparently there were not only Russian troops in Hungary but also technicians and it is said that a thousand of the technicians were murdered. There seem to have been massacres on both sides. The Russians had agreed to withdraw but came back when new developments took place in the rebellion. It is said, for example, that people were streaming across the border to help the rebels and that planes were landing in Hungary from outside the country to help the rebels.

I said that notwithstanding all this there was a clear act of aggression by Russia. This was evident from Nagy's appeals in the last few days. Nehru said he was not questioning that. I said I had not seen any mention of assistance from abroad in any of the newspaper despatches I had read. Any disputes about the facts of the Hungarian rebellion constituted an argument for the provision in the U.N. resolution on sending U.N. observers to Hungary.

In reporting this to Ottawa I said that Nehru had been fed these stories by the Soviet Government. It was not until years later when I read K. P. S. Menon's book on his ambassadorship in Moscow that I learned that Nehru's remarks to me must have been based on the ambassador's telegram to Delhi reporting on his call on Zorin of the Soviet Foreign Ministry on 5 November. This was the call which Nehru had on 2 November instructed him to make. In accordance with his instructions Menon told Zorin that Nehru was 'deeply worried and depressed' over the situation in Hungary. He added in language that may have represented a toning down of his instructions that India '*normally*' was 'against the stationing or use of foreign troops in a country without its consent' and 'recent events in Hungary were, *on the surface*, a violation of the Five Principles . . .' (italics added). Zorin then gave the Soviet version of events in Hungary.² It was bits of this version which Nehru passed on to me at the airport.

In my cable to Ottawa of 6 November reporting on this talk I tried to explain why Nehru had appeared to be so ready to accept the Soviet version of what had happened in Hungary. I said that Nehru had attached great hopes to the de-Stalinization process within Russia and in Russia's relations with its eastern European satellites and to the relaxation of international tension which followed. Indeed, his whole approach to foreign policy had, for the past two years, been based on his belief in the reality and permanence of the more liberal trends in Russia. He was now going through an intense internal struggle. Like any other man similarly placed he was tempted to grasp at any straw which might make it possible for him to postpone a complete re-examination of his foreign policy. I concluded my cable to Ottawa as follows:

I wish it were possible to fly to India immediately for the express purpose of seeing Nehru about four of the active leaders of the abortive Hungarian rebellion. It would be best if the group included a Communist, a Socialist, a member of the Smallholders Party and a non-party man and if one of the members were a poet, one an artist and one a university student. Nehru might sense in them the kind of people who fought beside him for Indian independence. With his feeling for history he might also sense the continuity of the Hungarian Rebellion of 1956 with the Hungarian Revolution of 1848, both of which were put down by the armed forces of reactionary Russia. He must be helped to realize that the ancient forces of nationalism in Europe are as worthy in themselves as the new forces of nationalism in Asia and that the nations of Europe have as great a right to national freedom and independence as the nations of Asia.

The American chargé d'affaires called on me the day after I had sent this telegram. I mentioned this suggestion to him and he seemed very attracted by it. We agreed that it would be less invidious if a similar mission went to Eisenhower; it was essential that the missions be secret and not used for propaganda, and that the sole purpose should be to present to Nehru and Eisenhower the facts of the Hungarian situation. In order to ensure that Nehru had confidence in the mission perhaps the Austrian Socialist Party might be asked to select the members and to guarantee their bona fides. The American chargé passed this suggestion on to the State Department but nine days later when the Canadian embassy in Washington spoke to the State Department about it the State Department was still 'actively discussing' it with other agencies of the American Government. Nothing emerged from this active consideration. If the United States had had in India a first-rate ambassador with access to the White House he might have persuaded Eisenhower to take immediate action on the proposal. If Pearson had, on receiving my telegram of 6 November making this proposal, instructed the Canadian Ambassador in Washington to call on Eisenhower to urge him to act on the proposal, Eisenhower might have taken immediate action.

The other suggestion I made to the American chargé when he called on me was that the State Department should furnish Nehru with a blow-by-blow account of what had been happening in Hungary since the outbreak of the revolt. Nehru had no up-to-date sources of information in Budapest which he would trust. The reports of the Indian chargé d'affaires in Budapest took at least six days to reach Delhi. Nehru would discount the reports of the British and French diplomats in Budapest since he would suspect Britain and France of trying to whip up his passions over Russian misdeeds in Hungary in order to divert his attention from their misdeeds in Egypt. Canada had no diplomatic mission in Budapest. There were no Indian newspapermen in Budapest and Nehru would discount the reports of western newspapermen. Because of the firm opposition of Eisenhower to the Anglo-French aggression in Egypt Nehru was likely to give credence to a United States account of what had been happening in Hungary. When I mentioned to the American chargé the importance of the United States giving such an account to Nehru he said he had already recommended this to Washington. The United States did not, however, give Nehru such an account until the middle of November.

(Nehru committed his great blunder over the Hungarian revolt in a speech in Calcutta on 9 November. Krishna Menon committed his great blunder the same day in his vote in the U.N. General Assembly. It is possible, even probable, that these blunders would not have been committed if Nehru had, before giving that speech, learned that he would shortly be receiving a delegation of the Hungarian rebels and if he had received a United States account of events in Hungary which would, at the very least, have cast doubt on the veracity of the account which he had received from the Soviet Government and which he made the basis of his speech.)

I was depressed by what Nehru said to me at the airport on 6 November. I was astounded by the news that India had abstained from voting on the first U.N. resolution on Hungary passed by the U.N. General Assembly on 4 November. This resolution had called on the Soviet Union 'to withdraw all of its forces without delay from Hungarian territory'. The resolution was passed by 50 in favour, 8 against (the Soviet bloc) and 15 abstentions. The abstainers were India, 12 other Asian and Arab countries, Finland and Yugoslavia. I had told Ottawa that Nehru had instructed the Indian delegation to vote for a resolution calling on the Soviet Union to withdraw its forces from Hungary. It was not until later that I learned of the explanation of how Nehru had countermanded his instructions. This explanation was given two weeks after the event by Mrs Pandit, then India's High Commissioner in London, to the Canadian High Commissioner in London. Mrs Pandit said that she had been with Nehru at his house in New Delhi when a call came through from Krishna Menon in New York at about half past one in the morning of 5 November (three in the afternoon of 4 November in New York). Nehru was tired and swamped with papers. Her impression was that the vote in New York was to be taken in a matter of minutes. What Nehru had said to Menon was simply, 'You will have to use your own judgement.' When she learned later how Menon had voted and how Nehru had publicly taken full responsibility for Menon's vote, she had written to Nehru reminding him of the circumstances in which he had taken Menon's call, how he had relied on Menon's judgement and discretion and how he had allowed his own real feelings and India's to be misrepresented by Menon.

India's abstention on this resolution caused great resentment in western countries. In Canada the resentment was profound. James Eayrs, in his book on Canada in world affairs from 1955 to 1957 published under the auspices of the Canadian Institute of International Affairs, said that in the eyes of many Canadians the abstention appeared 'a cynical and shameful betrayal of the moral unity of the Commonwealth and indeed of all free nations'.[3]

A few hours after my talk with Nehru at the airport on 6 November I called on Pillai. He had just come from a discussion with Nehru about the messages which Bulganin had, the day before, sent to Eisenhower, Eden, Mollet (the Premier of France) and Nehru. Bulganin had proposed to Eisenhower that the United States should join the Soviet Union in naval and air action backed by the U.N. to stop the Anglo-French aggression in Egypt. In his messages to Eden and Mollet, Bulganin referred to his message to Eisenhower and warned them that if they did not end hostilities immediately they risked attack by a stronger power capable of committing rocket weapons. 'We are filled with determination to use force to crush the aggression and to restore peace in the [Middle] East. We hope you will show the necessary prudence and will draw from this the appropriate conclusions.' Pillai said to me, presumably reflecting Nehru's views, that the situation created by the Soviet Government's messages was one which the great powers would, no doubt, settle among themselves; India had no influence. I disagreed and I urged that India should use its influence with the Soviet Government immediately since clearly there was danger of a world war breaking out. Could not the Soviet Ambassador be called immediately to the External Affairs Ministry and told that in India's view there was no justification for Soviet intervention? My parting shot as I was leaving Pillai's office was: 'If I were in India's position I would do this even if it were just so that the last document in the Indian Government white paper on the outbreak of the third world war might begin with "I summoned the Soviet Ambassador and told him . . ."'

That evening Pillai had a long talk with Nehru and Nehru then wrote a reply to the message from Bulganin. His reply was a strong criticism of the Soviet message to the British and French governments. Nehru said:

While we entirely agree with you that aggression of all kinds must be put an end to we feel strongly that any step that might lead to a world war would be a crime against humanity and must be avoided. . . . I agree with you fully that the situation [in Egypt] is serious and delay may lead to disaster. Urgent and effective measures have to be taken.

But I earnestly hope that they will be measures to bring back and ensure peace rather than to enlarge the circle of war and disaster.

If I had known when I called on Pillai on 6 November that Nehru was likely to send a message of this kind I would have been less depressed by what Nehru had said to me at the airport. I had hoped that his reference to Hungary in his Unesco speech, muted though it was, marked the beginning of a move towards accepting the almost unanimous condemnation by the non-Communist world of Soviet action in Hungary. He had taken two steps forward. His remarks at the airport seemed to indicate that he was taking three steps back. I therefore decided that it might be helpful if I were to send Nehru a memorandum incorporating the report which I had made to Pearson of what I had said to Pillai in our talk at midnight on 4–5 November. I told Pillai of my decision when I saw him on 6 November explaining that I was acting without instructions from Pearson because my communications with him were slow and events were moving fast. Pillai saw no objections to what I had decided to do and I sent the memorandum to him later that day for transmission to Nehru.

I had passed on to Ottawa on 5 November Pillai's suggestion to me at our midnight talk on 4–5 November that St Laurent send a message to Nehru which I would deliver to him. St Laurent did send me a message to Nehru on 7 November, but it did not reach me until 9 November and by then Nehru had left for a meeting in Calcutta of the All-India Congress Committee so I could not use the message as an occasion for calling on him but had to give the message to Pillai for transmission to him. Moreover the message was not the kind of message Pillai and I had suggested. We wanted a message which would urge Nehru to support certain defined actions which might be taken within the U.N. on both Hungary and Suez. The message from St Laurent did express appreciation of the way the delegations of India and Canada in New York had co-operated on the Suez issue but the sole reference to Hungary was banal—that St Laurent had 'read with great interest the references in your statement at the opening session of Unesco to the recent tragic events in Hungary'. It is just conceivable that if I had received on 8 November the kind of message Pillai and I had suggested and had delivered it personally to Nehru, Krishna

Menon and he might not have made the blunders they did make on 9 November.

When I saw Pillai on 9 November shortly before these blunders were made I gave him not only St Laurent's message to Nehru but also a message from St Laurent which I had given to Rajagopalachari. In this message St Laurent said that he would be extremely sorry if Rajagopalachari felt that they should not belong to the same club. 'The Commonwealth Club does provide us with opportunities for helpful exchanges of views and, even when our views do not coincide ... such honest divergence of views, so long as they are sincere, should not make it necessary for us to part company.' Rajagopalachari replied to St Laurent five days later in a letter in his own handwriting.

The Commonwealth Club as you put it is a good club. I would love to be in a club where the members are mostly decent.... But can any unit of the Commonwealth retain connection if Britain carries on war against a friendly country.... I can imagine a war against the U.S.S.R. and some units of the Commonwealth remaining neutral and yet continuing in the Commonwealth. But this wholly and universally condemned war against Egypt is different.... Do we want a Commonwealth Club going without the slightest meaning whatsoever?

Rajagopalachari's letter to St Laurent was mild in comparison with a public speech which he gave two days after he had written to St Laurent. What Britain had done to Egypt was rape. The Commonwealth was 'odious hypocrisy' and 'not a reality'. It had become 'an instrument of aggression'.

I also gave Pillai on 9 November for transmission to Nehru St Laurent's reply of 5 November to Eden's second letter to him. I had no instructions to do this. I did it because the reply went much further in its criticisms of British conduct than anything the Canadian Government had said publicly; this would be evidence for Nehru that the Canadian Government shared his revulsion at the British aggression against Egypt; the more Nehru could be convinced that Canada shared his revulsion the better the chances of his deciding that India should remain in the Commonwealth. In this message to Eden, which Pearson quotes in his memoirs, St Laurent said:

It is unfortunate that the events in the Middle East have cloaked with a smoke screen the renewed brutal international crimes of the Soviets. Many felt their satellite empire was crumbling and that they would not dare challenge world public opinion alone by resorting to the use of their military force against their neighbours to reverse that trend. ... The opportunity for comparisons [between Soviet action in Hungary and British action in Egypt] ... handicaps us in using world opinion as a check upon their outrageous conduct.[4]

Later in the day on which I gave Pillai this message from St Laurent to Eden, Nehru successfully opposed at the meeting of the All-India Congress Committee in Calcutta a resolution in favour of India severing its relations with the Commonwealth. Whether Pillai had given Nehru by telephone a summary of St Laurent's message to Eden I do not know, but in his speech opposing the resolution, Nehru used as one of his arguments against India withdrawing from the Commonwealth that other members of the Commonwealth (presumably Pakistan and Ceylon) were also very vigorously opposed to British policy on the Suez canal issue and there were other members of the Commonwealth (presumably Canada) who, while not opposing this policy openly, opposed it privately. Nehru's knowledge of the extent of the Canadian Government's opposition to British policy on Suez must have been a factor in his decision that India should remain in the Commonwealth. It may have been the determining factor.

Nehru's speech at Calcutta on the Commonwealth was encouraging. The other speech he gave that day in Calcutta was profoundly disturbing. In it he accepted as valid the Soviet defence of their actions in Hungary which he had received from Bulganin the previous day. He said that as far as Egypt was concerned 'every single thing that happened is almost as clear as daylight. There are no hidden facts.' The key sentence in his reference to Hungary was, 'what appears to have occurred in Hungary is a civil conflict'. At the beginning of his speech he said that he had at first found the situation in Hungary 'very confusing except for some basic factors'. Bulganin had at his request sent him an account of the facts as the Soviet Government knew them. He first protected himself by saying that the Soviet account might be called a partial account but then, forgetting this, he included in his explanation of what had happened in Hungary the 'facts' which the Soviet Government had given him. In the 'civil conflict' in Hungary there had been 'mutual killings' running into thousands including a fair number of Russians. The Soviet forces had been called in, then withdrawn from Budapest, and 'at this stage—something that is not quite clear—the [Hungarian] Government almost ceased to function, split up, and one faction—maybe the bigger faction —called itself the government and pushed the smaller faction and the Prime Minister out'. The new government invited Soviet forces to come back and quell the disturbance. At this point in his speech Nehru said, 'I am giving the facts without any comment.' He went on: 'Soviet forces thereupon came back and dealt with people who were rebelling against the new government with a heavy hand. This so far as I know is the story. Details I do not know.' The Soviet Government had stated 'that they went back to Budapest with great reluctance and want to draw back as soon as possible, as soon as order is established—that is their statement—and then to discuss with governments [presumably of Poland and Hungary] total withdrawal from their countries. I give the facts as I know them.'

On the same day that Nehru gave this speech (9 November) Krishna Menon in New York voted against a resolution of the U.N. General Assembly calling for the withdrawal of Soviet troops from Hungary and for free elections in Hungary. Yugoslavia was the only other country outside the Soviet bloc to vote against the resolution.

(Nehru by his speech and Menon by his vote demonstrated how remote they were from the feelings at the time of people with whom they would normally have been *en rapport*. On 5 November the Asian Socialist conference, meeting in Bombay under the chairmanship of the Prime Minister of Burma, demanded the immediate withdrawal of Soviet forces from Hungary. On 6 November, Jean-Paul Sartre, Simone de Beauvoir and Vercors protested against the Russian use of 'guns and tanks to break the revolt of the Hungarian people'. Even communists had been attacking the Soviet action in Hungary. Thus the communist *Daily Worker* of New York in an editorial on 5 November attacked the Soviet Union's use of force in Hungary.)

I read Nehru's speech with horror on Saturday, 10 November

and immediately asked for an appointment with Pillai. When I called on him the next day at eleven in the morning he said as soon as I entered his office that no useful purpose would be served by my speaking to him about the Indian vote in New York. I said I wished to speak to him in my personal capacity and not under instructions from my government about something even more difficult and embarrassing—Nehru's references to Hungary in his Calcutta speech.

In Canada the speech will I am afraid have a deplorable effect. My guess is that in the United States the effect will be even more deplorable. One statement which is likely to cause deep resentment is that 'what appears to have occurred in Hungary is a civil conflict'. I can imagine someone like Walter Lippman writing 'I understand that Indians have had difficulty in agreeing on a term to describe the fighting which occurred in India ninety-nine years ago. Some have been calling it the first war for Indian independence instead of the Indian mutiny. Now Nehru has provided the correct term. It was no doubt the Indian Civil War of 1857. Certainly at that time the British were supported by Indian forces when they repressed the rebellion. Perhaps also the massacre at Jallianwala Bagh in Amritsar in 1919 might in future be described in Indian history books as an incident in an Indian civil conflict.'

I went on to quote those passages in Nehru's speech in which he had said that he was giving the 'story' of what had happened in Hungary when in fact he was giving the Soviet version of what had happened. I concluded by saying:

I am making no request even in the most unofficial and personal capacity. I am merely expressing my own strong personal hope that Mr Nehru may find it possible in his statement in Parliament next week to correct what I am sure was not the impression he had intended to convey in his Calcutta speech. It is not that in Parliament he need accept the western version of what has been happening in Hungary but can he not show that even while he is withholding final judgement he realizes with what deep emotions we in the West are gazing in impotence at what seems to us to be the martyrdom of a gallant nation?

The following day (12 November) Malcolm MacDonald, the British High Commissioner, asked me to drop in to see him for a talk. He said he wished he could speak to Nehru to try to convince him of the deplorable effects on the West of the Calcutta speech and the Menon vote but his position in Delhi was now so weak because of the British aggression on Egypt that there was no use in his speaking to Nehru about this. He hoped I would speak to Nehru since I was the only western ambassador in Delhi who was in a position to speak frankly to him.

I had told Ottawa in advance of what I was going to say to Pillai and I was prepared to say much the same thing to Nehru with whom I had an appointment on 13 November but just before I called on Nehru I received a telegram from Pearson in which he said that he considered that it would be unwise for me to continue my campaign on the Hungarian question any longer and that I was not to take any further initiatives except on express instructions.

The purpose of my call on Nehru on 13 November, which I made on instructions from Ottawa, was to pass on to him information which the Canadian Government had secured about Soviet troop movements into Hungary. I told Nehru that the tentative conclusion of the authorities in Ottawa was that the timing and pattern of these movements, which had begun at least as early as 25 October, and the necessary logistical preparation for them, showed that the Soviet Union was prepared to take drastic action to cope with the Hungarian situation if it got out of hand at least four days before the Israeli attack on Egypt and five days before the Anglo-French ultimata. The Anglo-French action against Egypt could not therefore be considered as the primary motivating factor for the Soviet leaders. Nehru said that for some months there had been two groups within the Soviet Government pulling in different directions. One group was prepared to allow the trends towards liberalization in Poland and other eastern European countries to continue; the other considered it dangerous to let these developments get out of hand. The mere fact that the Soviet military build-up against Hungary had begun at least as early as 25 October did not necessarily mean that the tougher group in the Soviet Government had won out by then. 'When opinion within a government on a critical issue is divided it is often necessary for a government to authorize preparations for action which would have to be taken if the government finally came down on one side or the other.' The implication of Nehru's remarks was that the Soviet decision to crush the revolution in

Hungary was not made until after the Soviet Government had learned of the aggression by Israel, France and Britain against Egypt and that this aggression might well have been the determining factor in the Soviet decision. (Most authorities now agree that the Soviet decision was not made until late on 31 October or on 1 November, a day or two after the British and French ultimata of 30 October.)

On 12 November, the day before this call on Nehru, I had at long last made progress in my efforts to get to Nehru an account of what had been happening in Hungary which he would consider authentic. The Swiss Minister, Clemente Rezzonico, called on me that day to express his great concern over the inability or unwillingness of Nehru to see what was happening in Hungary and asked if I thought there was anything he could do. I said that because of Switzerland's special position Nehru would be likely to be greatly influenced by an account by the Swiss Legation in Hungary. He said he would immediately telegraph his government asking them to send him for transmission to Nehru the account of events in Hungary which had been maintained by the Swiss Legation. His government acted immediately. He and his staff worked at top speed for long hours deciphering the cables from Berne and on 17 November he handed to Pillai two reports from the Swiss Minister in Budapest. One was written about 2 November, the other about 13 November. They were first-hand eye-witness accounts of what had actually happened in Budapest. When I read them I was not surprised that Pillai had told the Swiss Minister that he would immediately give them to Nehru. They reached Nehru two days before he spoke in Parliament at the opening of the debate on foreign policy. The United States version of what had happened in Hungary reached Nehru at about the same time.

I had on 5 November warned Pearson against Krishna Menon. I said that Menon's inclination had been to hold that the eastern European states had no right to national freedom and independence since the Soviet Union had a right to have satellites on its western borders. This, combined with his violent antipathy to the Americans, might well result in his refusing to co-operate wholeheartedly in a resolution demanding the immediate withdrawal of Soviet troops from Hungary. I recommended to Pearson that if this happened he should send me a telegram recounting the situation in the U.N. General Assembly, giving chapter and verse about Menon's attitude, and quoting remarks made by Menon to him which would be more appropriate to a second-year university student scoring points in a university debating society. The telegram might end with a statement that he (Pearson) was hoping to see Menon again and to persuade him to change his position. The telegram should not be accompanied by an instruction to take it up with Nehru or Pillai since it might be less embarrassing to Nehru if I could say that I was acting without instructions. 'As you know Nehru has an inexplicable trust in Menon and he is apt to flare up if other countries criticize him.' On 11 November I cabled Pearson that perhaps the time had come for him to send me this telegram. On 14 November my second-in-command came into my office in great excitement. 'Here,' he said, handing me a telegram, 'is the telegram we have been waiting for about Krishna Menon.' It was certainly just what I had suggested. On the face of it, it was a report to Ottawa from the Canadian delegation to the U.N. in New York but I was amused at seeing how carefully it had been tailored to meet my requirements. It was a most convincing and damaging account of Krishna Menon's behaviour during the debate and voting on the resolutions on Hungary.

The telegram had taken four days to reach me. It was dated 10 November, two days before the telegram saying I was not to take further initiatives except on express instructions. Moreover it was so clearly what I had asked for that I assumed that the instruction to pass it on to Nehru or Pillai was implicit. I therefore sent it immediately to Nehru under cover of a secret and personal letter saying that I was sending it to him on my own responsibility since the telegram had not been accompanied by any suggestion that I show it to him. I have not been able to discover whether Pearson intended me to give the telegram to Nehru. I was not, however, reprimanded for doing so and three years later a memorandum prepared in the Department of External Affairs in Ottawa said that it remained a matter of speculation whether Menon's change of tone in his references to Hungary which took place within a few days of my giving Nehru the telegram might have been the result of Menon receiving explicit instructions from Nehru. It is also, in my opinion, possible that the telegram was one of the factors which led to Nehru's forthright condemnation of the Soviet Union in his speech to Parliament on 19 November.

On 12 November I had recommended to Ottawa that, in the interest of making India aware of the implications of what was happening in Hungary, St Laurent or Pearson should, during the weekend of 17-18 November, give a speech ostensibly directed to the people of Canada but in fact directed 'to all those in the world who love freedom whether they live in Russia or India or Hungary or Canada' and I outlined the kind of speech that was likely to be most effective in India. Whether my telegram had any influence I do not know, but three days after I sent it, St Laurent did give a speech which contained an implicit appeal to Nehru to condemn the Soviet intervention in Hungary. St Laurent said:

It would be idle to deny that the Middle East crisis did serve to obscure in the minds of many people around the world and especially in nations of Asia the enormity of the vicious Soviet intervention in Hungary during these past weeks when courageous men and women, yes even children, unaided by any outside sources were striving so hard and so heroically to throw off the yoke of tyranny which is the nature of the Soviet colonial system. It did tend to make more difficult the mobilization of the full weight of world opinion in favour of national freedom and against foreign domination in Hungary and Poland. It is also true that such an outcry of world opinion is, short of war, the most effective form of political assistance which we can at this time provide to the valiant forces of freedom which are stirring in those parts of the Soviet empire.

A 900-word summary of the speech containing this passage reached me on the morning of 16 November and I immediately sent it to Nehru saying that I thought he might like to read it before giving his speech in Parliament.

I had called on Nehru the day before not to discuss Hungary but, on instructions from Pearson, to request him to try to persuade Nasser to withdraw his objections to Canadian forces being included in the United Nations emergency force for the Middle East on the ground that Canada was too closely associated with Britain. Nehru saw me within thirty minutes of my requesting an interview. He said that he had three or four days before heard about the possibility of Nasser objecting to

Canadians being included in the international force and he had immediately sent a message to Nasser that he was much distressed to hear this since Canada would be a good choice. Krishna Menon had also a day or so later sent a very strong message to New Delhi from New York with a copy for the Indian Ambassador in Cairo. Thus India had already made two approaches to Nasser, and he would now make a third. Within an hour of my leaving his office he had sent a telegram to the Indian Ambassador in Cairo instructing him to see Nasser. Pillai told me later in the day, 'The Prime Minister has gone as far as he possibly can.'

In my talk with Nehru I said, with reference to Nasser's contention that Canadian forces should not be included in UNEF because Canada was too closely associated with Britain, that Nehru knew not only of the public attitude which Canada had taken ever since the Suez crisis had broken three months before but he also knew of what we had been doing in private in London to try to restrain the British. He had seen St Laurent's second letter to Eden and I read him passages from the first letter. Nehru said with a smile, 'You don't need to convert me.' My talk with Nehru took place the day after he had received from me the telegram from New York about Krishna Menon. Neither of us referred to this telegram but it was with a somewhat malicious glint in his eyes that Nehru referred at least four times to the very strong language in the urgent message which Krishna Menon had sent in an effort to persuade Nasser to withdraw his objections to a Canadian contingent and he said that no doubt our people in New York were aware of this.

Many factors must have gone into the decision which Nehru made, possibly as late as the weekend of 17–18 November, that when he spoke in Parliament on 19 November he would disavow the pro-Soviet line on the Hungarian revolution which he had taken in his speech at Calcutta on 9 November. He must have weighed the evidence about what had been happening in Hungary which he had received from Switzerland, the United States and Yugoslavia. He probably dismissed many of the attacks on him by westerners as motivated by a dislike of him or of India or by anger at his forthright denunciation of the aggression by Britain and France against Egypt but he must have pondered over the many appeals he had received from friends and admirers throughout the world and he must have been shaken by the attacks on him by respected leaders in India.

Stanislas Ostrorog, the perceptive French Ambassador, told me on 14 November that never during his five years in India had the press of India been so united in openly expressing its difference of opinion with Nehru on foreign policy. A distinguished elder statesman of India, V. T. Krishnamachari, the Vice-Chairman of the Planning Commission, said to me sadly on 11 November, 'If Gandhi were alive he would not have spoken as Nehru has. He would have attacked what Russia has done in Hungary.' Jaya Prakash Narayan who, along with Nehru and Vinoba Bhave, had inherited a part of Gandhi's mantle and whom Nehru had for many years wanted as his successor, speaking in Bombay on 9 November, said that if Nehru had spoken as strongly about Hungary as about Egypt the course of events would have been changed. On 11 November, two days after Nehru's Calcutta speech, Narayan issued an 800-word formal statement attacking the government for having applied a double standard to Egypt and Hungary. This double standard was unworthy of India and the sooner India renounced it 'the better for India's honour, for the peace of the world and for goodwill among nations'. The 'Hungarian struggle for freedom had started on 22 October' but it was not until 5 November 'when the curtain was being rung down on the last act of the Hungarian tragedy that Mr Nehru spoke out at the Unesco conference'. 'It was a futile gesture because it was too late.' It had taken Nehru 'two weeks to make up his mind about an event the significance of which should have been clear to any person acquainted even slightly with the situation in eastern Europe'. Narayan went on to attack Nehru's 'astonishing' speech at Calcutta on 9 November based on information which Bulganin had given him. Nehru had spoken in that speech of the stronger wing of the Hungarian government having asked for Russian help to suppress disorder when 'all reports have agreed that Nagy had the overwhelming support of his people'. 'The crowning piece of the shameful story' of Nehru and Menon was India's opposition to the U.N. resolution of 9 November and Menon's speech on that day. 'A more perverse and false view of the situation could have hardly been imagined. As an Indian I hang down my head in shame.' Narayan's statement was published in full in many Indian newspapers and lengthy summaries were published in many others. I was told that when many influential Indians read this statement they said, 'There is the authentic voice of Gandhi.'

The debate in Parliament on Monday, 19 November, and Tuesday, 20 November, was the first real debate in Parliament on foreign affairs since my arrival in India four years before. I have little doubt that it was the first such debate ever held in the parliament of free India. Nehru opened and closed the debate. I heard his speeches, Acharya Kripalani's devastating attack on him and much of the rest of the debate.

On 16 November, the Friday preceding the debate, Nehru had read a statement to Parliament on Krishna Menon's votes in New York on the resolution of 9 November. Nehru could make no defence of Menon's abstention in the vote on the paragraph in the resolution which called on the Soviet Government 'to withdraw its forces from Hungary without any further delay'. He put forward two arguments for India's vote against the resolution as a whole. The first was that it demanded that the free elections which should be held in Hungary were to be 'under United Nations auspices'. India was in favour of free elections but not of their being held under U.N. auspices since this would 'set a bad precedent which might be utilized in future for intervention in other countries', meaning Kashmir. Realizing that this could justify no more than an abstention in the vote on the resolution as a whole Nehru added his second argument.

It seemed to us that this resolution, apart from the basic objection we had to a part of it, would not prove helpful to Hungary at all. We were trying to get the Soviet forces withdrawn from Hungary. What was proposed in this resolution would come in the way of that withdrawal and an attempt thereafter to intervene with armed force would have led to a major conflict. It might well have led to Hungary perishing in the flames of war. The people of Hungary had already passed through a terrible ordeal and it was the duty of other countries to rescue them from further warfare and destruction.

Nehru wisely did not attempt to explain why of all the members of the U.N. outside the Soviet bloc it was only India and possibly Yugoslavia which believed that the resolution would come in the way of the withdrawal of Soviet forces and that therefore they should vote against it. As for the reference to an attempt thereafter to intervene with armed force, Nehru and every other informed observer knew by 9 November when the resolution came to a vote that there was no possibility of any country other than the Soviet Union intervening with armed force in Hungary and thus no possibility of Hungary perishing in the flames of war as the result of intervention. As for the implication that India had voted against the resolution because of its duty to rescue the Hungarians from further warfare and destruction this clearly made no sense, and Nehru must have known it. M. O. Mathai, who was at the time Nehru's principal private secretary, states in his memoirs that Nehru sent Menon a telegram instructing him to abstain in the vote on the resolution; that Menon claimed that the telegram arrived too late but that this was a lie.[5] Whether or not Mathai is correct in this statement it is clear from Nehru's telegram to Menon of 11 November sent two days after Menon's vote that Nehru considered that Menon should have abstained on the resolution instead of voting against it.

There is much feeling in AICC circles that our attitude in regard to Hungary has not been as clear as it might have been. There is naturally great sympathy for the Hungarian people and resentment at the use of the Russian army in strength to suppress them. It is recognized that the position in Hungary has been different from that in Egypt; but nevertheless it is felt that we have not been quite clear in our declarations. From the legal point of view and because of lack of full information, our statements can be justified. But the fact remains that large bodies of Soviet forces have suppressed a nationalist uprising in Hungary involving terrible killing and misery for the people. Events move fast and it is not possible to have consultations. Generally speaking, it appears better to abstain from voting on resolutions containing some objectionable features and moving amendments, rather than voting against it.[6]

The importance of Nehru's speeches in Parliament on 19 and 20 November lay not in his reiteration of the half-hearted and unconvincing defence of Krishna Menon which he had made on 16 November but in his retreat from his Calcutta speech of 9 November. This speech had been based on a communication Nehru had received from Bulganin. The Socialist Opposition in Parliament referred to Nehru's retreat from the Calcutta speech as the 'debulganisation of the Prime Minister'. Nehru did not speak from a written text and his language was not always precise but the following extracts from his two speeches demonstrate the extent of his debulganisation:

There is little doubt that the present movement in Hungary ... [has] the great masses of the people behind it, with the workers, with the young people in it.... Undoubtedly the Government in Hungary [before the revolt] was not a free government, was an imposed government.... The Soviet armies were there against the wishes of the Hungarian people.... The majority of the people of Hungary wanted a change, political, economic or whatever the changes were, and actually rose in insurrection ... to achieve it but ultimately they were suppressed.... If in the course of ten years [of an imposed Communist government in Hungary] the people could not be converted to that particular theory it shows a certain failure which is far greater it seems to me than the failure of the military coup [the Hungarian revolution]. It indicates that all of us, whether we are Communists or non-Communists or anti-Communists, have to think afresh.... All these events have powerfully affected the prestige of the Soviet Union. ... That is a much more precious commodity—the respect that a country, its government and its policy has—than anything else.... So far as Communism is concerned, quite apart from the military adventure which it has indulged in, ... it has done something which has uprooted even the deep faith of many Communists....

All this except the final sentence comes from Nehru's speech at the opening of the debate. In my report to Ottawa on the debate I said that by following this line in his opening speech Nehru may have thought that he would be taking the wind out of the sails of the Socialist Opposition but if so he underestimated the intellectual level and the debating skill of the Socialist spokesmen, Acharya Kripalani, Asoka Mehta and H. V. Kamath. They were quickly able by emphasizing Menon's speeches and votes in New York and the pro-Soviet line Nehru had taken in his Calcutta speech to push Nehru into a corner. Kripalani in his speech pricked Nehru with his rapier four times. Each time Nehru jumped up to protest and Kripalani worsted him three times out of four.

To anyone who was present at the debate in Parliament it was obvious that Nehru was suffering humiliation at the hands of his critics. He had never before been so humiliated in Parliament. He was not going to be so humiliated again until the successful Chinese invasion of India in 1962. Perhaps it was the memory of this humiliation which led him to write to his sister Mrs Pandit three months later:

Krishna has often embarrassed me and put me in considerable difficulties. If I speak to him, he has an emotional breakdown. He is always on the verge of some such nervous collapse.[7]

In my report to Ottawa on the debate in Parliament I said:

I do not think that Mr Krishna Menon's enemies in India, and especially within the Indian cabinet, will be depressed by the debate in Parliament. My impression is that they think they have Mr Krishna Menon on the run and that they will eventually be able to bring him down. How long it will take is another matter. In the short run much depends on Mr Menon's behaviour in New York and on the speed with which the British and French get out of Egypt. Much also, of course, depends on how careful the western delegations in New York are not to give Mr Menon some excuse which Mr Nehru can make sound not too unreasonable to the Indian people, for refusing to vote with the West on resolutions on Hungary.

Immediately after Nehru had spoken in Parliament on 19 November I cabled extracts from his speech to Pearson and he used one passage in his address to the U.N. General Assembly that day. He said:

The leaders of some of the great countries of Asia have added their voices to the demand that the Hungarian people be allowed to decide their own future and their own form of government without external intervention. We have had much Communist talk in this discussion that this heroic Hungarian uprising was merely the result of reactionary and fascist gangs. . . . [The uprising] was well described by the Prime Minister of India on 19 November. Mr Nehru said: 'It is a national uprising, and also one thing is clear. The Soviet army was there against the will of the people.'

The debate in Parliament on 19 and 20 November marked the end of Nehru's wavering on Hungary and Krishna Menon immediately fell in line.

In order to get a first-hand report by Indian officials of the situation in Hungary, Nehru sent to Budapest at the beginning of December a special mission composed of K. P. S. Menon, the Ambassador in Moscow, who was also accredited to Budapest, and J. N. Khosla, the Chargé d'Affaires in Prague. They found that Budapest was an occupied city with Soviet guards stationed even along the corridors leading to Premier Kadar's office in the Parliament Building. In the revolt about 25,000 Hungarians and 7,000 Russians had been killed, and the damage to Budapest was heart-rending; it was on the scale of what happened in time of war. A few hundred people might have entered Hungary to support the revolt; some supporters of the revolt could be called reactionaries; but these constituted a very small part of the national uprising. The fighting had ended but there was still a considerable measure of peaceful resistance reminiscent of the days of civil disobedience in India. The people of Hungary were a heroic people, defeated and dispirited, without hope and without any national leader.[8]

In his speech in Parliament on 13 December Nehru indicated his acceptance of this report. His debulganisation was complete. He had now accepted the western version of the Hungarian revolution and he had denounced the Soviet-enforced counter-revolution. But his conversion to the western view came too late to restore his reputation in the western world. It had been damaged permanently. Years later Frank Moraes wrote in his article on Nehru in the *Encyclopedia Britannica*, 'Internationally Nehru's star was in the ascendant until October 1956. . . .' What was more important than the damage to Nehru's international reputation was that his conversion to the western view of the Hungarian revolution came too late to affect the course of Soviet policy. He believed, as he said to me on 13 November, that in October there had been two groups within the Soviet Government pulling in different directions and that the more liberal group was prepared to allow the trends towards liberalization in Poland and other eastern European countries to continue. The Soviet Government considered that it was important to maintain good relations with India and Nehru. This had been demonstrated by the two-week-long visit which Krushchev and Bulganin had made to India in December 1955, just eleven months before the outbreak of the Hungarian revolt. No other country outside the Soviet bloc had been favoured by such a visit. Hugh Gaitskell, the leader of the British Labour Party, on 27 October, two days after Soviet tanks had opened fire in Kossuth Square in Budapest, deplored 'the ruthless intervention of Soviet tanks and troops against the Hungarian workers'. He saluted 'the heroism of those who have given their lives in the battle for freedom' and he declared that what the Hungarians desired was 'the democratic socialism for which the Labour Party stands'. This statement was made two days before the Israeli invasion of Egypt and three days before the British and French ultimata. If on the following day Nehru had in a private communication to Krushchev and in a public speech supported what Gaitskell had said, he would have strengthened the more liberal group in the Soviet Government. Whether this would have made any difference to the decision which the Soviet Government made late on 31 October or on 1 November to suppress the Hungarian Revolution no one can say. Even after that decision had been taken, firm and consistent support by Nehru for the Hungarian Revolution might have moderated Soviet policy. On the bigger issues of foreign affairs statesmen seldom deal with certainties. They deal with possibilities and probabilities. Their task is to do their best to help turn probabilities of bad developments into mere possibilities, possibilities of good developments into probabilities. Nehru did not in the autumn of 1956 help turn probabilities of bad developments in Soviet policy towards Hungary into mere possibilities, possibilities of good developments in Soviet policy towards Hungary into probabilities. The Hungarian revolt brought him to a test. His attitude to the Hungarian revolt demonstrated his weaknesses not his strength, his flaws not his touches of greatness.

CHAPTER TWELVE
KRISHNA MENON

Preceding chapters have told the story of how during my posting in India from 1952 to 1957 the special relationship between India and Canada which had taken root in the first years of Indian independence from 1947 to 1952 had flowered and had then begun to fade. Krishna Menon helped the special relationship to flower. He helped it to fade. He was a partner with Lester Pearson in the long-drawn-out difficult negotiations which led to an armistice in Korea in 1953. Pearson and he worked together at the Geneva Conference in 1954 to bring peace to Indo-China. At U.N. General Assemblies in 1952, 1953 and 1954 they co-operated on many other questions. In 1955, chiefly because of increasing differences over Indo-China, co-operation between Menon and Pearson became more difficult and Menon's behaviour in 1956 and 1957 over the Hungarian Revolution and Kashmir put an end to it.

Messages which Pearson and I exchanged highlight the changes. At the end of 1952 Pearson in a message which he sent me to give to Nehru spoke of Krishna Menon's 'skill, integrity and patience' in handling the issue of Chinese prisoners of war in Korea at the U.N. General Assembly. To me at this time Menon was a brilliant, constructive negotiator and draftsman. In August 1954 I paid tribute in Nehru's presence to Menon's holy obstinacy in pressing at the Geneva Conference for a peaceful settlement in Indo-China. But by April 1956 I was warning Pearson that negotiations with India on the supervisory commissions in Indo-China and on any other matter in which Menon took an interest were going to become increasingly difficult because Menon was becoming more and more arrogant and was asserting mis-statements of fact as self-evident truths. Four months later Pearson told me that his attempts to talk business with Menon at the recently concluded meeting of Commonwealth prime ministers in London had been frustrating. 'He was inclined to be both ignorant and irritable in respect of the subjects, like Indo-China, which we brought up.' At the beginning of November when the crisis over the Hungarian revolution was at its height I warned Pearson that Menon had been inclined to hold that the eastern European nations had no right to national freedom and independence since the Soviet Union had a right to have satellites on its western borders and that this and his violent antipathy to the Americans might well result in his refusing to co-operate wholeheartedly in a resolution demanding the immediate withdrawal of Soviet troops from Hungary.

By the beginning of March 1957 Menon's behaviour at the U.N. General Assembly since 1 November 1956 had resulted in Pearson losing all confidence in him. In a personal letter to me of 8 March he wrote as follows about Krishna Menon:

[His] usefulness to the cause of good international relations has, so far as I am concerned, disappeared. I recognize that at times he can be most helpful and conciliatory, as he was, for instance, over Cyprus, but on the whole he is a bad person to have at the United Nations as the spokesman, not only of India but on many occasions of Asia. The contrast between his moral lectures to us about the Middle East, his wavering on Hungary, and his tough realistic approach to Kashmir was too glaring to do anything but detract from India's reputation.

There were two explanations which I gave at the time of what seemed to Pearson and me to be the deterioration from 1952 to 1957 in Menon's approach to Indian foreign policy and diplomacy. One was his increasing antipathy to the United States, the other the corrupting effects on him of his increasing influence over Indian foreign policy and diplomacy.

The increase in Menon's antipathy to the United States from 1952 to 1957 was understandable. Even in western democratic countries allied to the United States most leaders of public opinion had at this time profound misgivings about American foreign policy, particularly American policy on Asian issues such as Korea, Indo-China, and relations with the Communist government in Peking. In India these misgivings were intensified by American arms aid to Pakistan and by American refusal, as in the case of the proposed Indian membership in the Geneva Conference in 1954, to accord to India what virtually all the democratic allies of the United States considered to be

India's rightful place. Krishna Menon's reaction to American policy was more violent than that of other Indian leaders because he started with more antipathy to the United States and he was often unfairly attacked by leading Americans.

Thus at the end of 1952 Dean Acheson, then Secretary of State, attacked him for his activities at the U.N. General Assembly which had contributed so greatly to the passage of the constructive resolution on Chinese prisoners of war in Korea, activities which most other leading western observers considered were extremely helpful. Pearson in the summer of 1954 characterized United States opposition to Indian membership in the Korean conference as 'almost pathological' and as 'due in part to their feeling that India and Krishna Menon are the same thing at international conferences'. Menon must have known of this and also that the American government was at this time helping to finance a publication in India which attacked him with even greater vigour than that with which he attacked the United States.

The second explanation which I gave at the time of the deterioration in Menon's approach to Indian foreign policy and diplomacy was the corrupting effect on him of the power which resulted from his increasing influence over Indian foreign policy and diplomacy. By January 1954 it had already become so great that, according to Pillai, there was no one in the Indian Government, whether cabinet minister or official, other than Nehru himself who could exercise effective control over Menon.

By the time I left India on home leave in April 1955 Krishna Menon had no rivals in New Delhi as principal adviser to Nehru on foreign policy. Panikkar had lost his influence. Mrs Pandit had left New Delhi for London to be high commissioner there. R. K. Nehru was about to leave New Delhi to be ambassador to China. (I was told that he did not welcome this appointment and that he suspected that one reason for the appointment was that Krishna Menon, with whom his relations were bad, wanted to get him out of the way.) As for Pillai, he told me in September 1954 that he had said to Nehru that, much as he respected and liked Menon, there was not room in the External Affairs Ministry for both of them. He therefore asked Nehru for permission to accept the offer of appointment as Governor of the Reserve Bank (the central bank of India) which C. D. Deshmukh, the Minister of Finance, had made to him. Nehru had agreed but without enthusiasm, and six months later he persuaded Pillai to stay on as Secretary-General at least until the end of 1958. (He stayed until 1959.) Presumably Nehru did this at the urging of Menon who feared that if Pillai left he would be succeeded by R. K. Nehru (as he was four years later) and for Menon, Pillai was a lesser evil than R. K. Nehru.

When I visited Washington in September 1955 on my way back to India after home leave in Canada I found myself constantly pressed by officers of the State Department to give them my opinion of Krishna Menon. I reported to Pearson that I had had to develop my thesis on Menon about seven times,

my thesis being that the key to understanding him is that he thinks much more as a member of the left of centre section of the British Labour Party than as an Indian, that he has his roots in Great Britain and not in India and that his role is that of a Colonel House or a Harry Hopkins.

In my very last talk with Krishna Menon before I left India in 1957 he demonstrated his lack of knowledge of India, as well as his capacity to be rude and arrogant. I had by this time acquired some understanding of proper Indian modes of address in polite conversation and I liked to display my knowledge. At the end of my last talk with Menon in his office in the External Affairs Ministry he walked with me down the corridor to my next appointment which was with Anil Chanda, the Deputy Minister of External Affairs, who was a good friend of mine. When we entered Chanda's office I said, 'Good morning, Anil Babu.' Menon exclaimed, 'Oh, he's been in India more than four years and he still does not realize that Babu is a term of contempt used by the British.' I replied, 'Anil has taught me the proper way to address an intellectual from Bengal and that is why I called him Anil Babu.'

Dag Hammarskjold whom I saw in New York in September 1955 told me that he agreed one hundred per cent that the key to understanding Menon was that on most matters he thought as a member of the British Labour Party. In his opinion Menon's greatest weakness was his pathological vanity. Hammarskjold added that President Eisenhower had told him that on both times Menon had visited him, Menon had rubbed him the wrong way; he could have stood the intellectual arrogance but not the mock humility which accompanied it; the antipathy which Menon had aroused in Eisenhower made him useless as a diplomatic envoy from Nehru to Eisenhower.

Another of Menon's weaknesses was his fondness for putting on public exhibitions of laying down the law to foreign diplomats. He did this once to me in front of cameras at the New Delhi airport where we were greeting some distinguished visitor. He had the day before made a statement in parliament which misrepresented the position of the Canadian government on the subject of the Canadian component of the U.N. Emergency Force in Palestine. I knew that this statement would cause irritation in Ottawa and I wanted to give him an opportunity to explain it away. I therefore asked him for an interview. He put me off. At the airport he told me that he had faithfully represented the views of the Canadian government and, with a sweep of his arm, 'If the Canadian government want to protest let them protest.' He gave me the impression that he was dismissing my request for an interview. I phoned Pillai after I got back to my office and told him what had happened with the result that within a few minutes Menon was asking me to call on him. The next morning when I saw him in his office with no cameras and no reporters he was extremely reasonable. Not only did he explain away what he had said in parliament but he gave sensible advice to Pearson on how to deal with Egypt in discussions about U.N.E.F. He said, as I reported to Ottawa:

The Canadians and others still appeared not to realize the extent of the sensitivities of coloured people who had in the past been conquered by the West. If they did, they would take care to dress up their proposals to a body such as the Advisory Committee on U.N.E.F. so that the proposals would appear to strike an equal balance between Egypt and Israel even though in their working out the proposals would not constitute as great an intervention in Israeli administration as in Egyptian administration.

Menon's vanity, arrogance and bad manners could lead him to commit serious diplomatic blunders. The new Prime Minister of Canada, John Diefenbaker, came to New York during the autumn session of the U.N. General Assembly in 1957. He gave a dinner to which he invited the heads of the Commonwealth delegations to the Assembly including Selwyn Lloyd, then the British foreign minister, and Krishna Menon. Menon had shortly before had an accident and walked with a cane. Knowing Menon's touchiness I was apprehensive when before dinner I saw Lloyd taking the cane from Menon and putting on an imitation of Menon walking with it. Menon was visibly annoyed. At dinner Lloyd was given the place of honour at Mrs Diefenbaker's right and Menon sat on her left. Perhaps Menon's annoyance at Lloyd was compounded by the failure to treat him as the guest of honour. Whatever the cause he sat silent throughout the whole dinner. Diefenbaker who was devoted to his wife was angered. I saw my hopes for good relations between the new Canadian government and the Indian government being frustrated. My apprehensions increased when I discovered that the new foreign minister of Canada, Sidney Smith, perhaps as a result of Menon's rudeness to Mrs Diefenbaker, had taken the initiative in arranging talks with the heads of all the Commonwealth delegations to the Assembly except Menon. When I protested he sullenly agreed that he would see Menon if Menon asked to see him. I had a long private talk with Menon. I persuaded him after considerable argument that he would agree to my telling Sidney Smith that he wanted to have a talk with him. I also told Menon that unless relations between Canada and India were to be soured he must be on his best behaviour when he met Sidney Smith. He was, but this did little to offset the bad impression he made on Sidney Smith and the other Conservative members of parliament on the Canadian delegation to the Assembly by what seemed to them to be his tedious, intransigent speeches on Kashmir before the Security Council.

In 1956 and 1957 Menon consolidated his position as Nehru's principal adviser on foreign affairs. In February 1956 he at long last realized his ambition to be a member of the cabinet. At first he had no portfolio but Nehru put him in charge of Indian policy in the U.N. and this included such important questions as Kashmir, Goa, the Middle East and the supervisory commissions in Indo-China. Using this as a basis he quickly extended his power so that Pillai confessed to me eight months later that it was only when Menon was away from New Delhi that he had any influence on Nehru. Menon had a serious setback at the end of 1956 because of his attitude to the Hungarian revolution. But the setback was temporary. By the early months of 1957 he had more than recovered his previous position by what was considered by Nehru and by Indian public opinion generally as his brilliant defence of India's case in the debate on Kashmir before the U.N. Security Council. One senior Indian official later said to me that though Menon did not persuade anyone outside India that India had a case on Kashmir he persuaded Indians that India had a case. This made it possible for Nehru after the general elections of March 1957 to make him minister of defence and a member of the inner cabinet which consisted of Nehru and twelve of the cabinet ministers.

When I called on Menon shortly after his appointment as minister of defence he showed me a secret note from Nehru stating that as far as the External Affairs Ministry was concerned, he would continue to be responsible for Kashmir, Goa, Suez and U.N. affairs. Menon told me that he intended to continue to use his office in the External Affairs Ministry and not to move to the Defence Ministry. I said to Ottawa in a despatch at the end of April 1957:

Thus Menon gets a portfolio and does not lose his position in the External Affairs Ministry. He has his cake and eats it too. . . . Nehru clearly believes, though it seems incredible, that Menon was a first-rate advocate for India in the United Nations on the Kashmir issue. . . . Menon's power has increased and is increasing. I am afraid he is the kind of man who is corrupted by power. Nehru seems blind to this. Indeed, so far as Menon is concerned, Nehru seems to live in an unreal world.

I went on to say that Menon might take a mis-step which would start him down the slippery slope to the sort of political oblivion which had so suddenly engulfed his rival, Panikkar. Perhaps he had had in the past three or four months more popular success in India than was politically good for him. He was not accustomed to the adulation of crowds or to recognition in India of what he considered to be his merits. He was now getting both. There were signs that this was going to his head. For the last week, for example, almost every morning the newspapers had reported another public speech by him. Nehru might not like this competition. Menon was also more inclined than in the past to give the impression in conversation that he ran the Prime Minister. 'Most people don't like having the impression conveyed that they are run by someone else and I should think that Prime Ministers are no exception.' It used to be clear to everyone, including Menon, that he had no political strength in India and that his position in India depended entirely on Nehru. It had been assumed that once Nehru departed from the political scene, his shadow, Menon, would also depart. This was no longer as certain as it had been and Menon might now indeed be thinking that he had a chance for the greatest prize of all, the prime ministership. If Menon's eyes were fixed on the prime ministership and Nehru did not want him to be prime minister, Nehru might in time begin to feel that he would have to take Menon down a peg or two.

There is, however, the possibility which cannot be discounted, although at the moment it seems most improbable, that Mr Nehru may be thinking of Mr Menon as a possible successor. Mr Nehru has for long had an infatuation for Mr Krishna Menon. The infatuation has become lately almost an obsession. I have been told that at a recent meeting of the Congress Parliamentary Party he referred to Mr Menon as having one of the five or six greatest brains in India and that he had gone on to say that at the United Nations when Mr Vishinsky was alive everyone used to listen to him; and now Mr Menon has taken Mr Vishinsky's place. Mr Nehru has, I have been informed, told his sister, Mrs Pandit, that she is never to mention Mr Krishna Menon in his presence since he knows she would like to get her knife into him.

In April 1957 just before I left India I paid farewell calls on eight of the twelve members of the inner cabinet and also had long talks with the three senior members of the External Ministry, Pillai, Subimal Dutt and M. J. Desai. In my talks with the cabinet ministers I knew well and with Pillai, Dutt and Desai I brought up indirectly or fairly directly, depending on the person, the damage which Menon had done to India's interests abroad. In reporting on this to Pearson I said that my formula had been to mention the many crises or difficulties India was going through and to comment that it was unfortunate that these were coming to a head at a time when what seemed to the West to be inconsistencies between recent Indian policies on the Middle East, Hungary and Kashmir had aroused irritation and resentment among many even of India's best friends in the West. I had then, I told Pearson, when the ice was strong enough, gone on to speak along the lines of his letter to me of 8 March in which he had said that so far as he was concerned Menon's usefulness to the cause of good international relations had disappeared.

While those I talk to are naturally very cautious there is, I think, little doubt that most of them would subscribe entirely to the views you expressed in your letter to me. With only one exception, however, they gave me the impression that virtually nothing could be done to shake Mr Nehru's blind faith in Krishna Menon. Indeed, some have suggested that the more Menon is criticized, the stronger becomes his position with Mr Nehru. One man, however, suggested that the only person who could talk with Mr Nehru on the subject of Krishna Menon with any possibility of effect was Mr St Laurent. He said that only a prime minister could talk to Mr Nehru about Menon and that the only one of the Commonwealth prime ministers who would be listened to by Mr Nehru would be Mr St Laurent. The reason was that Mr Nehru had a special feeling of respect and affection for Mr St Laurent. He was clearly hoping that Mr St Laurent would speak very privately to Mr Nehru during the Prime Ministers' Meeting in London.

Before the Commonwealth Prime Ministers' Meeting took place St Laurent's government was defeated in the general elections on 10 June and it was John Diefenbaker who represented Canada at the Meeting, not St Laurent. Whether St Laurent would have spoken to Nehru about Menon I do not know. Whether it would have done any good I do not know.

I do not now recall with certainty which cabinet minister it was who suggested that St Laurent should speak to Nehru about Krishna Menon. I think it was probably T. T. Krishnamachari, then minister of finance. My reason for thinking this is a conversation I had with him in New York six months later. I was attending the U.N. General Assembly. He was in New York discussing India's financial needs with leading American bankers. He had just been in Washington discussing these needs with the United States government. He invited me to have breakfast with him and the secretary of the Finance Ministry, H. M.

Patel, at the Waldorf-Astoria hotel. He said to me that there were three main obstacles to the United States government doing very much more for India. The first was the general desire of Congress to cut down on expenditure; the second was the Pakistan lobby; the third was his colleague, Krishna Menon. Whatever Krishna Menon's merits or demerits, he was becoming a psychological obsession with many Americans in authority.

When in April 1957 I attempted in a final despatch to Ottawa to assess the strengths and weaknesses of Indian foreign policy and diplomacy I said that in the first seven or eight years of independence Indian diplomacy had suffered from the traditional defects of generous youth or gifted amateurs—reading lectures and self-righteous sermons to the world; offering simple solutions to difficult problems; dissipating one's influence over the policies of other countries by trying to exert influence over too wide a field instead of conserving one's influence for matters directly affecting the national interest; trying to do good in matters not of direct concern to one's own country, but of very direct concern to other countries. I went on to say:

In the last two years or so Nehru has offended much less often in these respects. His principal spokesman, Krishna Menon, has continued to offend. His offence is compounded by bad temper and sophomoric sallies. He also has a suspicion of the United States and a blindness to Russian crimes and ambitions which Nehru does not possess, or possesses to a much more limited degree.

# PART FOUR

CONCLUSION

CHAPTER THIRTEEN
SOME PUBLIC FIGURES

Vijaya Lakshmi Pandit

One reason for the ascendancy which Krishna Menon had secured by the beginning of 1954 on those issues of foreign policy in which he became involved—and these normally were issues that were being discussed by the U.N. General Assembly —was the paradoxical one that Mrs Pandit, his rival on Indian policy in the U.N., had become President of the General Assembly and Nehru maintained that as President she was an international official and should not be involved in discussions of Indian policy in the U.N. This seemed to me to be a specious argument. I am sure that Krishna Menon put it into Nehru's head. It was certainly an argument which Lester Pearson would have repudiated; he was foreign minister when he was President of the Assembly and he did not subject himself to any such self-denying ordinance. Nor did other foreign ministers who served as presidents of the Assembly.

Mrs Pandit was guarded in speaking to me in 1954 about Menon but he had no similar inhibition. In speaking to one ambassador he referred to Mrs Pandit as a 'glamour puss' and when she was speaking at a reception given in her honour as President of the Assembly by the Indian Federation of U.N. Associations he kept making loud disparaging remarks about her speech to my wife who was sitting next to him. A few minutes later he was prevailed on to speak as a result of Mrs Pandit's urgings and when she walked up with him to the platform they acted as though they were close friends.

I reported to Pearson that a long talk which I had had with Mrs Pandit at the beginning of January 1954 had confirmed in my mind what I understood was Pearson's view that Mrs Pandit was now a much wiser and more moderate adviser on foreign affairs than she had been seven or eight years ago. Such influence as she possessed over Nehru was, I said, on almost all questions a moderating one. She had gone out of her way on 23 December 1953, in her first speech to parliament after her return from the U.N. General Assembly in New York, to state that she did not believe the world was in danger of American expansionism, an obvious rebuttal of the thesis which Krishna Menon was advancing at the time. When she was appointed as High Commissioner to London I wrote to the Canadian High Commissioner in London about her. I said:

My strong impression is that she is one of the few people surrounding the Prime Minister who is not afraid to give him frank advice even though it may be distasteful to him. Moreover, her advice can almost always—if not always—be depended upon to be a counsel of moderation. How great her influence over the Prime Minister is, I do not know. I doubt whether it is as great as Krishna Menon's. But it is, I think, substantial. Certainly I think that the two people Mr Nehru is fondest of are Mrs Pandit and his daughter, Indira Gandhi.

I also explained to him that Pandit was pronounced pundit; and that her family and friends called her Nan. I did not try to explain why so many Americans called her Madam Pandit instead of Mrs Pandit.

Mrs Pandit would have much preferred to be minister for external affairs or the Chief Minister of U.P. than high commissioner to London. Girja Bajpai told me in November 1953 that Nehru had recently told him that he wanted to appoint a foreign minister, but he asked who was available. He knew that ambassadors in New Delhi consulted Mrs Pandit on Indian foreign policy but he would be criticized if he appointed his sister. Bajpai said to me that he did not rule out the possibility of Mrs Pandit becoming foreign minister. Krishna Menon wanted the position but Bajpai did not think he had a chance. He was unpopular with the Congress Party which had been annoyed even by his election to the Upper House of Parliament, the Council of States.

Sardar Panikkar

At the beginning of 1954 a rival to Krishna Menon appeared in New Delhi, Sardar K. M. Panikkar, India's first ambassador to Communist China from 1950 to 1953 and ambassador to Egypt in 1953. He was brought back to New Delhi to serve on the States Reorganization Commission. Panikkar was ambassador to China when I took up my appointment in New Delhi and I found out in my introduction to Indian diplomacy that he aroused intense dislikes and suspicions. I had a talk with Pillai about Panikkar at the end of December 1953 just after it had been announced that he would be returning to New Delhi. Pillai said that he was afraid of the influence which Panikkar would exert. Krishna Menon advised the Indian Government to exercise moderation in dealing with colonial issues but Panikkar pressed Nehru into extremist policies on these issues. I reported to Ottawa in January 1954 that Panikkar's return to New Delhi would enable him to exert greater influence on Indian foreign policy and that it was generally believed among western diplomats in New Delhi that Panikkar was an evil genius of Nehru. I suggested that it was possible that Panikkar and R. K. Nehru might find themselves on the same side on many issues. Two and a half months later I told Ottawa that my gloomy predictions appeared to have been accurate. I went on to say that I had been informed by a reliable source in the External Affairs Ministry (I cannot now recall whether it was Pillai or someone else) that within a few weeks of Panikkar's return to New Delhi R. K. Nehru was relying on him more and more for advice on almost all the questions of foreign policy with which he was concerned, that he was showing him many reports and despatches, and that he was even consulting him on appointments of heads of mission. I quoted 'a reliable and high source in the Ministry of External Affairs' as saying that the influence of Krishna Menon and Panikkar on Prime Minister Nehru was so great that he had been advised that it was worse than useless to criticize them adversely in any way when speaking to Nehru. He said that the current phrase was 'the Prime Minister has an infatuation for Krishna Menon and an admiration for Panikkar'.

During 1954 I became a member of a small dining club called the Bahadurs which Panikkar had founded. It consisted of five ambassadors or high commissioners and five Indians, none of whom could be members of the External Affairs Ministry. At the end of the first meeting which I attended after being elected to the club, I must have looked somewhat overwhelmed by the evening for Malcolm MacDonald, who had been a member of the Bahadurs for some time, said to me, 'It's always the same at every meeting. For the first half of the evening everybody talks and nobody listens. During the second half, Panikkar talks and everybody listens.' Panikkar had a beard like Lenin's and cultivated a likeness to Lenin. At meetings of the Bahadurs he discoursed with equal facility, vigour, assurance, wit and brilliance on subjects about which he knew much and on those of which he knew almost nothing. He also told stories about his victories in repartee, some of which were probably inventions and others exaggerations. Thus he told me a couple of years later when he was ambassador to France that when he had presented his credentials to the President of France and the President had said, 'How extraordinary of India to appoint as ambassador to France a man who speaks no French', he had replied, 'India will appoint an ambassador to France who speaks French when France appoints an ambassador to India who speaks Hindi.'

Panikkar's influence over Nehru was short-lived. By the spring of 1955 he was no longer even being kept informed on questions concerning Indian foreign policy though he still pretended to be knowledgeable about these questions.

Indira Gandhi

When we first came to India in 1952 Indira Gandhi was thirty-five years old. She lived at the Prime Minister's house with her husband and her two young sons. She was recognized as the Prime Minister's hostess. She had been, for example, the hostess at the state banquet I had attended in January 1950 which Nehru had given at Rashtrapati Bhavan in honour of Rajagopalachari. But though she was *de jure* the Prime Minister's hostess, her aunt, Mrs Pandit, would, I think, sometimes give her the impression that she was behaving at functions at the Prime Minister's house as if she were hostess. Sometimes, too, I think Rajan Nehru (Mrs R. K. Nehru) might give her the same impression.

My wife and I and Indira Gandhi got on well together from the beginning of our stay in New Delhi. We were soon on first-name terms. We liked her and she, we felt, liked us. She would come to informal dinners at our house as, for example, on my birthday. I never thought of her during the first part of my assignment to New Delhi as being politically ambitious. When in 1979 I read T. N. Kaul's memoirs I found that his description of her in 1954 tallied with my memory of what I then felt about her: 'She was shy, unassuming, aloof and quiet and did not show much outward interest in party politics.'[1]

I did not at the time suspect the dislike which existed between Indira Gandhi and Mrs Pandit, which went back to Indira Gandhi's childhood. And I did not know that there was an unresolved dispute between them over who had official precedence over the other. This failure of perceptiveness put me once in an embarrassing position. My wife and I were giving a farewell lunch in honour of George Allen, the American Ambassador. We invited Indira Gandhi and Mrs Pandit. Both accepted. It was my social secretary's task to draw up a seating plan for the lunch based on the official Indian order of precedence. If there were problems about relative precedence she would consult the protocol division of the Ministry of External Affairs. She came to me in some distress because the junior officer in the protocol division with whom she dealt was not being helpful over the seating for this lunch. I said that I would phone the Chief of Protocol. I said to him, 'We are having problems over the seating at the lunch we are giving tomorrow for George Allen. Mrs Pandit and Indira Gandhi are coming.' There was a long silence at the other end of the phone and then, 'Escott, you shouldn't have done it.' I said that unfortunately I had and what was I to do now? Who would sit on my right at lunch—Mrs Pandit or Indira Gandhi? The Chief of Protocol refused to give an opinion. Finally when I pressed him he said the best thing for me to do was to make George Allen co-host but I would have to decide without benefit of advice from him who should sit on my right and who on George Allen's right.

By the spring of 1955 Mrs Pandit's departure for London and Rajan Nehru's for Peking where her husband had been appointed as ambassador left Indira Gandhi as undisputed hostess, *de jure* and *de facto*, at the Prime Minister's residence. It was not until my talk with Dag Hammarskjold in New York in September 1955 that I realized that Indira Gandhi's victory over Mrs Pandit and Rajan Nehru was probably related to Krishna Menon's victory over Panikkar. Hammarskjold told me that he had learned on what he considered good authority that Menon's influence with Nehru stemmed in part from the support which Indira Gandhi gave him and that this was related to the rivalry between Indira Gandhi and Mrs Pandit. By the spring of 1957 Indira Gandhi was beginning her rapid rise in the hierarchy of the Congress Party which culminated two years later in her election as President of the Party.

M. O. Mathai

Krishna Menon and Pillai came from Kerala, which was then the smallest state in India, the most densely populated and possessing the highest proportion of literates, Christians and Communists. M. O. Mathai, Nehru's principal private secretary, also came from Kerala. (According to Subimal Dutt, Mathai, 'by the time he resigned early in 1958, was probably one of the most influential persons in Delhi'.[2]) When Nehru went to London for the 1956 meeting of Commonwealth prime ministers he took only three advisers with him: Menon, Pillai and Mathai. I saw Pillai and Mathai shortly before they were to leave. I said that if Indian newspapers were like newspapers in most other democratic countries they would have carried stories about how strange it was that these three advisers all came from a state which contained only about three per cent of the population of India and they would have talked about 'the Kerala gang' which surrounded the Prime Minister. The next day I received a parcel from Mathai containing the kind of Kerala costume which Krishna Menon wore in India—a flowing white *dhoti* with embroidered edges, a long white shirt without collar and a stole with embroidered edges. With the parcel came a note, 'This will qualify you to join "the gang which forms a ring around the Prime Minister".'

I wrote to Pearson who would shortly be seeing Mathai in London that a few days after I had received this gift from Mathai he had come to family dinner at our house and that I had worn the Kerala costume in his honour.

Perhaps as a result of this Mathai became more communicative than on previous occasions. He was also somewhat indiscreet. . . . Mathai professes a most profound admiration for Krishna Menon's intellect and intelligence. On the other hand, he makes great fun of him for being, as he says, so 'frightened' of Mr Nehru. He is also happy to do his best to destroy the legend that Menon has known Mr Nehru intimately for many years. He says in all they have 'known each other for only two months' and that Mr Nehru himself is responsible for this statement.[3] I assume what he means by this is that over the many years during which Mr Nehru and Menon have been acquainted the number of days on which they have seen each other, other than casually, totals only about sixty. Mathai is a great admirer of Pillai. This may be partly local patriotism, but I think it is also partly affection and genuine respect. He has repeated to me firmly on more than one occasion that there is no civil servant in whom Mr Nehru reposes greater trust and confidence than Pillai.

Leonard Brockington, the greatest Canadian orator of his generation, came to Delhi in November 1956 as head of the Canadian delegation to the Unesco conference. Among the famous orations which he had delivered in Canada was an eulogy of Gandhi delivered over the Canadian radio on the occasion of Gandhi's death. Brockington, Mathai and I had dinner together at the end of the conference. I was still convalescing from jaundice and was off alcohol. They each had a couple of whiskeys before dinner, wine at dinner and brandy after. At the brandy stage the conversation got around to Gandhi. Through one ear I heard Mathai declaiming that it was fortunate for India that Gandhi had been assassinated soon after Independence because his influence on Indian policy would have been bad with his preaching of cow worship, his opposition to modern methods of contraception, his fanatical advocacy of Hindi, linguistic states, prohibition and cottage industry.[4] Through the other ear I heard Brockington repeating his eulogy of Gandhi. Neither heard a word the other said.

Rajagopalachari

Krishna Menon, during my stay in India, became corrupted by power and by public adulation, and his judgement became increasingly distorted by his dislike of the United States and his obsession with the danger to India from Pakistan. Chakravarti Rajagopalachari, commonly known as Rajaji, the elder statesman of India in my time, was becoming towards the end of my stay in India corrupted by the loss of power. Rajaji had a sense of humour and a malicious wit which Krishna Menon lacked. The first time I met him was at the banquet which Nehru gave in his honour in January 1950, two days before he ceased to be Governor-General. In those days, in India as in Canada, women curtsied when presented to the Governor-General. Before the dinner we were all lined up around the vast drawing room so that the Governor-General could walk along the line and meet the guests. I was standing beside Lady Nye, the wife of the British High Commissioner. When her turn came she made a deep, deep curtsey. Rajaji said, in his piping high voice, 'That will be your last opportunity to do that, my dear.'

When St Laurent came to India at the beginning of 1954 Rajaji was Chief Minister of Madras. Charles Ritchie of the Department of External Affairs and I accompanied St Laurent on his call on Rajaji at his office in Fort St George. We were received by an array of photographers and newspapermen. We were shown into an office where Rajaji had gathered to meet us, not his cabinet, but his six leading civil servants. More pictures were taken. There was some discussion with the civil servants of the development plans of Madras State. Rajaji led us out of this meeting into the hall again. More photographers, more interviewers. Then he escorted us into his private office. The photographers followed. They took pictures. They withdrew. The four of us were left alone: St Laurent, Rajaji, Charles Ritchie and I. Rajaji broke the silence. 'Prime Minister,' he said, 'people always think that when people like us get together for a private talk, we have something to talk to each other about. Actually, of course, we haven't.' I have always felt that I failed in my duty by not having warned St Laurent that Rajaji was capable of such an escapade. Rajaji had never played this kind of trick on me but he had on the United States Ambassador, George Allen, and George Allen had told me the story. Allen was making his first visit to Madras and the programme included a call on Rajaji. Allen was ushered into the Chief Minister's office. They shook hands. They sat down. Rajaji turned to him and said, 'And now, Mr Ambassador, I suppose we shall embark on an exchange of the usual platitudes.' I do not now remember how the conversation between St Laurent and Rajaji went after Rajaji's unusual opening gambit. My guess is that it went about as well as such conversations usually go. St Laurent wrote to Rajaji two years later that he had never forgotten the impression of Rajaji's realism which he had got from his interesting conversation with him, of which he had such agreeable memories.

I paid my last call on Rajaji in January 1957. He was then living in retirement in Madras. I reported to Ottawa:

> Mr Rajagopalachari was looking much older than when I had seen him last, two years ago when I accompanied the Prime Minister on his call.... His mind, however, is very clear, his wit is still mordant, but I am afraid he has succumbed, as I understand Lloyd George did in his later years, to a temptation which besets men who have had great power and have lost it—the temptation to strike about rather wildly in all directions. Mr Rajagopalachari has lately been leading campaigns against the Commonwealth, Hindi, nuclear bombs, the method which has been adopted for currency reform, B.C.G. (compulsory vaccination against tuberculosis), the anti-Brahmin movement in the South, and reforms within Hinduism.

Radhakrishnan

Sarvepalli Radhakrishnan was Vice-President of India during the whole of my term as High Commissioner. He, like Rajaji, was a Brahmin from Madras but unlike Rajaji he was a philosopher (and a very distinguished one) not a politician, he was a Hindu liberal not a Hindu conservative, and he had never been a member of the Congress Party. He had for a while been a professor at Oxford and he had been knighted by the British. He would have made an excellent director-general of Unesco. I suggested this to Pearson in the spring of 1956.

Soon after my arrival in India I got into the habit of calling on Radhakrishnan every few months. He would invite me to tea at his house. During about my third call when we were drinking tea and talking about India and its problems it suddenly dawned on me that the atmosphere was that of a tutorial at Oxford. Radhakrishnan was my tutor supervising my study of India.

Radhakrishnan was fond of my wife. Sometimes they found themselves at the same table at dinners in the Prime Minister's house and I would be at the Prime Minister's table. From Radhakrishnan's table we would hear outbursts of laughter.

Nehru would look a bit puzzled, perhaps jealous because his table was usually subdued. My wife accompanied me on my farewell call on Radhakrishnan in April 1957. This, I think, encouraged him to pour out to us his sorrows and disappointments. In my report to Ottawa I said that I thought it so probable as to be virtually certain that Nehru had told Radhakrishnan some months before that he would be elected President of India in the elections at the beginning of May. Rajendra Prasad refused to retire, however, and he apparently had the support of a large number, if not of a majority, of the Congress Parliamentary Party. Most of the members of the Congress Parliamentary Party, being conservative Hindus, preferred Prasad to Radhakrishnan because Prasad was a conservative Hindu. Radhakrishnan was so put out by this that for a time he refused to permit his name to be put forward for the vice-presidency. He finally agreed at the Prime Minister's pleadings. He kept asking me,

What is there to do in the Vice-President's job? What useful purpose is served by my staying in it? All I do is to address public meetings and open Canadian art exhibitions. The Prime Minister seldom comes to talk to me about his problems. I have to take every advantage of opportunities to take him aside at public functions in order to argue with him.

Radhakrishnan, I said, was particularly upset by Krishna Menon's elevation to the portfolio of Defence Minister. When some time ago Nehru had brought up the question of the inclusion of Krishna Menon in the Cabinet, an objection had been raised that Menon was a bad administrator and careless about financial matters. Nehru had replied that this would not matter since he would not be given a portfolio. Now he had got one.

The second Indian general elections had taken place shortly before my farewell call on Radhakrishnan. The Congress Party on the whole had done well. Its share of the popular vote which had been 45 per cent in the first general elections in 1951 had risen to 48 per cent. The anti-Congress vote was split among many parties. The one with the most popular support was the Praja Socialist Party but its share of the popular vote fell from 16 per cent to 10 per cent. The second most important anti-

Congress party was the Communist; its share of the popular vote increased from 5 per cent to almost 10 per cent. In the Lok Sabha the Congress Party had almost exactly the same number of seats as in the previous house—365 out of 500. Congress governments were returned to power in every one of the fourteen states except Kerala where the Communists won and Kashmir, which returned the National Conference Party, an ally of the Congress Party. But in the elections the forces of communalism and caste were pervasive. Muslims tended to vote for Muslims and Hindus for their own sub-caste regardless of party labels. In our conversation in my farewell call, Radhakrishnan said that he was depressed by what had happened in the elections—not only the coming into power of a Communist government in Kerala but also the demonstration of the strength of communalism and caste. I said in my report to Ottawa of my talk with Radhakrishnan:

What the Congress Party needs, he said, is fresh blood at the top and an intensive drive against corruption. If it does not make such a drive then in the next election there may be five Keralas—five states in India which go Communist. The Communist government in Kerala is doing two things—putting down corruption and raising the salaries of low paid officials in the villages. These low paid officials are school teachers, administrative officials and the police. This is the same thing which the Congress Party had done when it first came into power in the provinces in the thirties. This is the surest way of building up strength in the countryside. One difficulty is that the Prime Minister is himself without guile or a capacity for intrigue and he does not recognize guile and intrigue in the people around him, nor does he know how reactionary some of his Cabinet Ministers are. One man Dr Radhakrishnan mentioned by name was Pandit Pant, who is in order of precedence third-in-command of the Cabinet and in practice second-in-command. Dr Radhakrishnan said that Pandit Pant was so reactionary that when one of his junior colleagues in the Ministry, a fellow Brahmin, Mr Malaviya, permitted his daughter to marry a non-Brahmin, Pandit Pant went up to him and said, 'You should be ashamed of yourself.' According to the theory of the Congress Party, this is the kind of remark which so clearly demonstrates caste prejudice that it should constitute a disqualification from being even a Congress candidate.

Radhakrishnan came from a non-Hindi-speaking state. He was opposed to the efforts of the Hindi-speaking north of India to make Hindi the national language in the whole of India. As I got up to go from my farewell call I said to him that I supposed it would not be necessary for my successor to be able to speak Hindi but perhaps it would be necessary for my successor's successor. Radhakrishnan said, 'I don't see why. I don't speak a word of Hindi and I have no intention of ever learning Hindi. If I don't have to learn Hindi, why should an ambassador?'

Morarji Desai

Morarji Desai was Chief Minister of the State of Bombay when I came to India and he remained Chief Minister until he became a member of the central government in the autumn of 1956 as Minister of Commerce and Industry. Even before he came to New Delhi he was, as I wrote in a despatch to Ottawa in February 1955, 'generally considered to be the most likely successor to Mr Nehru as Prime Minister of India'. I had met him a number of times in 1953 and 1954 but I did not have a long talk with him until February 1955. He had just returned to Bombay after a two-week's absence during which he had been attending the annual meeting of the Congress Party. I had a fifty-minute conversation with him in his office. In my report to Ottawa I said:

Mr Morarji Desai is fifty-nine years old. He is opposed to alcohol, gambling, horse-racing and ostentatious living. He has not, however, the thin mouth or the repellent personality which one associates with fanatics on prohibition and simple living. He has a great deal of charm in conversation and has a humorous mobile mouth. He is said to be cordially disliked by most sections of the community but he is a powerful figure in Indian politics. He gave me the impression of great confidence in his own future as well as in the future of India. I think he believes he is likely to become Prime Minister of India.... Mr Maurice Zinkin... has told me that he thinks that the closest thing in recent British political history to Mr Morarji Desai and others like him in the Congress Party are the non-conformist middle-class Welsh Liberals of the end of the nineteenth century. They too had simple ideas of right and wrong and they had a hatred of alcohol and gambling and believed in simple living and hard work. I thought of this when at the end of our conversation Mr Morarji Desai said that he was confident that everything was going to work out for the good of the world. He shares, I think, the belief of the old non-conformist Welsh Liberal not only in the inevitability of progress but in Divine Providence.

Much of our conversation was directly or indirectly about Nehru. I thought at the time that some of his remarks about Nehru were strangely indiscreet. Here he was hoping to be Prime Minister, realizing presumably that Nehru's support for his ambitions would be helpful but nevertheless in his first serious conversation with me making remarks about Nehru which if Nehru heard of them would annoy if not anger him. Thus Morarji Desai suggested that Nehru had not only been born with a silver spoon in his mouth (which was true) but that he had had extraordinary luck in reaping where others had sown and in getting credit for the work of other people. He made it clear that he was referring not only to the usual story that when Nehru first became President of the Congress Party in 1929 at the age of forty he was chosen not because of his own qualities but because he was the son of his father, Motilal. Morarji Desai meant also that it was Mahatma Gandhi who had secured the independence of India and Nehru who had reaped the reward of becoming the first prime minister. Similarly it was Sardar Patel who had forced the princely states of India to join the Indian Union. Morarji Desai said that Nehru could not have done what Sardar Patel did; Nehru was not ruthless enough.

Early in our conversation when speaking about American foreign policy, Morarji Desai said that one difficulty with the Americans was that they had never known defeat in war. They had always fought their wars to virtually unconditional surrender. The same was true of Nehru. He had never known defeat. He had never in his life met with anything but success. 'Mr Nehru is an American.' He had never told Nehru this and he was sure it would annoy him to be told. But he had told a number of Americans, including Adlai Stevenson. He had suggested that Americans would find it easier to get on with Nehru if they realized how alike he was to them.

He said he had, however, been frank in telling Nehru that the bad relations between India and the United States could not be blamed wholly on the Americans since it took two to make a quarrel. He thought that one problem was that Nehru had in the years before independence, and for a short time after, known that he was the idol of the American people. Now he was attacked viciously in the United States. Nehru believed, however, that he had not changed. Morarji Desai made it clear that he himself was not so certain that Nehru had not changed in the previous eight or nine years. He did not say this directly but he did bring up the whole question of the effect of power on the holders of power. My impression was that he accepted the orthodox explanation that the reason that power so often corrupts is that the powerful man is surrounded by people who tell him what he wants to be told because they want something out of him and that Nehru had been corrupted in this way. Some time after our theoretical discussion of the problem of the effect of power Morarji Desai said, 'Mr Nehru is the most powerful man in the world today. He is powerful because he is the idol of all the people of India who love him even when he is abusing them.'

Morarji Desai said that one source of Nehru's strength was that he was willing to change his mind. All the Congress leaders when they were in opposition during the struggle for independence had made irresponsible statements and had committed themselves to unrealistic programmes. Many of them now tried to pretend that their present policies were consistent with their previous statements. Nehru made no such pretence. Thus in the middle thirties by the exercise of a great deal of persuasion he got Mahatma Gandhi to support the proposal that when India became independent it should break completely with the Commonwealth. Now Nehru was a wholehearted supporter of the Commonwealth connection.

I said that I had been struck by the fact that Nehru had lately been attacking caste and communalism more forcefully than when I first arrived in India. It seemed to me that he must be worried about the increasing strength of communalism and caste. Morarji Desai said that the explanation was the exact opposite. The reason Nehru was now attacking caste and communalism more directly than before was that they were weaker and he now felt strong enough to go over to the attack. 'In twenty years' time caste will have disappeared from India.'

Boshi Sen

In Almora we met an agricultural scientist, Boshi Sen, who was as close to being a saint as anyone I have ever met. He was a devout Hindu, a disciple of Vivekananda. He told me stories of his own life and of the lives of people he knew which had the resonance of some of the sayings of Jesus and of the stories of the way in which Jesus gathered together his disciples. Boshi Sen said that he might have become, like other Bengali intellectual nationalists of his generation, an assassin of British officials but for a question put to him by the man who subsequently became his guru, his spiritual adviser. This man said to him, 'How many British are there in India?' He replied, 'I suppose about two hundred thousand.' His interlocutor said, 'How many Indians are there in India?' He replied, 'Three hundred million.' His interlocutor said, 'Are the British in India because of our weakness or their strength?' Vivekananda had once said, 'You can't preach religion to empty stomachs', so Boshi Sen, after he became converted, gave up pure science to go in for agricultural research in order to fill empty stomachs in India and thus make possible the spread of religion. He told me that Vivekananda's first disciple was the station master at the terminus of the railway line which pilgrims took who were going to the holy places of Hardwar and Rishikesh. His custom was to give the pilgrims a little something to eat. One night he dreamt of a pair of penetrating eyes. The next day he saw those eyes in a pilgrim getting down from a third-class railway car. He invited the man to come to his house for a meal. Then he went to his office, cleared up his papers, locked them away, changed out of his uniform and went up to the pilgrim and said, 'Will you take me as your disciple?' Just like the disciples of Jesus leaving their fishing boats. The pilgrim was Vivekananda. The station master, years later, became Boshi Sen's guru.

CHAPTER FOURTEEN
INDIA'S PROSPECTS

I had three farewell talks with the Nehru family in April 1957 just before I left India, all of them at the Prime Minister's house. The first was with Indira Gandhi, the second with Nehru, and the third a farewell lunch at which there were present only Nehru, Indira Gandhi, Mrs Pandit and my wife and I.

We had two pieces of Eskimo sculpture by Oshaweetuk which we were very fond of. We decided to present them as farewell gifts to Nehru and his daughter. I gave the walrus to Nehru and my wife gave the musk-ox to Indira Gandhi. My last words to her when we were leaving after lunch were, 'Please don't repeat this to anyone but note the resemblance between the sculptures and two of the cabinet ministers. The walrus looks like Pandit Pant, the musk-ox like the Rajkumari Amrit Kaur.' Sixteen years later when she was Prime Minister we met at dinner at the Prime Minister's house in Ottawa. She said to me, 'Do you remember your last words to me before you left India?' I looked blank and she said, 'About the Eskimo sculptures'. I wondered if, with so retentive a memory, she also remembered what I had said to her in our hour-long private talk a week before the family lunch. We had been talking about the weaknesses of the Socialist Party. I said, 'It seems to me what the Socialist Party should do is to pick at random a dozen villages out of the half million villages in India. The villages should be ones dominated by the Congress Party. The Socialist Party should send to each village a couple of people to live there for three months or so and uncover as many incidents as possible of corruption, bad treatment of Harijans, police brutality and so on. Then the Socialist Party would publish the results, village by village, over weekly intervals. Surely this would be an effective way of weakening public support for the Congress Party.' (If I had visited India during the emergency which she proclaimed I would have reminded her of this and suggested that she use this technique to find out what was happening under the emergency.)

In my farewell talk with Indira Gandhi I went over some of the ground which I intended to go over with Nehru when I saw him a few days later. I hoped she would tell him and that this might mean that he would be better prepared for the discussion with me. I started my talk with Nehru by saying that I had just returned from Ranikhet and that he ought to take a holiday there soon since the view of the Himalayas was now at its loveliest. He told me that he was planning to take four or five days in the mountains above Mussoorie. He congratulated me on my ability to take a holiday just before leaving. I said it was not a holiday since I had been working on a farewell speech which I was to give to the Rotary Club of New Delhi, an article for the Indian newspapers and, what was much more difficult, a confidential despatch to Ottawa summarizing my views about India. I went on to say that trying to do this despatch had impressed on me how little I knew about India. I recalled that when I had first called on him he had said he had not himself finished his voyage of re-discovery of his own country. I said I hoped he would not think it impertinent if I were to ask him to let me go over with him some of the ideas which had occurred to me in attempting to cast a balance sheet of India's liabilities and assets. He said he would be happy if I were to do this.

I said that the first liability which occurred to me was that independent India had inherited an economy in decay; that in the twenty-five years or so before independence the population had been increasing faster than production with the result that the average standard of living had been going down. Nehru said he would put it that independent India had inherited a 'stagnant economy'. There had been advance in some sectors. The two world wars, for example, had stimulated industrial growth. Gandhi's insistence on reviving handloom weaving had improved the lot of cottage industry. It was difficult to generalize about the conditions of the mass of the people. (Nehru was right, as I later discovered, in saying that independent India had inherited a stagnant economy not an economy in decay: in the twenty-five years from 1921 to 1946 population and gross national product had increased at the same rate.[1])

I suggested that a second liability was the climate of India;

that the heat for four months of the year brought on lassitude. He did not consider this an important liability. The climate, he said, was certainly better than the climate of Ceylon, Burma and Indonesia. Moreover, in those countries it was too easy for the people to scratch a living. Was it not also true that up to two or three centuries ago most of the civilizations of the world had arisen in warm river valleys? He admitted, however, that north Indians were more energetic and hard-working than south Indians, though, to put against this, the per acre production in parts of south India such as Madras was higher than in the north. I said I had intended to compare the climate of India not with Ceylon, Burma or Indonesia, but rather with the climate of such countries as China, Russia and the United States, and that perhaps the more India became industrialized the greater would be the problem presented by the heat since conditions in factories in the summer would lower production. He did not take up this point but returned to the question of the effect of excessive heat on the villagers. He said that the demands on the villager's energy because of the necessity of the peasant working harder in order that agricultural production in India should go up could be offset by better living conditions. At present, for example, peasant women in many villages had to waste an enormous amount of time in going miles to get water.

The third liability that I pointed out was the Indian scruples against doing things which would be the economical, the sensible thing to do, such as killing the 50 million or so useless cattle in India and killing the monkeys. There were also the scruples against eating certain types of food, scruples which the Chinese peasant, for example, did not have. He did not take me up on the first two examples I gave but he did take me up on food habits. He said it was important to remember that the scruples against using certain types of food were confined mainly to the upper castes and that, moreover, they varied from one part of India to another.

The next liability was one which he had been particularly emphasizing lately. This was caste. I said, 'It seems to me, Prime Minister, that you are more worried about this now than you have been for some time.' He said that caste had been breaking down in India in social matters. There was now much more inter-dining between castes than there used to be. It was taking longer to break down the conventions against intermarriage. While caste was breaking down socially it seemed to be getting stronger politically. A caste, he said, was a sort of petrified occupational group. The struggle between castes was, therefore, in part a class struggle. What had been happening in the last elections in Bihar, for example, was that people of lower castes and the Harijans (the former untouchables) had been urged to vote against members of all the upper castes. A constituency for the federal parliament had an average population of 750,000. Such constituencies normally contained many different sub-castes. There was, therefore, not much advantage in choosing a member of any particular sub-caste as a candidate. On the other hand, in the constituencies for the provincial legislatures, which on the average had a population of about 100,000 people, one sub-caste might be dominant. Every political party had to take account of this in its choice of candidates. The opposition parties, particularly the Communists and the Socialists, had been very careful in choosing candidates who belonged to sub-castes which were dominant in the constituency.

I had a long list of other liabilities but we were taking so much time on liabilities that I said I felt we should proceed to assets. Nehru's comment was that none of the liabilities I had mentioned were, in his opinion, permanent. I asked him what important items he would add to my list. He said that he would add the tendency of Hindu society to 'live and let live'. He said this tolerance had helped to hold the country together but on the other hand, if carried too far, it worked against the homogeneity of the country. He developed this point at some length but I found it difficult to follow his argument. I said that I understood that some people considered that one aspect of the 'live and let live' philosophy of India was an unwillingness to be ruthless with people who were inefficient, to let the inefficient producer go to the wall, or to impose drastic penalties on a man found guilty of corruption because this would break the hearts of his aged parents. Obviously one of the sanctions against corruption was that if a man was found guilty it would break his parents' hearts. He said this kind of obstacle in India to dealing with the corrupt was not as strong as it had been in China before the Communist revolution. (It must have been very strong in China.)

We passed on to assets but before I had a chance to mention the first asset I had listed, Nehru mentioned India's great asset, the feeling of the people of India through centuries that they belonged to a common culture. He said this feeling had throughout history been stronger in India than it had been in western Europe even in the Middle Ages when the unity of Western Christendom was at its greatest. I said that another asset which I had listed was the fact that India was a natural political unit, much more so, for example, than Russia or the United States. He agreed. I went on to suggest that a third asset was that the British by their conquest had unified India politically and had bound the sub-continent together by railways, a national civil service and also, was I not correct in saying, by creating a homogeneous upper class throughout the country? He agreed, emphasizing the fact that the British had created a political unit. He went on immediately to say that they had also created political unity in India in opposition to their rule. I said that I was going on to mention that the British had, in a sense, created the Congress Party. The Congress Party had become a disciplined body with mass support throughout the whole country and was, therefore, able to play after independence the essential role of a political party in a country such as India—that of a broker between conflicting interests.

This led him off on one of his hobby-horses. He spoke of the rootlessness of Pakistan compared with India. Pakistan had grown out of Jinnah's insistence on the two-nation theory. Jinnah's argument was not that there were two regions in India and that those in one region owed their allegiance to that region; it was that there were two religions in India. The result was that since Pakistan had to take the form of a region the government of Pakistan did not have its roots in a region. This had led the government of Pakistan to look to the Middle East and to Pan-Islam. Pan-Islam was non-existent and had always been non-existent. It had been the invention of Abdul Hamid at the beginning of the twentieth century. There was certainly a sympathy between Islamic countries but this sympathy was never strong enough to override national interest. It was comparable to the sympathy between Christian countries but this sympathy had certainly not led to the unity of Christian countries nor had the sympathy between Islamic countries led to the unity of Islamic countries. There was no national unity in Pakistan other than that based on an appeal that the religion of Islam was in danger. The Pakistan government was based on landlords and the civil service.

Since it was getting late I broke the conversation off preparatory to getting up to leave. As Nehru came to the door with me I said that I had not mentioned one of the assets in my list of India's assets and that was himself.

There were many other liabilities and assets of India which I did not have time to mention in my talk with Nehru. I dealt with these (as well as the ones I had discussed with Nehru) in the farewell essay which I sent to Ottawa in which I attempted to hazard an opinion on India's prospects. I said that it was with hesitation and humility that I undertook this task. I had been in India for four and a half years. This was a long time for a diplomat to serve in India; it was a very short time for a westerner to get to know much about India.

India is composed mainly of illiterate, ill-clad, hungry peasants living in mud or straw huts but the Indians whom the westerner, and especially the western ambassador, gets to know are almost all members of a small governing class which constitutes less than one-quarter of one per cent of the population, and is not representative of the mass of the people from whom it is divided by a deep gulf.

Another reason for caution was that I was making my assessment of India's prospects at a period of low ebb in India's fortunes and it was difficult not to let recent developments bulk too large in my assessment. The last general election had demonstrated the strength of the divisive forces of caste, communalism and factionalism. The Communists had secured a beachhead in Kerala from which they could expand if the Congress Party did not have a virtual rebirth. The failure of Nehru to strengthen his cabinet by getting rid of some of the reactionaries and incompetents and by bringing in new blood aroused apprehensions that his normal lack of ruthlessness and guile added to his fatigue and increasing years might mean that he would not lead the Congress Party to a rebirth. India was facing an agricultural crisis because of its inability to increase production beyond the level reached three years before. India was so short of foreign exchange and domestic resources that unless it received foreign aid on a scale larger than that which appeared likely it would have to slow down the rate of its economic progress to a pace which might be politically and socially dangerous. There was also grave danger of inflation which was also politically and socially dangerous. The Indians might not fully realize the dangers to them of all these developments. Indeed, one of the most serious aspects of the present crisis was the complacency of almost all the Indian leaders. They were complacent about Kerala; they were complacent about the failure of their agricultural policy; they were complacent about the dangers of inflation. The leaders of the Congress Party had been jolted by the results of the recent general elections but most of them now seemed to be sinking back into the rut of their usual complacency.

Having issued these caveats I went on to discuss some of India's liabilities which I had not discussed with Nehru. Indian society, I said, suffered from a persistent and pervasive feudalism. It was reflected in the importance attached to status, in the arrogance of superiors to subordinates, in the servility of many subordinates to their superiors. Since most Hindu sub-castes were regional, and the religious minorities tended to be concentrated in certain regions, the existence of sub-castes and of communalism strengthened the divisive force of regionalism in India, a force already strong because it was based on language and tradition and differences of economic interest. Then there was factionalism. It was said that wherever four Indians were gathered together there would be two factions and each faction would intrigue against the other. Villages were often divided into two factions. The provincial Congress parties were divided into factions. Civil servants were likely to be split into factional groups in each department.

Another thing which retarded India's progress and weakened the fabric of its society was corruption. India presumably had the normal kind of political corruption which we used to have in Canada: a contractor, to get a contract, had to be on the patronage list, and he had to pay the regular tariff on the contract to the party funds; politicians got jobs for party workers; politicians persuaded or intimidated civil servants into doing favours for deserving constituents; the complaisant civil servant was promoted. But Indian corruption was more pervasive than this. Corruption had not been as bad during the last hundred years of British rule. British administrators in India had not been subject to the same temptations as the Indian politicians and administrators who succeeded them. The British weren't members of a sub-caste to which they owed loyalty. They didn't need to raise party funds. They could pay their 'party workers' with titles from 'Rai Bahadur' to knighthoods. Presumably they steered government contracts to 'loyal' Indians. Presumably their 'slush funds' for buying newspaper support and so on came out of one of the many 'secret service' appropriations. The British civil servant was much better paid than the Indian civil servant now was. Under the British, bribery, corruption and petty oppression were rife up to the district magistrate level, but not beyond. Now they had reached higher levels and the higher the level that was reached, the more grasping and oppressive did the man at the bottom get. Yet it was necessary to keep a sense of proportion. It was easy for an Anglo-American to exaggerate the comparative extent of corruption in India. Maurice Zinkin, who had known India for over twenty years, first as a civil servant and then as a businessman, asserted in his latest book that India was less corrupt than most European countries and that, in spite of nepotism and corruption, the Indian bureaucracy was the best government service between Paris and Vancouver. And he meant going east from Paris to Vancouver across the Eurasian land mass.

Undoubtedly, however, caste, communalism and corruption weakened the administrative machine and they weakened the machine where it was weakest, in the states. Mediocre men were appointed and promoted. First-class men lost heart.

Here is an impressive, though by no means complete list of the forces in India which are divisive, corrosive or retrogressive. There are others: unemployment, particularly white-collar unemployment, under-employment, a propensity to resort to violence, police brutality, the importance attached to leisure rather than to other goods, a business ethic inherited from petty trading rather than from an instinct of good workmanship, a distaste for permitting the inefficient competitor to be driven to the wall, a failure to appreciate the role of profit in any kind of economy, capitalist, socialist or mixed; an underrating of the importance of monetary rewards as an incentive.

I then went on in my farewell despatch to deal with the question which was basic to any assessment of India's prospects: how important was it to the continued existence of India as a united independent nation for India to achieve and maintain a relatively rapid pace of economic progress? The orthodox argument was that India was faced with a revolutionary movement of rising expectations and that stable democratic government could not long survive if these revolutionary demands were not met. The demands were in part the result of the promises made by the Congress Party when it was in opposition to the British. These promises went further than the ordinary promises of ordinary opposition parties because the governing party was foreign, because the opposition party had never been subjected to the moderating influence of holding power at the national capital, and because the opposition party was revolutionary, and a revolutionary party was apt to use revolutionary language. A minority view was that the peasant had for centuries been submissive to misery and injustice and that he was still submissive. There was, therefore, no pressing political need to raise his standard of living, though it was probably politically essential to do something for the unemployed or underemployed or badly paid educated middle class. My own guess was that though the mass of the hundred and ten million working peasants was still resigned or apathetic, the leaven of discontent was working rapidly, and that if within five or ten years their lot was not improved, the bulk of the peasants would withdraw their allegiance from the regime.

In one way, satisfying the peasant will be easy. Oblivious to the competition between India and China which the world sees, the peasant will be content if every year he knows that he is a little less hungry, that officials are a little less corrupt and the police a little less brutal. Satisfying the middle-class intellectual is going to be more difficult. Like the peasant, he will have to have more material security. But he will also need to know that his society values him; and he in turn must see sufficient virtues in his society to reject the quick and brutal solutions which China offers to India. Failure to satisfy these two groups will be dangerous, particularly if, as it probably would, a withdrawal of the peasant's allegiance from the regime were to coincide with mounting discontent among the unemployed or poorly employed white-collar workers, especially university graduates. These could provide the leaders. The unemployed or under-employed urban workers living in the slums of the big cities could provide the mobs. Indian mobs resort easily to violence. Indian police resort easily to beatings and firings. The Indian people, as the last election showed, are becoming increasingly angered by police firings. If hopes of reasonably rapid economic progress are frustrated, and even more so if there are economic setbacks, all the divisive and corrosive forces in Indian society are strengthened. If, on the other hand, the mass of the Indian people come to believe that their economic and social condition has improved and is likely to continue to improve, they will have more confidence in themselves and in their leaders and in their country, and the more confidence they have, the easier it will be for them to withstand the divisive forces of regionalism, language, religion and caste and the corrosive forces of under-employment, un-employment, sickness, hunger and hopelessness.

Substantial economic progress in India might thus be a political necessity. Was it, however, a possibility? In an attempt to answer this question I cited some of the main conclusions of an economic mission of the World Bank which had visited India in the summer of 1956. India, the mission said, had a large domestic market and diversified resources, and its labour skills were developing satisfactorily. The climate for foreign investment in India compared very favourably with that of most other Asian countries. In the long run India could probably become a major manufacturing country and a supplier of industrial goods and equipment to Asia and Africa. There seemed to be no reason why the expansion of agricultural output at an average rate of two to three per cent a year should not continue for many years. Proper application of known techniques, in conjunction with the possible expansion of irrigation and the cultivated area, could increase India's agricultural output four or five fold. For some time India should be able to raise its national income at an average rate of four or five per cent a year, though eventually, as higher income levels were attained, there might be some decline in this rate. Such an average annual rate of economic growth should enable India to keep well abreast of the increase in population which would be somewhat over 1.5 per cent a year in the next five years and might rise above 2 per cent in the following decade.

My conclusion was that if in the next two or three years a steady upward march of agricultural production was resumed, and industrial production continued to increase at a rapid rate it would be reasonable to conclude that independent India had been able to reverse a fifty-year trend of economic stagnation and decay. Grave doubt would be cast on the validity of the thesis that since independence India had been coasting along on the momentum given it by the British and using the efficient administrative machine built for it by the British. This argument was summed up in the description of Nehru as 'the last British Viceroy'. It was contended that when the British-inspired momentum ran down, when the administrative machine deteriorated, and when Nehru had gone from the scene, India would sink back into the rut of its lumbering bullock-carts. While a longer trend than that of the last six years would be required to disprove this thesis, the economic trends of the past six years certainly threw considerable doubt on it in spite of the disquieting failure to increase agricultural production during the previous three years.

My relative optimism is bolstered by my memory of how far India has advanced in the last ten years, not only in political and economic matters but in social matters. . . . In ten years of independence more has been done to eradicate the evils of Indian social life than was done in the previous hundred years under the British regime. Caste in its social aspects has been greatly weakened. The position of women who have been the despised and rejected of Hinduism has greatly improved. More children are going to school. India has done all this. It has also achieved political miracles: the welding together of the 500 princely states with the rest of India; the division of India into linguistic provinces; the successful holding of two general elections. This has been done by a country which was at the beginning faced with difficulties which must have appeared to outsiders as being almost overwhelming—the mass murders and the mass migrations of the partition period. . . . Compared with all the other countries in Asia between Turkey and Japan which are of any size and are not in the Russo-Chinese bloc, India's liabilities are small, its assets large, and its political stability and its economic and social progress remarkable. India probably has much the best administrative machine of any of those countries. It has a strong, heterogeneous national party. It has a dominant national leader of genius. It is almost alone among these countries in possessing the great advantage of a broad-based popular national government.

But I added a note of caution. I said that India's prospects compared with China's did not appear bright. China had great advantages over India. It did not have the pitiless tropical sun of India and its climate was more conducive to hard work. Its people worked harder than Indians. The Chinese did not suffer as did the Indians from religious inhibitions about certain foods. They ate anything that was eatable. They were not stopped by religious scruples from killing useless cattle or destructive monkeys. They used night soil as fertilizer. China did not suffer as did India from the divisive forces of caste or linguistic nationalism. China had a strong central government which could make its writ run in all the regions of China; it was not inhibited by a division of legislative powers with the provinces under which the provinces alone had the right to legislate on such matters as agriculture, forestry and education. China, moreover, could take the short cuts of totalitarianism, whereas India had to take the winding, democratic path of government by discussion and persuasion.

It is not surprising, therefore, that with every year that passes more and more Indians of the governing classes become more and more concerned with the possibility that their great northern neighbour, China, will soon outstrip them in the race for economic and social betterment. And the implications of that for India, for the other countries of Asia and for the world are enormous.

CHAPTER FIFTEEN
NEHRU

(This chapter consists in the main of a slightly abbreviated version of an assessment of Nehru contained in a farewell despatch which I sent to Ottawa on 3 May 1957. I have added material from other despatches and have made a few stylistic changes. In the next chapter, 'Reconsideration', I examine the assessment made in this chapter.)

Nehru dominates the scene in India. India today is Nehru's India. He has been a leader of India for thirty-five years. For sixteen years before independence came in 1947, he was second only to Gandhi in the eyes of the Indian people. Since Gandhi's death nine years ago, he has been second to no one. When Patel was alive, Nehru had to share power with him. Since Patel's death seven years ago, Nehru has reigned supreme. There is no one since Napoleon who has played both so large a role in the history of his country and has also held the sort of place which Nehru holds in the hearts and minds of his countrymen. For the people of India, he is George Washington, Lincoln, Roosevelt and Eisenhower rolled into one.

He plays many roles in India. He is an Old Testament prophet, an inspired teacher who proclaims the truth. He is an Elisha who has inherited the mantle of Gandhi, the Elijah. In his role as prophet he castigates India for its shortcomings, its sins, its whoring after the strange gods of linguism and caste instead of following the pure gospel of Gandhi. He calls India to repentance. He shows India apocalyptic visions of future greatness. He is a high priest of the new India. As high priest, he officiates at the opening of a new dam or factory or community project. These ceremonies are to him the sacraments of the new India, the outward and visible signs of a new inward and spiritual grace. He is king as well as prophet and priest for he is the symbol of the unity of India; he is the spokesman of

India, the head of its government. Sometimes he behaves as if he were also the leader of the opposition.

He possesses immense nervous energy and staying power. He had a month's holiday trekking in Kashmir shortly after he was released from jail for the last time in 1945. For twelve years after that he has not had more than a day or two's holiday in any year. He has not, since becoming prime minister eleven years ago, spent one day in bed ill. He considers ordinary illness a crime. He has occasional bad colds but never takes time off because of them. Up to this year he used to work solidly from about eight every morning till one the next morning. Now he gets to bed at midnight and does not get up till seven or seven-thirty. He works seven days a week, fifty-two weeks a year. He is constantly giving speeches, attending public functions, travelling around India, being interviewed by foreign newspapermen, writers, distinguished visitors, the premiers of the provinces, Congress Party workers. He scarcely ever eats alone. At breakfast his only guests are his house guests, but he often has house guests. He almost always has guests to lunch. He must almost never dine alone or only with his daughter. He seems to find it impossible to relax for more than a few hours at a time. Thus when he had a chance to take a four days' holiday in April 1957 he refused to do so. Instead he spent two of the four days attending a conference of development commissioners.

The visiting prime minister or cabinet minister who calls on him always finds him gracious, apparently relaxed, unhurried, the personification of moderation and sweet reasonableness. Occasionally to other callers he will behave as if a thick wall of glass had fallen between him and his caller. His mind will not be in the room. His habit when asked a direct question on a difficult problem is to reply, 'In order to answer that question you have to go a long way back', and then he goes back ten years, or 100 years, or 1000 years, and does often succeed in giving perspective to the problem. Another gambit of his, when asked if he agrees with some generalization about some aspect of international affairs, is to say, 'That is, I think, too simple an approach to a highly complicated situation.' Then he proceeds to unsimplify the approach. Sometimes this is helpful. Usually it is not. Indeed, Nehru's determination to see every problem in perspective and his refusal to accept generalizations advanced by people other than himself mean that his contribution to discussions with his peers is often from such a height that his view is cloudy.

He delights in giving speeches. He doesn't like listening to speeches. Usually at public meetings when someone else is speaking he appears to relax. His appearance of relaxation is often so complete that he looks as if he were asleep. He is much less abrupt, much more considerate of the people who work for him, whether officials or servants, than are most Indians. Those who work under him serve him with a passionate devotion. As a host, he is gracious, considerate, gay. He dislikes talking shop at lunch or dinner. If he has a distinguished guest with whom he wants to talk seriously, he will take him aside after the meal for a tête-à-tête. He likes the company of good-looking, amusing women. He has great personal charm. He is very conscious of this. He has probably always been charming. All the arts of the charmer come naturally to him and appear, and perhaps are, spontaneous. He uses these arts just as kings used them in the past. There is an elegance about him. Not just his well-fitting Indian clothes and his red rose, but the way he smokes a cigarette, the way he greets a visitor or sees him off at the door of his home.

He often gives the appearance of being an arrogant aristocrat. Sometimes he is rather arrogant even in the chit-chat of dinner table conversation. He will say abruptly and challengingly, 'What do you mean?' He will dismiss someone else's opinion out-of-hand and lay down the law himself. Within half a minute he will make some remark which constitutes a sort of apology for his brusqueness. I once said to him, at a lunch party for a distinguished Canadian visitor who was about to visit Agra and Fatehpur Sikri, 'Prime Minister, which do you think is the loveliest mosque in India? My own favourite is Fatehpur Sikri.' 'What?' he said; 'why, of course, it is the Jama Masjid' (the great mosque in Delhi). A few seconds later, he said, in an almost puzzled, hesitating way, 'You know, it's twenty years since I've seen the mosque at Fatehpur Sikri.'

He can be impatient over trifles. He can lose his temper when a microphone doesn't work, or when baggage doesn't appear when it should. Like other people, he can get out of the wrong side of the bed in the morning and look for something exasperating in order to give him a chance to explode. He does not give the impression of being a humble man. He seems to like flattery and praise provided they are kept within the limits of good taste. He doesn't like flattery and praise laid on him with a shovel. He doesn't seem to mind it being laid on India with a steam shovel. When introductory speeches or addresses of welcome to him are too flowery, he will angrily tell the unfortunate speaker to shut up. He is an actor like those who have to live a good deal of their lives in public with the spotlight turned on them, and who have to exercise charm in order to get their way. When the spotlight is on him, he puts on his actor's mask—handsome, smiling, alert, young for his sixty-seven years.

In his pride and sensitiveness he reflects the pride and sensitiveness of India. Since he is not only the spokesman but in a very real sense the symbol of India it is not surprising that he interprets snubs to himself as snubs to India. Since he is much the most important statesman in the whole of non-Communist Asia, it is likewise not surprising that he interpets snubs to himself as a demonstration of failure to recognize the profound changes which have taken place in Asia since the war, and thus as snubs to Asia.

He is a very lonely man. He is a shy man. Since the death of Gandhi, there has been no one really close to him except his only child, his daughter Indira, a woman of thirty-nine who is his hostess. Perhaps his closest friends are the Mountbattens. In India he has no intimate friends. He has old and valued colleagues for whom he has respect and affection. He has subordinates and a host of friendly acquaintances. Power does not always corrupt. It often ennobles. But power always separates. Power has made Nehru more lonely, but he must have been a lonely man before he rose to power. He himself wrote twenty years ago that he finds it easier to open his heart to a large crowd than to one or two people. He suffers from a refusal or inability to discuss his problems with his equals. Thus he never discusses his problems with the President, Rajendra Prasad. He seldom discusses them with the Vice-President, Radhakrishnan. Each in his own way could be helpful to him.

His wife died twenty years ago when he was forty-six. He considers that he failed, until it was too late, to appreciate his wife's qualities and her desire to be his partner. It would have been good for him if he had had his wife's companionship throughout his life. It is possible that he has suffered from having had a dominant, brilliant, strong-willed father whom he has always admired and of whom he was frightened when he was young. His father became one of the two or three top leaders of the Congress Party. Nehru knows that when he was first elected chairman of the Congress Party in 1929, at the age of forty, many people said that he owed his election to being his father's son. Similarly, he knows that people say that he did not become the first Prime Minister of India because of his own merits but because Gandhi chose him; and that moreover, he was prime minister in name only until death removed Gandhi and Patel. Perhaps one reason he got into the habit of driving himself so hard was to try to drown his feeling of guilt about the failure of his marriage and to prove to himself and his critics that he deserves to be Prime Minister of India because of his own merits, not because he was born with a golden spoon in his mouth, or because he was the spoiled favourite of Gandhi.

The person who has had the greatest influence on him is Gandhi. Gandhi was his 'guru', his master; he was Gandhi's favourite *chela*, his disciple. He was no slavish follower of Gandhi, no blind devotee. He often thought Gandhi mistaken. He often quarrelled with him. The relationship between them was much more complex and subtle than the relationship between the younger man who is the practical politician and the older man who is the saint who is above politics. Gandhi was a very shrewd, practical politician with an acute and brilliant sense of political salesmanship and showmanship. He was also, if not a saint, very close to being a saint. Gandhi was greatly concerned with the problem of ends and means: a good end not only should not be achieved by evil means; a good end cannot be achieved by evil means. Nehru is distressed by the difficulty of reconciling this principle with the fact which he has become more and more aware of the longer he is prime minister, that the choice before a prime minister is so seldom between good and evil; it is usually between a greater evil and a lesser evil. But he refuses to seek refuge in a shallow utilitarianism which judges every act merely by its consequences here and now—whether it results in the greatest good to the greatest number. He knows there is a limit to the acts which a moral man can do or condone no matter how expedient they may seem to be. He keeps remembering that Gandhi emphasized the necessity of distinguishing between the evil thing and the evil-doer. The evil thing must be hated; the evil-doer must be loved. In the struggle for independence, the Indians should hate the evil of imperialism, but they should have no bitterness or hatred in their hearts for the individuals who served that evil thing. He often recalls that it was the obedience of so many Indians to this teaching of Gandhi—plus, he is always generous and honest enough to add, the very moderate way in which the British used force to suppress the independence movement, and their decision to leave when they did—which made it possible for the final parting between India and Britain to take place 'gracefully, graciously and with a minimum of bitterness'. Perhaps the greatest single force which kept him from becoming a Communist in the twenties and early thirties was Gandhi's emphasis on means as well as ends, and on the necessity of reducing the use of force to a minimum. It has been the persistence of Gandhi's influence which has, ever since India became independent, prevented him from accepting the regimes in Russia or Peking China as really 'good' regimes. No regime can be 'good' which relies on Stalinist terror or which suppresses with ruthlessness a revolt of a whole Hungarian nation. He says there is 'too much coercion and suffering' in the 'methods employed in certain Communist societies' and these are 'not the right methods'.

The highest term of praise he uses in speaking of someone is that he is a 'good man'. 'Mr St Laurent is a good man.' I think he believes that Eisenhower is a good man. U Nu of Burma is more than a good man because he possesses in addition to goodness an inner radiance. He would never even in his most bitterly anti-western moods describe Krushchev or Bulganin as good men. What he means by a good man is, I think, a man whose conduct is governed by moral considerations; who is not consumed by personal ambition; who is not a time-server or intriguer; who is 'serious'; who considers his fellow men as objects of sympathy, not as instruments or pawns or abstractions.

He is thoroughly westernized. He probably dreams and

thinks in English. The things in India which make him impatient are the things which make westerners impatient: the microphone which doesn't work; the concert that goes on and on; the speeches that go on and on; shoddy workmanship; unnecessary filth and smells. He is a westerner who has consciously and deliberately gone native. Thirty-five years ago he embarked on a voyage of rediscovery of India. In his jail days when he had leisure, he read deeply in Indian history and philosophy. In his approach to religion he has been a late nineteenth century western liberal sceptic. He has the sceptical westerner's contempt for such aspects of orthodox Hinduism as sadhus, cow worship and astrology. (It is almost as if a French-speaking prime minister of Canada were not only anti-clerical but were contemptuous of the sanctity of marriage and of Thomist philosophy.) Lately he has been making a distinction between religion and spiritual force or spiritual truth. He is more and more attracted by the teachings of the Buddha. He is a socialist of the Stafford Cripps school, but his is not an intellectual socialism. He is not at home in socialist theory. His socialism is in the tradition of the nineteenth century Christian socialism of Great Britain and Ruskin socialism. His socialism is in large part the socialism of the generous-hearted and imaginative aristocrat in a poverty-stricken country who is revolted equally by the vulgar conspicuous consumption of the rich and the filth and misery of the poor. He has the suspicion, the superior attitude, the lack of understanding of the United States which most upper class leaders of the British Labour Party had in the late twenties and which some still have—not much more, not much less. In general, he shares the *New Statesman*'s approach to the United States. When he likes an individual American he says he is unrepresentative of the United States. It is reported that in New York on his second visit to the United States in December 1956, he quoted with approval a remark someone had made to him, 'America is a country one should never visit for the first time.' He should have added, 'as Prime Minister'. The pity is that he did not spend a year in the United States as a private citizen in the middle thirties when the New Deal was in full flower. This would have given him a much truer picture of the United States than he now has in his mind.

He is essentially a liberal. He loathes McCarthyism. The

four-year-long detention of the Sheikh Abdullah in jail in Kashmir without trial is repugnant to him. He admires the zeal, the discipline, the material accomplishments of the totalitarian regimes of Russia and China but he dislikes the drabness and uniformity and conformity of totalitarian countries. He says, 'I do not like dictatorships. I do not like authoritarian regimes.' He knows better than anyone else the difficulty of pushing the largely inert mass of largely reactionary Indians up the steep, twisting democratic path of economic and social progress. He must constantly be subjected to the temptation to take the short cuts of totalitarianism, but he rejects these temptations. He believes that democracy is better for India in the short run and in the long run.

He judges the West and Russia by different moral yardsticks. He also believes that public denunciations of the failings of the West may help to change western policies for the better, whereas public denunciations of the failings of Russia and China will do no good and may do harm. He does not appear to realize that his failure to denounce the misdemeanours and crimes of Russia and China weakens the force of his denunciations of the mistakes of the West. He also does not seem to realize that it is dangerous because it does not help to correct the false picture of Russia and China which exists in the minds of so many Indians. His constant turning of a blind eye to the misdemeanours and crimes of Russia and China flows in large part from his identification with the independence movement. It was the British whom the Indians had to struggle against, not the Russians. It was the British type of imperialism and racial arrogance which the Indians knew at first hand, not the Russian. Western imperialism is to Nehru a familiar enemy. It is easy for him to discern its lineaments. In 1956 he recognized it right away in the crisis over the Suez canal. The reaction of Britain and France to Nasser's nationalization of the canal was to him a clear example of a reversion to the nineteenth century gun-boat imperialism of the whites against the coloureds. British justifications smelled to him of sanctimonious nineteenth century British sermons on the white man's burden. It is not so easy for Nehru to discern the lineaments of Russo-Chinese imperialism or expansionism. In 1956 he took an unconscionably long time to recognize it in Hungary.

Indian foreign policy and diplomacy under Nehru, though

at times exasperating to India's friends in the West, has a record of solid achievement to its credit. In the first place, it has not divided India, it has united India. In a country afflicted by such strong divisive forces, this in itself is a notable achievement. Secondly, India has helped to ease relations between the West and Peking and to find solutions to problems on the periphery of China—Korea, the coastal islands and Formosa, and Indo-China. In Korea and Indo-China it has borne a heavy burden in helping to implement solutions. Thirdly, India has exercised a useful, moderating influence on the extreme demands of most other members of the Afro-Asian group on colonial matters and on such questions as Cyprus and Israel. The fourth achievement is the greatest. Nehru has argued in season and out of season that it is an extreme over-simplification of a highly complicated situation to present the problem before the world as one of Communism versus anti-Communism. Equally important or more important are the demands of colonial peoples for self-government, the demand of coloured races for racial equality, and the revolt of two-thirds of mankind against its poverty, its disease and its illiteracy. All these, he has insisted, have created a revolutionary ferment in the minds of millions of people in Asia and Africa. How to deal with this ferment is at least as important as how to deal with Communism. By his insistence on this Nehru has helped to restore a sense of balance to the thinking of the West, which has been so conscious of the dangers of Russian expansionism that it has failed to attach sufficient importance to these other dangers to the peace and welfare of the world.

These are great accomplishments. But they are more than offset by Nehru's failure to achieve the most important goal of any realistic Indian foreign policy, the establishment of good relations with Pakistan. The stumbling block has been Kashmir.

Nehru is essentially an optimist. He believes that the forces of common sense and goodness are likely to win in the long run both in the West and in Russia and in China. 'There is in me', he said recently, 'a sense of confidence in the future; in India's future; in the world's future. A confidence which I cannot justify by any reasoning . . . I have a sense of adventure and joy in life; in work and in doing things in general.'

His way of life, the traditions of India, the pressure he works under mean that he cannot live anything approaching a normal life. Once I mentioned to him the abbreviated version of his book, *The Discovery of India*. He was surprised and annoyed. 'I never heard of it.' I said it was displayed prominently in every bookshop in Delhi. He paused and then said, as if surprised, 'You know I haven't been inside a bookshop in India for four or five years.' He probably hasn't been in any shop in India for seven or eight years. He probably never pays for anything with his own hands. Somebody else makes all payments on his behalf, big and small. He hates the precautions the police take to protect him and those in charge of his security have to try to conceal from him the measures they take for his protection. He insists on the minimum number of plainclothesmen and uniformed police. He occasionally breaks away from them when they hedge him off from the people. He walks through the police cordon right into the crowd. Sometimes he finds he has jumped from the frying pan into the fire for people in the crowd will come up to him and bend down and touch his feet as a mark of their respect. He hates this.

He lives in constant danger of assassination. There is in every land the ordinary sort of lunatic who holds a prime minister personally responsible for some act of real or imagined injustice done to him. In India there are 400 million people, and so India has many more of these lunatics than most countries. Moreover, tens of millions of the more orthodox Hindus in India consider that Nehru is a traitor to the traditions of Hinduism. Their feeling about this Brahmin who is forcing Hindu code bills through Parliament to clean Hinduism of some of its barnacles is much more bitter than the bitterness of a fellow Groton and Harvard man against Roosevelt. Gandhi was assassinated by one of these reactionary Hindus. At least once in the past four years, possibly twice, possibly more often, one of them has tried to assassinate Nehru. But though he lives in constant danger of assassination, he appears not to live in fear of it or in any event he shows no fear. As Churchill has said of him, he has mastered fear and conquered hate. He seems to have no bitterness against the British though he struggled against them for twenty-five years, though they kept him in jail for a total of ten years, and though almost all his loved ones were imprisoned by the British and some were beaten by their police. He seems to have no hatred or bitterness against any group of people—except perhaps the extremist Hindus, the kind who murdered Gandhi. His motto is, confidence begets confidence. In order that someone may have confidence in you, you must show him that you have confidence in him. He says that this works with the masses of India. He carries this thesis over to international affairs. If Eisenhower wants his confidence, Eisenhower must show that he has confidence in him.

His speeches normally sound much better than they read. He almost never talks in public from notes. He usually does not think out in advance what he is going to say. He relies on the inspiration of the moment. His speeches are usually a sort of stream of consciousness. He says what comes into his mind. He wanders into by-paths. He is diffuse. At his worst in public speeches—but he is fortunately rarely at his worst and probably never when he is talking to an audience of hundreds of thousands—he is repetitive, dull, obscure. At his best, sometimes in after-dinner speeches, sometimes at great public meetings, he can persuade, move, flatter, establish what he himself has called 'a sense of communion' with his listeners. For he will appear to them to be paying them the rare tribute of opening his heart and mind and soul to them in intimate, informal, heart-to-heart talk. This flatters his immediate audience. But the audience of a great prime minister of a great country is not only the people who are physically present. It also consists of people all over the world. And for a prime minister to think aloud on foreign affairs before a world audience can, sometimes, have unfortunate results in causing offence—often unnecessarily —to friendly foreign countries. Nehru might well reply that he likes giving public speeches, that he is good at it, that it is his recreation and that he comes back to his desk strengthened and exhilarated by speaking to tens and hundreds of thousands of people. He could also reply that by going around the country showing himself to millions of people every year he helps to pull the country together. It is not only that in his speeches he attacks the divisive and centrifugal forces which are at work in India, but that he preaches the positive gospel of a united India in which each part of India, each community, feels itself the heir of the great traditions of all the other parts, all the other communities of India.

I heard Nehru preach this gospel at a ceremony in New Delhi to commemorate the nineteen hundredth anniversary of the martyrdom of St Thomas the apostle. In his speech he said that it was a tradition of the Christian church in South India that St Thomas had brought Christianity to India soon after the death of Christ and that he had been martyred near Madras. Whether this was historically accurate or not was unimportant. 'Things which did not happen and which have influenced history are more important than things which did happen and which have not influenced history.' Whether or not Christianity had come to India with St Thomas, the belief that it had, had influenced the history of South India. In any event, Christianity had certainly come to South India by the third century. Christianity had been brought to northern India by the European conquerors. But Christianity had existed in South India for seventeen hundred or possibly nineteen hundred years. Now that India was united the north of India inherited the traditions of the south. 'The North should therefore realize that Christianity is one of the great ancient religions of India.'

In his speeches Nehru tries to communicate to the people of India his feeling of excitement at what he considers to be the high adventure of economic development in which they are engaged. Nehru understands the profound truth about economic development in an under-developed country such as India; that economic advance is not only good in itself, it is good because it gives the people of India more confidence in themselves and in their country. And the more confidence they have, the easier it is for them to withstand the divisive forces of regionalism, language, religion and caste, and the corrosive forces of under-employment, unemployment, sickness, hunger and hopelessness. Nehru therefore realizes how important it is not only that there be economic advance in India but that as many Indians as possible realize that economic advance is taking place, and that they have a feeling of personal pride in the new monuments of national development—locomotive works, fertilizer factories, dams, power plants.

Nehru said recently in an interview, 'My chief business ... has been ... to speak to [the people of India] as a schoolmaster, to try to explain things to them in as simple language as possible ... trying to get them to think and to understand.

... In India the approach by public meeting is still the biggest approach.'

Nehru loves being Prime Minister of India. He revels in relentless activity. He basks in the spotlight and in the flattering way in which the great and powerful of the world pay their pilgrimage to Delhi to see him. He gains strength from the adulation of the masses. He has a sense of mission, and it is only in fulfilling what he considers to be his mission that he can fulfil himself and find satisfaction if not happiness. He delights in the endless adventure of politics. He finds it exciting to be the creative, practical politician who prods, pushes, pulls, cajoles and leads India out of the bullock-cart and cow-dung age into the age of jet airplanes and nuclear energy. Because he is the leader of India in a high adventure of national development, he lives in a pleasurable state of whirling, restless activity, a state which he himself has called 'continuous excitement'.

He could be a much better leader for India than he is. He would, for example, be a better leader if he were to devote more of his time and energy to domestic affairs and less to international affairs. He should be more ruthless in eliminating colleagues who have got old or tired, no matter how much he or India owes to them. He should be ruthless in stamping out corruption within the Congress Party and in the administration from top civil servant to village official. He should then devolve more responsibility on his colleagues. He should not allow himself to be represented in discussions with other countries by a man [Krishna Menon] who, in spite of his ability, has conclusively demonstrated that he loses many more friends for India than he gains and creates many more opponents for India's case than he gains supporters. He has only about five years left in which to leave his imprint on India and he should conserve his time and energy for matters of first importance by not giving so many public speeches or appearing at so many public functions. He should never speak extempore in public on difficult or delicate international questions. He should realize that the most important task before him in domestic policy is to get India to double its agricultural production in ten years and his most important task in international policy is to get a settlement with Pakistan on all the deep and difficult issues which divide the two countries and, to get this settlement, he should be prepared to use all his powers of leadership to persuade India to accept the necessarily unpalatable compromises. He should be scrupulously careful never to lay himself open to the accusation of applying a double standard of morality to the Russo-Chinese bloc and to the Anglo-American bloc. He should long ago have selected the best possible successor and have been training him to take over.

His weaknesses are many. But in spite of his weaknesses he is great. He is one of the ten or so great political leaders of the last one hundred years. He ranks with Mutsuhito, Lincoln, Bismarck, Sun Yat-sen, Lenin, Gandhi, Roosevelt, Churchill and Mao Tse-tung. His tragedy may be the tragedy of Roosevelt: to remain leader of his country for a year or two after he has lost his grip and thus damage his own reputation and his country's interests. The damage which Roosevelt might have done to his country by staying on too long and by not training a successor was averted by the providential accident that the Vice-President turned out to be a good President though he had not been selected or trained for the job. India may not have the same providential good fortune.

Sometimes I have had the feeling watching Nehru that he is a magician who conjures up a vision of a united, progressive India and that when he passes from the scene, the vision will disappear. It is a vision which he conjures up and he conjures it up deliberately. He doesn't do it to mislead the foreigner. He does it because he knows that India can advance only if it can see visions and dream dreams, if it draws on the best in its past, if it breaks with the worst.

He genuinely returns the respect, the adulation and the love of the Indian people for him. One of his favourite theses is that the peasant of India, though illiterate, is not ignorant. The peasant, he says, knows by heart parts of the Hindu holy book, the *Ramayana*; he is steeped in the rich mythology and folklore of India; this enriches his mind, his understanding and his imagination. Nehru, when he is talking like this, may be somewhat idealizing the Indian peasant. But it is better for a leader of men to idealize his fellow citizens than to despise them as Mussolini despised the Italians. He loves India in a poetic, almost mystical way. He loves the land of India, and it is a land which is easy to love. He grows rhapsodical about India, the mountains, the plains, the backwaters of Travancore, the ancient monuments and the lovely shrines. He is enchanted by the great vistas of Indian history. Whenever he mentions Banaras, he talks of how moving it is to any Indian to walk in a city which for three thousand years has been a holy city of India. He loves drawing attention to all the persistent indications of the days when Hindu kingdoms ruled South-East Asia and Indonesia; the temples of Angkor Wat, the dances, the Sanskrit names of most of the present leaders of the whole area. As an Indian living in 1957, he is patriotically proud of the Buddha who died 2500 years ago, whom he calls India's greatest son.

He is kind and generous and imaginative and sympathetic. He feels for the misery of the people of India. Their misery hurts him. It makes him impatient. It makes him angry. Perhaps it is these virtues above all which make him the undisputed leader of India and the darling of the Indian people: his affection and respect for the people of India, his confidence in them, his love for the land of India, his enchantment with the history of India, his hurt and anger at the misery of the people of India. And it is the defect of these virtues which is his weakness. He shows his kindness, generosity, imagination and sympathy to the inefficient and corrupt by not dismissing them or imprisoning them. His own lack of guile, his own dislike of intrigue, mean that he is blind to guile and intrigue in others.

He will go on as Prime Minister of India until he is assassinated or until he drops in his tracks from exhaustion. He will become more lonely, more dependent on manifestations of the love of the Indian people for him, more impatient, more in a hurry, more tired, more unwilling to do the thing which will hurt his friends or old colleagues but which is essential for the country's good. He will become even more conscious of his place in the history of India and of the world. He must already know that he will be ranked with India's two great rulers of the last 2500 years, Ashoka and Akbar, that if India succeeds he will be called the creator of modern India, and that whatever happens, he will go down in history as one of the great men of the world.

Anyone who tries to describe Nehru must feel very much the

way he felt when he tried to describe Gandhi. He said recently of this, 'It's always difficult to describe a man who is rather unusual and a tremendous personality, and who gave an impression of enormous strength and inner reserves of power.... And then his career was one of success... in moulding the Indian people... in making them better than they were, stronger, braver, more disciplined.'

CHAPTER SIXTEEN

RECONSIDERATION
EPILOGUE

My wife and I spent the winter of 1978-9 in India. We wanted to see old friends and acquaintances. We wanted to visit again some of the places in India we especially love. And I wanted to try to find out how far the events of the twenty-two years since I had ceased to be Canadian High Commissioner to India had served to confirm or qualify the opinions I had expressed in my reporting to Ottawa from 1952 to 1957. This was not the first time I had been back in India since 1957. I had visited India in 1963 and 1964 as director of the South Asian and Middle Eastern Department of the World Bank. I was in India for an unofficial conference in December 1971 during the war between India and Pakistan over Bangladesh and again in 1974, on holiday.

I had had hints in letters from Indian friends of what I might expect to find when I revisited India. My correspondents had been or still were senior officials in the government. One wrote two months after Indira Gandhi's government had been defeated in the general elections of March 1977, 'While we cannot expect miracles from the new government, what we have avoided, at least in political terms, is something for which we can be truly grateful to the wisdom of the common man in the country.' Another, a few months later, wrote, 'We in India have gone through times of hope, frustration and disappointment. If the British have left any legacy behind, it is the ability to muddle through. We are doing that at the moment, and if there is no bright light at the end of the tunnel, there is always the hope that it may be due to a bend in the tunnel and that sooner or later it will become visible.' After the Janata Government had been in office for a year another friend wrote, 'On the most exposed political level, the Janata Government have, I'm afraid, achieved little. But, in the economic field, their experimentation in a modern way with the old Gandhian ideas seems interesting and is well worth watching.' Waiting for me when I arrived in New Delhi in December 1978 was an impassioned cry from a recently retired senior public servant, 'What a different India it is today from the one we dreamed of when you were Canadian High Commissioner!'

Poverty, Population and Production

I soon discovered that the principal error I had committed in my reporting as Canadian High Commissioner was that I had underestimated the inertia of the poor in rural India. I had said in my final despatch from India in May 1957 that, though the mass of the working peasants was still resigned or apathetic, the leaven of discontent was working rapidly and if within five or ten years their lot was not improved the bulk of the peasants would withdraw their allegiance from the regime. I meant by this not simply that they would vote a government out of office but that they would repudiate the whole political, social and economic system under which they were governed. The peasant, I said, would consider that his lot was improved 'if every year he knows that he is a little less hungry, that officials are a little less corrupt and the police a little less brutal'.

I found in the winter of 1978-9 from reading the draft sixth five-year plan and articles in Indian newspapers and periodicals and from talking to economists, officials and politicians that there was general agreement that the conditions of life of the poorest two-fifths of the people in rural India had not improved in the preceding twenty years or so; it was indeed possible that their conditions had worsened. It was probable that they were just as hungry. It was possible that they were hungrier. It was probable that the officials they had to deal with were more corrupt and the police more corrupt and more brutal. One reason the conditions of life of the rural poor had not improved was that, on balance, they had not benefited from the land reform legislation enacted since Independence. In spite of this they had not withdrawn their allegiance from the regime, though they had in 1977 voted Indira Gandhi out of office because of the excesses committed by her government during the emergency which she had proclaimed in 1975. And I was told that what was true of the poorest two-fifths of the people living in rural India was likewise true of the poorest two-fifths living in towns and cities: their conditions of life had probably not improved in the preceding twenty years or so. The failure to improve the conditions of life of the poorest two-fifths of the people of India was failure on a massive scale. Two-fifths of the people meant about 260 million people, more than a quarter of the billion poorest people in the whole world. Robert McNamara, the President of the World Bank, has called these billion people, the 'absolute poor', those 'severely-deprived human beings struggling to survive in a set of squalid and degrading circumstances almost beyond the power of our sophisticated imaginations and privileged circumstances to conceive'. Rabindranath Tagore called them 'eternal tenants in an extortionate world, having nothing of their own'. (Evidence in support of statements in this paragraph is set forth in Annex A, 'The poorest forty per cent of the people of India', pages 283 to 285.)

I was at fault in my reporting from India in the fifties in not realizing that the social, economic and political power of the rural élite was so great that they would be able to abort or distort measures for land reform and to divert to themselves the increases in per capita rural income so that the small and marginal farmers, the tenant farmers, the landless labourers and the village artisans would remain about as wretched as ever. It was, I learned, the lower peasant castes which now constituted the rural élite in most of India. They were 'determined to rule the villages by pushing out from the new power structure of the village the extremely poor and backward Hindu castes and the Harijans who are share-croppers and landless labourers'. These dominant land-owning castes were especially enraged by the resistance the former untouchables were beginning to show and 'given the limited reach of the law and order machinery of the state the Harijans cannot withstand the onslaughts of the ferocious peasant castes'.[1] When I read the article from which these quotations are taken I was reminded of what a leading cabinet minister had said to me in 1971 when we were discussing the failure of land reform, 'You must remember that the writ of the Government of India does not run in many [or did he say most?] of our villages.'

'In order to remove the poverty and misery of the Indian

people and to ameliorate the conditions of the masses, it is essential to make revolutionary changes in the present economic and social structure of society and to remove gross inequalities.' 1979 was the fiftieth anniversary of the passage of this resolution by the Congress Party. The Congress Party had been in power for thirty years after Independence. In those thirty years it had scarcely begun to give effect to the resolution it had adopted at Lahore in 1929.

In my farewell despatch in the spring of 1957 I had, by accepting as valid the forecasts of the Indian Planning Commission, greatly underestimated the rate at which the population of India would increase. I had said that the population would increase by somewhat over 1.5 per cent a year in the five years after 1956 and possibly by more than 2 per cent in the following decade. The actual annual rates of increase were 2.2 per cent in the five years after 1956, 2.3 per cent in the sixties, and probably about 2.1 per cent in the seventies. The errors made in the fifties in forecasting the growth of population were enormous. Thus in 1951, when the population was 361 million, the Planning Commission estimated that the population in 1976 would be 500 million. It was 618 million. In the twenty-five years after 1951 the population increased not by the 139 million forecast by the Planning Commission but by 257 million. In 1976 India had to try to feed, clothe and house 118 million more people than the Planning Commission had estimated in 1951. Independent India started off with 343 million people. Thirty-five years later, in 1982, it will have twice as many. India will have added to its population in a little over a third of a century more people than will be living in 1982 in the whole of North America (Mexico, the United States and Canada). Merely to maintain these additional hundreds of millions of people at the levels of living of their parents required a doubling of production, no easy task for a poverty-stricken country. India did more than this but what it did was not enough to raise the levels of living of the poorest 40 per cent of its people.

In my farewell despatch I had accepted the forecast made by the World Bank's economic mission in 1956 that the annual rate of increase in the national income of India should average four or five per cent 'for some time'. In the twenty years after I wrote that despatch, the years from 1956–7 to 1976–7, the average increase was only 3.37 per cent.[2] Since in that period the average annual increase in population was 2.14 per cent, the increase in average income a head was disappointingly low—about 1.2 per cent a year. At that rate it would take sixty years for average income to double, whereas if the annual rate of increase in national income had been five per cent, average income a head would double in twenty-five years.

One reason for national income increasing so slowly in the two decades after 1957 was that agricultural production had increased by only 2.5 per cent a year,[3] little more than the increase in population. This was discouraging. What was encouraging at the beginning of 1979 was the record of the previous five years, the years 1973-4 to 1978-9. In those years agricultural production increased not by a mere 2.5 per cent a year but by 4.1 per cent and the production of foodgrains increased even more rapidly—by 4.5 per cent a year. The poor did not, however, benefit. Their consumption of foodgrains remained almost constant. T. A. Pai, a member of parliament, declared at the end of March 1979: 'We have been able to build up stocks [of foodgrains] because millions of people go hungry for want of purchasing power',[4] and, he could have added, they lack purchasing power because they lack remunerative employment.

Though India by the end of the seventies was 'a major industrial power capable of producing any but the most ultrasophisticated of modern manufactures'[5] the rate of increase in industrial production in the twenty years after 1957 had not been impressive. In 1955 India had had the eighth largest manufacturing sector among the market-economy countries; by 1973 it had sunk to the sixteenth position.[6] During the second to the fourth five-year plans (1956 to 1974) the increases in production of the key items of coal, steel and cement were all at least 50 per cent short of the targets set in the plans, installed capacity for power was about 60 per cent short and fertilizer production reached less than 20 per cent of targets. Indian industry in 1979 was, I was told by experts, characterized by a pervasive obsolescence; heavy investment in modernizing industry was needed if this obsolescence were to be remedied and it was not clear that this heavy investment would be forthcoming. The kind of modernization that was needed extended from the renovation and replacement of over-aged and worn equipment in the cotton mills of Bombay to modest improvements in technology in other industries to the latest in sophisticated equipment. As in agriculture so in industry, the rate of increase in production in the twenty years after 1957 was discouraging, but the increase in more recent years was encouraging. In the three years from 1 April 1976 to 30 March 1979, industrial production had gone up by 7.1 per cent a year, almost double the rate in the years of stagnation from 1971 to 1975 (3.7 per cent) and substantially higher than the average for the twenty years after 1957 (5.9 per cent).[7]

One of the most distressing aspects of India's industrial development was, I learned, the slight impact it had made on India's tragic problem of the lack of productive, remunerative employment for tens of millions of its workers. The whole factory sector (large-scale, medium-scale and small-scale industry, including mining, quarrying and the generation of electricity) employed only about 6.5 million people out of a total labour force of 265 million, and it had been creating directly only about 200,000 new jobs a year. Even when the jobs created indirectly are added it was clear that the expansion of the factory sector was making little impact on a labour force which was increasing by six million a year. Village and cottage industries employed about 45 million people, seven times as many as the factory sector, but ever since Independence these industries had been declining or at least stagnating.[8]

Social Advance

In my farewell despatch I said that my relative optimism about India's prospects was based in part on the advance in social matters which India had made in the ten years since Independence. More had been done in those years to eradicate the evils of Indian social life than in the previous hundred years of British rule. Caste in its social aspects had been greatly weakened. The position of women had greatly improved. More children were going to school.

According to official statistics a considerable number of the developments which had taken place since I wrote this despatch justified my relative optimism. In 1960, 28 out of 100 children had died before reaching the age of five; by 1977 this had been reduced to 18. Life expectancy at birth had been 32 years in the forties; by 1961 it had gone up to 41 and by 1978 to 52, largely as a result of the fall in infant mortality, the extinction of smallpox and the reduction in the incidence of malaria and cholera. In 1962 there was one physician for every 5,840 people, in 1977 one for every 3,135. The number of hospital beds for every hundred thousand people had doubled from 1958 to 1977. In 1970 only a sixth of the population had access to safe drinking water; by the mid-seventies one-third had. In 1960 the adult literacy rate had been 28 per cent; in 1978, 35 per cent. From 1951 to 1978 the enrolment of students at the elementary level had risen from 32 per cent to 69 per cent of the relevant age group and at the secondary level from 5 per cent to 25 per cent.

Many of these statistics, however, had to be approached with caution. Dharam Vira, a former secretary of cabinet, in a lecture in January 1979, put the number of illiterates at 70 per cent, the number of 'half literates' at 20 per cent, and the number of real literates at 10 per cent, not the 35 per cent of official statistics.[9] The Minister of Education informed Parliament in May 1979 that three-quarters of the children in eight States had not been enrolled for elementary education.[10] This scarcely seemed consistent with the claim that in India as a whole 69 per cent of children of the relevant age group were enrolled in elementary schools. Moreover, what was significant was not enrolment but attendance and it was well known that many children enrolled at school dropped out very soon, and that a high proportion of the drop-outs came from the poorest families. One writer said that the drop-out rate of children in the first year of primary education was over 48 per cent;[11] another that 60 per cent of the children enrolled in primary schools left without achieving functional literacy.[12]

Like other statistics in India, some of the other social indicators doubtless masked the fact that the benefits indicated by them had largely gone to the upper and middle-income groups, not to the poorest 40 per cent of the people. What proportion of the children of the poorest 40 per cent died before reaching the age of five? What was the life expectancy at birth of these children? How many of the poorest 40 per cent had access to safe drinking water? Another deficiency of the social indicators was that they did not measure the social costs of the cancerous growth of the half dozen or so largest cities of India with their mile after sordid mile of slums and semi-slums.

As for caste and communalism, the daily newspapers in the winter of 1978–9 made sad reading. They were full of stories of attacks by caste Hindus on Harijans and the tribal people and of riots between Hindus and Muslims. They detailed at length every day stories of how Hindu sub-castes were struggling against each other for economic and political power within political parties and in the battles between political parties. Morarji Desai had said to me in February 1955, 'In twenty years' time caste will have disappeared from India.' Twenty-four years later he was presiding over a country much more racked by caste rivalries and disputes than when he had made this prediction.

I discovered that not all the experts on rural India were disheartened by the increasing number of atrocities committed by the rural élite against the Harijans and other underprivileged people. Thus B. G. Verghese, the former editor of the *Hindustan Times*, wrote in February 1978 that the disadvantaged had begun to challenge the established order and to offer organized protest.

As the challenge has grown so has the response from those 'threatened'. ... The very trends can be interpreted as symptoms of structural change in society with the long-established status quo coming apart as a result of the pressures of modernization. Seen this way, current tensions might be regarded as a positive sign of progress towards a new social order.[13]

The paradox was bitter: the more atrocities against the poor the more hope for the poor.

The increasingly successful demand of conservative groups within the Hindu majority to make the slaughter of cows illegal throughout the whole of India was a disturbing indication of a determination by a politically powerful group to impose Hindu taboos on the whole population, Hindu and non-Hindu alike. The only State governments to stand out against this demand were the communist governments of West Bengal and Kerala. While I was in India the saintly Vinoba Bhave was threatening to fast to death to persuade these two recalcitrant governments to fall in line. E. M. S. Namboodiripad, the general secretary of the Communist Party of India, Marxist (CPM), in a letter to Bhave reminded him that India was a secular state and that about 150 million of its people, about a quarter of the population belonging mainly to the minority communities, were not averse to eating beef. 'No secular-minded people can ignore the sentiments and food habits of these vast numbers of our population and adopt a policy based purely on the religious belief of the majority.'[14] It was ironic that it fell to one of the leading communists of India to defend secularism with the authentic voice of Nehru. A typical example of Nehru's attack on the advocates of legislation to ban the slaughter of cows was his speech in Parliament in September 1956 when he said that this legislation encouraged 'all kinds of animals [to] roam about eating up crops'; the advocates of this legislation cared 'too much for certain species of animals and less for human beings so that both suffer'.

The banning of the slaughter of cows strained relations between orthodox caste Hindus and the many other communities of India. The campaign to promote Hindi at the expense of English, Urdu and the regional languages strained relations between the Hindi-speakers of northern India and the rest of the Indian people. The non-Hindi States wanted to preserve English as one of the two official languages of the central government and as a link language, the language in which they would communicate with other States and with the central government. Many Hindi-speakers wanted Hindi to supplant English as the link language and as the working language of the central government. This would put at a disadvantage those whose mother-tongue was not Hindi and they constituted 70 per cent of the population.

Nehru had fought with all his strength, wisdom and charisma those who would weaken the unity of India by undermining its secular foundations. He had opposed the abolition of the slaughter of cows. He had defended English and Urdu against the attacks of the enthusiastic proponents of Hindi. He had protected the Muslims, the Christians and other minorities. India at the beginning of the eighties had no great national leader to fight the battle which Nehru had fought, unless Indira Gandhi took up the challenge. That was one of India's principal weaknesses, for in the plural society of India a victory of Hindi-speaking chauvinists would mean the break-up of the nation.

Administration

In my farewell despatch I said that since Independence caste, communalism, nepotism, corruption and political interference had weakened the administrative regime which independent India had inherited from the British. But I cited with approval Maurice Zinkin's assertion that, nevertheless, Indian bureaucracy was the best government service in the whole Eurasian land-mass east of Paris. Twenty years later the best a similarly sympathetic and well-informed foreigner could say was that 'as far as competence or corruption is concerned India's governments have a better record than those of many developing countries'.[15] This was certainly damning with faint praise. In those twenty years corruption had become more widespread and had reached higher levels as a result of the increase in the power of governments to control the economy; the extent of administrative discretion in the granting of money-making licences and permits; the spread over almost the whole of India of legislation prohibiting the sale of liquor and the slaughter of cows; the growth of black money; the demands of political parties for contributions from business; and the low level of the salaries of civil servants and members of the central and State legislatures.

Political interference in administration had increased vastly, especially in the States. Bihar was cited to me by a leading public servant in the Punjab as the most horrible example in India of maladministration. There, he said in tones of profound contempt, the politicans controlled the administration down to the pettiest detail; thus a minor functionary could not be transferred from one post to another without the approval of the State cabinet.

Dharam Vira in his public lecture of January 1979 painted a black picture of the decline of administration in India. He said that he had been to 'practically every important democracy in the world but nowhere is there so much blatant interference by the elected leaders of the country in the day-to-day functioning of administration as it operates in India today'. Officers were transferred and suspended 'merrily to suit the whims and fancies of individual politicians'. This resulted in feeble administration and in corruption. During the emergency from 1975 to 1977 'demoralization of the services became total and the naked play of politicial authoritarianism was complete and unabashed'.[16] I was told that relatively few public servants had then had sufficient integrity and courage to refuse to carry out orders from their political masters to commit improper or illegal acts; they had not even been prudent enough to insist that their political master put the order in writing. Their behaviour was regrettable but understandable. A public servant in New Delhi who was not complaisant was fortunate if all that happened to him was that he was shifted to another post in New Delhi. Others were transferred to unpleasant posts in remote areas or suspended or retired or subjected to minor or major harassments. Some were put in jail under the emergency legislation.

Fortunately for the reputation of the public service, not all public servants were complaisant during the emergency. N. K. Mukerji was Secretary of the Home Ministry when the emergency was proclaimed, and was about to be promoted to Cabinet Secretary, the highest post in the public service. Because he objected to carrying out an illegal order he was immediately transferred to another, less responsible, post where his integrity would not embarrass the government. When the Janata Government came to power he was appointed Cabinet Secretary. At the beginning of 1980 he was the only Indian Civil Servant in the service of the government. It is, as Nehru would say, in the fitness of things that the last I.C.S. officer to serve the Government of India is a man who during the emergency lived up to the highest traditions of the I.C.S.

Foreign Policy

In my farewell despatch I tried to balance the accomplishments of Indian foreign policy under Nehru in the ten years since Independence against its failures. I said that among its accomplishments were that it had not divided India but had helped to unite it; that India had assisted in easing relations between the West and Peking and in finding solutions to problems on the periphery of China—Korea, the coastal islands and Formosa, and Indo-China; that India had exercised a moderating influence on the extreme demands of most other members of the Afro-Asian group on colonial matters and on such questions as Cyprus and Israel; and, most important of all, that Nehru had helped the West to attain a more balanced approach to foreign policy by insisting that the demands of colonial peoples for self-government, the demand of coloured peoples for racial equality, and the revolt of two-thirds of mankind against its poverty, its disease and its illiteracy constituted at least as great a danger to to the peace and welfare of the world as Soviet expansionism.

Among the failures of Indian foreign policy I put Nehru's habit of judging the West and the Soviet Union by different moral yardsticks and of not balancing his denunciations of the failings of the West with denunciations of the failings of the Soviet Union. This exasperated opinion in the West, weakened the force of his denunciations of the West and did not help to correct the false picture of the Soviet Union and China which so many Indians had in their minds. The second great failure of foreign policy under Nehru was the inability of India to establish good relations with Pakistan; the stumbling block had been Kashmir; in order to hold the Vale of Kashmir, India had sacrificed immensely greater national interests. Kashmir had not only been a stumbling block to the establishment of good relations between India and Pakistan; it had embittered relations between India and the West. I discovered in the winter of 1978-9 that Jaya Prakash Narayan had said this in 1966 to Indira Gandhi, then the Prime Minister. He wrote: 'Kashmir has distorted India's image for the world as nothing else has done.'[17]

One principal weakness of my analysis in 1957 was that I failed to realize that Nehru might be mistaken in dismissing the possibility of a Chinese invasion of India. Nehru was right in so much of what he said at that time about China that I thought he was right in this. In January 1950 he already recognized, as the United States Government for years arrogantly refused to do, that the new Communist regime in China was firmly established and that what was important was not so much that a Communist government had come to power, but that, after thirty years of revolution and war, China had a powerful central government and that this was changing the balance of power in Asia and the world. He was well before his time in not only hoping for but foreseeing a break between China and the Soviet Union. He recognized two strains in Chinese behaviour: the Chinese, he said to me, were a very cold-blooded, unemotional, rational people, a little too cold-blooded for his taste; they looked down on foreigners as inferiors and they took offence easily at what they assumed to be slights.

The error Nehru made when he dismissed the possibility of China invading India was to take into account only the rational strain in Chinese behaviour, and he considered a Chinese invasion of India to be irrational, and to fail to take into account the non-rational strain, that the Chinese looked down on foreigners as inferiors and that they took offence easily at what they considered to be slights. Because they considered Indians to be inferiors they resented India's leadership of the Third World; they wanted that leadership themselves; they therefore sought an excuse to humiliate India and thus put India into its 'proper', inferior place. Because they took offence easily they were offended by Nehru's refusal to negotiate a compromise on boundary claims and by his issuing a public challenge to them over the boundary. One leading public servant told me in the winter of 1978-9 that he considered the Chinese had been so determined in the early sixties to humiliate India that if Nehru had not given them the excuse of his public challenge they would have found another excuse for invading India. A former leading public servant, on the other hand, told me that he believed the Chinese would not have invaded India if Nehru had agreed to negotiate on the boundary dispute. The negotiations would not, in his opinion, have led to an agreement since the only possible agreement then as now was one which neither Nehru nor Chou En-lai was politically powerful enough to agree to: that China would accept the McMahon line in the east in return for India's acceptance of the Chinese claims to Aksai Chin in the west. But the negotiations could have gone on and on.

The second main weakness in my analysis in 1957 of Indian foreign policy was that I failed to realize that India might in a crisis with Pakistan find that it had little support not only from

Western countries but also from Afro-Asian countries. This happened when rebellion broke out in East Pakistan in March 1971 and India was swamped by ten million refugees. India's isolation led it to conclude in August a friendship treaty with the Soviet Union. When in December Indian troops entered East Pakistan in support of the rebels India had to rely on the Soviet veto in the Security Council to protect it from an intervention by the U.N. which would have been supported by the great majority of its members. The tilt of the United States Government to Pakistan in December 1971 was thus accompanied by an Indian tilt to the Soviet Union so great that it involved a departure from the kind of policy of non-alignment which Nehru had moved to by the end of his life.

I found when I came to India in the winter of 1978–9 that the Janata Government had from its formation in 1977 been trying to create a greater distance between India and the Soviet Union and to narrow the gap between India and the United States. This it called the pursuit of a policy of *genuine* non-alignment. It had also tried to improve India's relations with China which had been bad ever since China invaded India in 1962. In these efforts it had met with some success, helped by the departure from power of Henry Kissinger and the downfall of the 'Gang of Four' in Peking. The pursuit by the Janata Government of a policy of genuine non-alignment did not, I was told, mark a sharp break with the policy which the Indira Gandhi government had pursued in its last three years of office, from 1974 to 1977; it too had been moving in this direction. The Janata Government speeded up the process.

I had the feeling at the beginning of 1979 that some of those concerned with the framing of Indian foreign policy hoped that it might sometime be possible to balance the Indo-Soviet treaty of 1971 with a similar treaty with China. There was indeed no logical reason why China and India should not, in the words of Article IX of the Indo-Soviet treaty, undertake 'to abstain from providing any assistance to any third party that engages in armed conflict with the other party' and to consult if one party was subjected to an attack or threat of attack 'in order to remove such threat and to take appropriate effective measures to ensure peace and the security of their countries'. Nor was there any logical reason why India should not try to have a treaty of this kind not only with China and the Soviet Union but also, the Senate consenting, with the United States. Then India would have pledged itself not to assist any country which was at war with the Soviet Union, or China or the United States. This would be a demonstration of genuine non-alignment.

The secession of Bangladesh from Pakistan in 1971 made India the clearly dominant power in South Asia. Political instability further weakened Pakistan. The result was that by the mid-seventies India was able to put aside the fear it had had in the mid-fifties and later of a Pakistan armed by the United States invading India. Indira Gandhi's government before and during the emergency was thus able to pursue a policy of reconciliation with Pakistan and the Janata Government continued this policy. The Janata Government also improved India's relations with its other immediate neighbours, Nepal, Bangladesh and Sri Lanka. The improvement of relations with Nepal and Bangladesh made it more likely that the three countries would co-operate in imaginative programmes to develop their water resources for power and irrigation and so raise the standards of living of their peoples. Thus India under the Janata Government had discussed with Nepal a project that would produce major irrigation works and power equal to about all the power produced in India in the 1960's. In these efforts to improve relations with Nepal, Bangladesh and Sri Lanka there was, my informants told me in the spring of 1979, little difference between the policy pursued by the Janata Government and the policy Indira Gandhi would have pursued.

Relations between India and Pakistan began to deteriorate towards the end of the seventies. The explanation which one distinguished Indian gave me in October 1979 was 'the Islamic resurgence and not only the possibility but the probability that Pakistan will be supported in a conflict with India with Islamic arms and OPEC dollars'. Another reason for renewed Indian anxiety about Pakistan was the possibility of Pakistan developing nuclear weapons and the means of delivering them. If Pakistan were to do this India would do likewise. The resulting balance of terror would be unstable. The unstable balance would have been purchased at the price of diverting resources from development. Both countries would suffer from their failure to conclude in the second half of the seventies an agreement to forgo the development of nuclear weapons and to ban the nuclear weapons of other countries from their territories. For this failure it seemed at the end of the seventies that India bore the major share of responsibility.

The Soviet invasion of Afghanistan in December 1979 created great uncertainties about the longer-run trends in the foreign policy of India, as of almost every country in the world. The invasion came only a few weeks before Indira Gandhi once again became prime minister after a spectacular victory in the general election. The invasion was followed by announcements by the United States of its intention to build up Pakistan's armed forces and by discussions on defence between the United States and China. The immediate effect of these developments was to tilt the foreign policy of the new Indira Gandhi government to the Soviet Union and away from a policy of genuine non-alignment.

What the longer-run effects are likely to be it is impossible for anyone, writing as I am in mid-January 1980, to predict. There are too many unknowns. What is clear is that the Soviet invasion of Afghanistan has made the world a more unstable, a more unpredictable, a more dangerous place. No one can, for example, be certain about the kind of changes which may take place in the eighties in the relations between the United States, the Soviet Union and China. The immediate effect of the invasion of Afghanistan has been to widen the gap between the United States and the Soviet Union and to narrow the gap between the United States and China. Other trends are possible in the eighties. If the Soviet Government were to become sufficiently frightened of China it might decide to try to make a deal with the West in order to be able to concentrate its forces against China. In 1980 a Soviet–Chinese pact to divide Asia seems incredible, but so in 1938 did a Soviet–Nazi pact to divide Europe and Asia.

Given the frightening unknowns of the perilous eighties it seems to me, as an outsider, that the wisest course for India is to do its best to maintain its freedom of manoeuvre. This means not committing itself to any one great power or combination of great powers. It means continuing in the eighties the policy of the second half of the seventies—a policy of genuine non-alignment.

Domestic Politics

I had expected when I left India in 1957 that Nehru would continue to be Prime Minister until he was assassinated or until he dropped in his tracks from exhaustion; I thought he had about another five years in which to leave his imprint on India. Nehru in fact continued as Prime Minister until he died, but he lasted seven years not five. However, in his last two years he made little imprint on India; his position in the country was weakened by the defeat by China and his health was not good. Nehru's tragedy turned out to be the tragedy I had feared for him and for India, that he would remain leader of his country for a year or two after he had lost his grip and thus damage his own reputation and his country's interests.

My forecast in the fifties of how the political party system might develop after Nehru's departure was that it was unlikely India would develop a system of government based on two main political parties which would alternate in office. Rather, I thought that the Congress Party would remain in power by shifting to right or to left in accordance with changes in public opinion. It would continue to be a party of consensus: if public opinion moved left, it would move left; if public opinion moved right, it would move right. It would not be a relatively homogeneous ideological party on a western European model but a national party on the traditional Canadian model, drawing support from a heterogeneous group of people across the nation and fulfilling the traditional role of a national party in a plural society by being a broker between conflicting interests in the nation.

By the end of 1979 I was convinced that I had been mistaken in my forecast of the development of the political party system in India. Instead of government by one national political party it looked as if India had been launched into a period of government by fluctuating coalitions of political groups. By the time the general elections took place in 1977 the Congress Party had split into three groups and two of these (one under Morarji

Desai and one under Jagjivan Ram) united with all the other non-Communist groups opposed to Indira Gandhi's Congress Party to form the Janata Government. After the elections Indira Gandhi's Congress Party split into two. In 1979 another re-alignment of political groups took place.

The general election of January 1980 once again changed the picture. Indira Gandhi's sweeping victory restored her Congress Party to the place her father's Congress Party had occupied in the fifties. The forecast which I had made in the fifties of how the party system in India would develop once again appeared to be well based. But the elections of 1977 and 1980 had demonstrated the unpredictability of Indian politics. Virtually no one had believed before the election of 1977 that Indira Gandhi would be defeated so ignominiously. Virtually no one had believed before the election of 1980 that her opponents would be defeated so ignominiously. Moreover, no one could forecast with certainty the likely political effects of continued failure by India to improve the conditions of life of the poorest forty per cent of its people.

Krishna Menon

I tried when I was in India in the winter of 1978–9 to find some satisfactory explanation of Krishna Menon's approach to international affairs and of why Nehru reposed such trust in him.

One former senior public servant who had worked closely with Menon told me that the key to Menon's approach to international affairs was that, by the time Independence came to India, Menon was no longer an Indian; he had become an Englishman; he had lived in London for eighteen years; he had been a student of Harold Laski for ten of those years; he had belonged to the extreme left of the British Labour Party and at that time, as George Brown, the former Labour foreign minister, has put it, the left-wingers 'despite all evidence to the contrary, and even if they themselves were not Communists, . . . believed that pretty well everything that came out of the Russian Revolution was somehow good, . . . that the Russians were "goodies" standing up to the "baddies" of all the rest of the world'.[18] Krishna Menon, my Indian informant went on to say, 'believed that nothing the Russians did was wrong and that everything the Americans did was wrong'.[19] These, he said, were the exact words which President Kennedy had used to Menon after he and Menon had discussed the situation in Laos at the White House in 1961.

I found general agreement that Menon's principal objectives in foreign policy were to weaken the links between India and the United States and to strengthen India's links with the Soviet Union. When I read the first volume of Sarvepalli Gopal's life of Nehru I came across an early example of how Menon went about this task. This occurred in the autumn of 1946. Nehru then held the portfolio of external affairs in the interim government. Acting as Nehru's personal envoy, Menon met Molotov, the Soviet foreign minister, to seek assistance in foodgrains. Going beyond his instructions he 'spoke to Molotov about the possibility of Soviet military experts visiting India'. Nehru had to caution him on this, and Menon received 'the first of over the years very many mildly-worded cautions from his chief'.[20] I found that a well-known writer such as Kuldip Nayar would casually refer to Menon as 'known for his pro-Communist views' and as 'the former pro-Communist Defence Minister'.[21]

On my return to Canada I re-read Michael Brecher's book on Menon based on his interviews with him in 1964 and 1965. His analysis of Menon's many references to the United States in those interviews led him to conclude that Menon had

an intense emotional antipathy [to the United States], as well as intellectual disdain. . . . 'American imperialism' is unquestionably the preeminent evil force. In fact, criticism of the Soviets is rare and inevitably mild. . . . The contrast between derision, disdain, accusation, and denunciation of the United States role, and rare, mild regret with reference to Soviet actions reveals an enormous bias in Menon's image of this key component of world politics.[22]

In the summer of 1953 Pearson believed that the opposition of the American government to Indian membership in the Geneva Conference was 'almost pathological . . . due in part to their feeling that India and Krishna Menon are the same thing at international conferences'. Krishna Menon's antipathy to the United States was likewise almost pathological. The interaction between these two almost pathological antipathies poisoned relations between India and the United States. It

Reconsideration

helped to produce in both countries diplomacies and foreign policies which did not serve the national interest.

Some of my Indian friends who had worked with Krishna Menon told me that in order to understand him and his influence on Indian foreign policiy it was essential to bear in mind that he had not just one set of prejudices—his antipathy to the United States and his sympathy with the Soviet Union—but that he had a second set of prejudices based on his hatred of Pakistan. The first set of prejudices he possessed as a brown Englishman who was an adherent of the extreme left of the British Labour Party. Why he possessed the second set of prejudices they did not know. What they did know was that, whenever before the Chinese invasion in 1962 there was trouble between India and China, Menon would try to divert attention from it by playing up some affair with Pakistan. The Chiefs of Staff had once drawn up a plan of defence against Chinese attacks in the North-East; Menon instructed them not to waste time considering such an eventuality. Brecher's book confirmed this analysis. Menon said to him in 1964 and 1965:

Our main enemy was Pakistan . . . [and] is Pakistan. . . . [Pakistan's] idea is to get a jumping-off ground to take the whole of India. . . . Pakistan will do anything and everything against us. . . . Our defence policy until the Chinese invaded us was intended to resist an attack from Pakistan.[23]

Some months after I returned to Canada from my 1978-9 visit to India I read the second volume of Sarvepalli Gopal's biography of Nehru, based on access to Nehru's private papers. This threw what was for me a new and revealing light on the relationship between Nehru and Krishna Menon. I was surprised by the volume of their personal correspondence. I was even more surprised by the tone of the correspondence.

Menon's letters to Nehru would, in Gopal's words, often blend 'fawning hysteria and plaintive self-pity'. In one letter to Mathai in August 1951 which he knew Mathai would show to Nehru he said that Nehru was 'the greatest man in Asia, maybe in the world' and that he might be driven to suicide if he did not possess Nehru's full confidence. Six months later in letters to Mathai and Nehru he again threatened suicide. Sometimes his letters to Nehru would be 'tearful', sometimes his questioning of a decision by Nehru on foreign affairs would be couched 'in presumptuous rhetoric' or would be sarcastic.

Nehru would reply not only with patience but with deep affection, ignoring the presumptuous rhetoric and the sarcasm. When he was compelled to chide Menon for an error which had seriously embarrassed him, such as Menon's vote against the U.N. resolution on Hungary of 11 November 1956, he would merely say:

Generally speaking, it appears better to abstain from voting on resolutions containing some objectionable features and moving amendments, rather than voting against it.

And in February 1953 when Menon complained to Nehru that he felt almost at the end of his emotional and mental tether because something had come between them Nehru replied:

The real thing is a basic affection and respect and a belief in the integrity of each other. Nothing has happened to shake that so far as I am concerned. I was happy to have you here and loved the talks we had. I was glad to know that there was a possibility of your coming to India for good, for I wanted you not to be far from me. So, please do not imagine something that is not there and do not distress yourself about it. Love. Yours affectionately, Jawaharlal.

I had not realized that Nehru must have known the extent of the deterioration of Menon's physical and psychological condition in 1951 when he was High Commissioner in London, a deterioration caused by or reflected in his 'living for years on the drug Luminal' and revealing itself in his 'speaking incoherently in public'. If Nehru knew of this behaviour in 1951 he must have turned a blind eye to a recurrence of it at the U.N. in the autumn of 1957. I was at the Assembly that year and heard some of Menon's incoherent speeches on Kashmir. I was told at the time that one explanation of the incoherence was that Menon was constantly taking drugs.

Nor had I realized when I was High Commissioner that Nehru's esteem for Menon was so great that he would have rated as his greatest failure in political relationships in 1953 and 1954 his inability to secure immediate agreement to Menon's entry into the cabinet and that his disappointment over this failure influenced his announcement in August 1954 that he would like to retire from office.[24]

I came across when I was in India in the winter of 1978–9 two examples of Nehru's obstinate refusal to face the fact that Menon's behaviour at the U.N. in New York damaged India's national interests. One was in a book by the distinguished Indian journalist, Frank Moraes. Moraes wrote that he had been at the U.N. in the autumn of 1956 during the debates on Hungary and Suez. On his return to India he had in a conversation with Nehru told him of 'the damage done to India's image by Krishna Menon's partisan performance at the U.N. [on Hungary]'. Moraes says that Nehru was so angered that from then on his relations with Nehru which had been cordial though not close were never quite the same.[25] The other example was given me in a conversation with a senior public servant who had been close to Nehru. He told me that he had warned Nehru again and again that whenever Menon went to New York for U.N. meetings he inflamed American opinion against India; Nehru refused to believe this and it was not until President Kennedy himself told Nehru this at a private meeting in 1961 that Nehru was convinced; even then, however, Nehru continued to believe, despite all the mounting evidence to the contrary, that Menon was a first-rate advocate for India in the debates at the U.N. on Kashmir.

The perplexing question is why Nehru accorded to Menon so special a place in his affection and esteem. Gopal gives the orthodox explanation:

Nehru relished his tart cleverness, the barbed wit, the astringent conversation. 'I have hardly come across a keener intelligence and brain.' Surrounded in Delhi mostly by small men with shallow minds, Nehru admired the quality in Menon's intellectual performance and recognized the mutual sympathy in their viewpoint on most matters. . . . [Menon was to Nehru] the man with the closest intellectual affinity.[26]

I find this explanation insufficient. It is impossible for me to believe that Nehru could not have found in India a friend and adviser, or two or three friends and advisers, who possessed Menon's good qualities but not his faults. There were certainly in India a few people who were as close or closer to Nehru than Menon. Menon never addressed Nehru as *bhai* (brother). Jaya Prakash Narayan and Homi Bhabha did.[27] They were indeed the only people outside Nehru's family who did. Narayan had a mass following in India which Menon had not. He knew the

United States which Menon did not. Bhabha was a renaissance man; he was a distinguished scientist and in addition he was, unlike Menon, a man of deep culture and wide interests. Gopal knows that his father, Radhakrishnan, excelled Menon in intelligence, knowledge, cleverness, wit and the astringency of his conversation. Vijaya Lakshmi Pandit was a much more persuasive advocate for India at the U.N. than Menon.

In a despatch to Ottawa in April 1957 I said that Nehru's long infatuation for Menon had become almost an obsession. There is to my mind no explanation for Nehru's attitude to Menon other than infatuation—infatuation in the sense in which Webster defines the word, that is, that Nehru was completely carried away by foolish affection for him.

The Special Relationship with Canada

The special relationship between India and Canada had ceased to exist many years before I revisited India in the winter of 1978–9. The relationship reached its high point in 1953 and 1954. The Korean armistice signed in July 1953 was in large part the result of a close partnership between India and Canada. Canada gave full support to the unsuccessful effort to have India included as a member of the Geneva Conference of 1954 on Indo-China and Korea. Just before the Conference took place Louis St Laurent, then Prime Minister, disassociated himself from the principal Western powers by publicly supporting Nehru's call for a cease-fire in Indo-China. At the Conference, India and Canada worked closely together. In the crises over the coastal islands and Formosa, Canada tried to moderate American policy and India Chinese policy. India and Canada co-operated in efforts to reduce the tension between the United States and China caused by the imprisonment of American airmen in China. In the first days of November 1956 India and Canada were associated at the U.N. in New York in efforts to find a peaceful way out of the Suez crisis. Nehru and St Laurent supported each other on many issues which came up at meetings of Commonwealth prime ministers. The Indians liked the way Canada went about giving aid under the Colombo Plan, in particular Canada's gift to India of an atomic research and experimental reactor. Nehru was pleased that Canada had completely removed by 1957 all Canadian legislation, federal and provincial, which discriminated against Canadian citizens of Indian origin. St Laurent received a warm welcome in India in 1954 and Lester Pearson in 1955. Nehru likewise received a warm welcome in Canada in 1956. A distinguished Indian scholar, M. S. Rajan, wrote in 1962:

One strange but fruitful development in post-war Commonwealth as well as general international relations is what has been called the 'Indo-Canadian *entente*' or 'the Ottawa–New Delhi Axis'.

and he called this development an 'improbable, but surprisingly real relationship'.[28] A Canadian scholar's assessment of Indo-Canadian relations from 1947 to 1957 is:

Behind the well-turned phrases of mutual compliments lay the reality of a relationship which admittedly had to be constantly nurtured but which kept both India and Canada engaged in a multi-state, multi-subject intercourse, keeping their national life more open and receptive.... The fact that India did not close itself off as Burma did is in some measure due to the effort and patience that Indians and Canadians put into their relations.[29]

There were, of course, strains on the relationship between India and Canada even when it was at its most cordial in 1953 and 1954, and the strains increased in 1955, 1956 and 1957. St Laurent and Pearson considered India to be intransigent on Kashmir and I assume that Nehru considered that they were prejudiced against India on this issue. St Laurent and Pearson believed that Nehru was unduly shrill in his protests against United States military aid to Pakistan and Nehru must have been disappointed that they did not attempt to dissuade the United States from giving this aid. St Laurent and Pearson were irritated by the warmth of the welcome which India gave to Krushchev and Bulganin in 1955. They were outraged by Nehru's reaction to the Hungarian Revolution in 1956. They were incredulous that Nehru continued to allow himself to be represented by Krishna Menon at U.N. meetings in New York. Nehru must at the same time have become increasingly aware of the misconceptions which he had held about Canada, misconceptions which Pearson warned me of in my talk with him just before I left Ottawa for New Delhi in September 1952— that Nehru exaggerated Canada's influence in international affairs and did not realize the limitations on Canada's freedom of action imposed by its position between the United States and Britain.

The principal cause of the erosion of the special relationship after 1955 was the joint membership of the two countries in the three supervisory commissions in Indo-China established by the Geneva Conference in 1954. By the time I left India in May 1957 the Indians were beginning to believe that Canada was serving American policy in Indo-China and that the United States was determined to undermine the settlement on Indo-China reached at the Geneva Conference by aborting efforts to hold elections in Vietnam. Krishna Menon was in charge of Indian policy in the Indo-China supervisory commissions from their establishment in 1954 until his fall from power after the Chinese invasion in 1962. I have no inside knowledge of what happened in the commissions from 1957 to 1962 after I left India but, knowing how apt Krishna Menon was to believe in the good faith of the Soviet Union and the bad faith of the United States, I assume that he instructed the Indian representatives on the Indo-China commissions to tilt to the governments of the Soviet Union, China and North Vietnam, just as the Canadian representatives tilted to the government of the United States. Both these tilts became more pronounced after the United States entered the Vietnam war in earnest in the mid-sixties.

My impression is that from the early sixties until the commissions came to an end in 1973 almost all the Canadian political officers who served on one of the three commissions came back to Canada firm supporters of United States policy in Indo-China and with profound distaste and contempt for Indian policy in Indo-China and for the Indians they had served with. An Indian writer has put it that the Canadians on the commissions 'were angered and exasperated with the Indians' and that the result was 'an accumulation of bitterness against India'.[30] A Canadian journalist who was at the time stationed in South and South-East Asia has written:

A constant source of amazement to Americans in Vietnam was the fact that Canadians with the international commissions, as individuals, were often more hawkish than many U.S. officers.... It was largely because of Indo-China ... that Canadian good will and encouragement toward India were transformed into bitterness and distrust.³¹

By 1973 nearly 200 Canadian foreign service officers had served on one of the commissions in Indo-China, about one-third of all the officers in the Canadian foreign service. Their influence on Canadian policy to India has been profound and remains profound.

The explosion by India of a nuclear device in May 1974 had a catalytic effect on Indo-Canadian relations. It demonstrated that so far as Canada was concerned the special relationship had ceased to exist. To some members of the Canadian foreign service it did more than this; it confirmed them in their belief that there had never been a special relationship. One of them in a letter to me in October 1977 put his argument as follows:

To my mind a special relationship should involve a reciprocal process by which each side takes account of the interests of the other. Without such reciprocity, any notion of a special relationship constitutes infatuation on the side of the one who perceives it. There is no evidence that during the period in which the special relationship was supposed to exist India ever modified its policies to suit the interests of Canada. What India did was to make demands which Canada and other western countries were to concede. The special relationship was entirely one-sided so far as it existed at all or, to put it another way, it existed in Canadian minds only. The Canadian reaction to the Indian test of a nuclear device in 1974 was the result of a realization on the part of Canadian cabinet ministers and the general public in Canada that they had been misled, of discovering that there was no community of interest between Canada and India. And it was a genuine countrywide reaction.

When the papers of Nehru, Krishna Menon and the Indian Ministry of External Affairs for the nineteen-fifties are made available to scholars it may be possible to determine how far, if at all, India modified its policies in the fifties as part of its contribution to nurturing a special relationship with Canada. My own belief is that India did modify its policies on a number of occasions, notably in the negotiations which led to the armistice in Korea. I also believe that the special relationship was one of the factors which went into the decision by Nehru that India should not withdraw from the Commonwealth after the British invasion of Suez, and that it is possible that the special relationship influenced Nehru finally to come out against the Soviet suppression of the Hungarian Revolution.

But it seems to me that the important question from Canada's point of view is not whether India modified its policies as the result of its relationship with Canada but whether the relationship which Canada had with India, special or not, promoted the national interests of Canada just as the important question from India's point of view is whether its relationship with Canada promoted its national interests. I believe that the relationship did promote Canada's national interests. Nehru's insistence at Commonwealth meetings and in talks with St Laurent and Pearson on the importance of the demands of colonial peoples for self-government, the demands of coloured races for racial equality and the revolt of two-thirds of mankind against its poverty, its disease and its illiteracy helped to correct the very natural concentration of Canadian foreign policy on the affairs of the North Atlantic countries and the cold war with the Soviet Union. This made Canadian foreign policy more attuned to the realities of the world than it otherwise would have been and thus more likely to promote the national interests of Canada.

It is relevant to speculate how much better off the United States and the world as a whole might be today if the United States had had the same sort of friendly relationship with India and Nehru in the nineteen-fifties as Canada had, and if it had been similarly influenced by Nehru's theses of the importance of what are now called North–South relations, and of recognizing that the Chinese Communists had established a strong, stable government and that it was in the general interest to encourage a split between China and the Soviet Union.

A specific example of the relationship between Canada and India promoting the national interests of Canada is the contribution which Pearson made from October 1952 to July 1953 to the achievement of an armistice in Korea. Had it not been for Pearson there might well have been no armistice in 1953 or for an indefinite period thereafter. As long as there was no armistice there was danger that the fighting in Korea might spread to China and thence to the Soviet Union and precipitate a third world war. The main argument for Canadian membership in the North Atlantic Alliance and for Canada spending over four billion dollars a year on defence is that this makes a world war less likely and so contributes to Canadian security. Pearson's role in reducing the chances of a world war breaking out in 1953 did as much for Canadian security as many billions of the defence expenditures by Canada since the Second World War. He could not have played this role if there had not existed a special relationship between Canada and India.

The special relationship may also have contributed to the strengthening of the unity of the Canadian nation. A Canadian journalist in an article in April 1978 contended that the idea of Canada as a nation with a mission in international affairs was, from about 1942 to about 1957, an externalized sustaining myth which helped Canadians define themselves as a people, helped them reach beyond themselves, helped to strengthen Canada's will to endure.[32] In my opinion one of the important components of that myth was the belief of Canadians that there was a special relationship between Canada and India.

If that special relationship is to be re-established the governments of India and Canada will have to ponder deeply how best to go about the task. The task will not be easy and progress will have to be by stages. Effort must be accompanied by patience. Disagreements over one issue such as nuclear proliferation must not be allowed to bar the way to attempts to discover areas of foreign policy on which the two governments can, if not reach substantial agreement, at least so modify their policies as to narrow the gap between them.

Perhaps the best way to start would be to launch a series of sustained dialogues between ministers and officials of the two countries on North–South relations. The starting point for the discussions might be the report of the Willy Brandt Commission on international development issues. This could lead into an exchange of views on what might be done to make multilateral intergovernmental institutions more effective, particularly the U.N. and the specialized agencies. Could anything be done to modify the undemocratic one-State one-vote system under which governments representing less than one-tenth of the population of the U.N. can pass a resolution in the U.N. General Assembly by a two-thirds majority? Might it, for example, be possible to add to the U.N. Charter a provision that resolutions on certain precisely defined subjects would be binding on all members of the U.N. if the two-thirds majority included States with at least half the population of the U.N. and States contributing at least half of the U.N.'s regular budget? Could anything be done to modify the system of weighted voting in the World Bank and the International Monetary Fund, which gives the populous poor countries too little influence in these bodies? Might it, for example, be possible to add to the existing votes of member States in the Bank and the Fund a certain number of votes for every million of their population? What else might be done in the Bank and the Fund to make these agencies less unequal partnerships between the rich and the poor countries? (In my book on the World Bank published in 1973 I put forward about a dozen suggestions on how the Bank might be made a less unequal partnership.[33]) If a dialogue between ministers and officials of India and Canada on questions such as these proved useful to both governments they might go on to discuss at a series of meetings such additional questions of common concern as the limitation and reduction of armaments (not just the issue of nuclear proliferation), Palestine, South Africa, Indo-China, the Islamic revival, Soviet policy in the Middle East and South Asia, and what can be done to promote human rights throughout the world.

The principal advantage to the governments of India and Canada of discussions such as these is that they would help to correct distortions in the views of the world as seen from New Delhi and Ottawa and thus lessen the danger that distorted views might result in policies which did not serve the long-run national interest. The discussions would also make it easier for the two governments to work together in the eighties as they did in the fifties during periods of dangerous international tension. The United States as a great power will be directly involved whenever there is such tension. The re-establishment of a special relationship between India and Canada would enable Canada at these times to bring a constructive influence to bear on United States policy, as it did in the fifties. It would not be that the Canadian Government knew more than the American Government but that because of its special relationship with India its angle of vision would be likely to be different and this would help to correct distortions in Washington's view of what was happening.

India and China Compared

In my farewell despatch I said that though India's prospects were bright compared with those of other Asian countries of any size which lay between Turkey and Japan and south of the Soviet Union and China, its prospects compared with those of China were not so bright. During the next seventeen years until the death of Mao most observers believed that China was making much more rapid progress than India both in increasing its production and in ensuring that the conditions of life of the poor were greatly improved. But in recent years, since the death of Mao, doubts have arisen about the reality of many of the proclaimed accomplishments of Communist China and it is no longer considered so certain that China's economic, social and cultural advance in the thirty years after the Communists came to power in 1949 has been much greater than India's in the same period.

R. H. Cassen in his book on India published in 1978 discussed in a brilliant eight-page essay the problem of attempting to compare the progress of India and China. He emphasized the difficulties of making any comparison, a principal difficulty being that Chinese statistics are highly unreliable. His conclusions can be summed up as follows. In agriculture it is unlikely that China's growth exceeds India's and India's may indeed have been better since the sixties. China's record in industrial growth has probably been superior to India's both in its rate of increase and in its character and 'unless India changes its ways it is difficult to believe that China's planned industrial expansion will not continue to be more effective than India's inefficient public-sector and rule-bound private sector'. The status of women is improving more rapidly in China than in India. China has been more successful than India in narrowing the gap between the conditions of life of the upper-income group and the poor: 'There is no evidence of anything in China resembling the differences between richest and poorest in India....' There is not in China 'the kind of widespread, severe poverty that exists throughout India'.[34]

In the two years or so since R. H. Cassen wrote this a good deal more information has come out of China. This information tends to narrow the gap which was generally perceived between the accomplishments of China and of India. The conclusion of an Indian writer, A. S. Abraham, in March 1979 is that the Chinese system does not seem to have performed much more efficiently than the Indian. He believes, and his belief seems to be well founded, that:

The educational restructuring under Mao ... put the clock back by years; the emphasis on ideology over expertise was as irrelevant as it was sterile; ... the urban-rural divide was only marginally reduced in favour of the latter; family planning was ... not very successful, and there was vast inefficiency, wastage and bureaucratic corruption. ... China is now discovering the necessity of opening out to the West; India has from the start shunned hermetic isolation. China is beginning to see the emergence of a democratic movement; India has run a democratic system for over three decades, except for one mercifully brief spell of authoritarianism.[35]

Nehru

The essay on Nehru which I sent to Ottawa in May 1957 (which is substantially the same as the preceding chapter) did not, I think, enhance my reputation in Ottawa. Rather, it confirmed the suspicion that I had been so captivated by Nehru as to be incapable of weighing judicially his demerits against his merits, his weaknesses against his strengths, his failures against his accomplishments. I was indeed captivated by Nehru. How far this affected my judgement of his policies is another matter. But in being captivated I was in good company. Arnold Toynbee in an obituary essay on Nehru used the word captivation to describe the effect Nehru had on him[36] and two years later he wrote: 'I took delight in Nehru as a beautiful living creature—one of the noble works of God's creation. He delighted me by his youthfulness of spirit and body, ... by his spontaneity, by his utter freedom from pompousness.'[37] Walter Crocker, who was for many years Australia's High Commissioner to India, wrote a book about Nehru in which he emphasized Nehru's misjudgements. He also said, 'Most people found Nehru captivating. I certainly did. ... Nehru was that rare man who is both clever and good ... the clever man wielding power who remained good. . . . Nothing can destroy his distinction. His supreme achievement was to have been Nehru, the fine spirit exercising power, the ruler who remained disinterested and compassionate.'[38] Asoka Mehta, economist and politician, in his book of reflections published thirteen years after Nehru's death, charges Nehru with four serious faults but he also writes, 'Effortlessly he communicated around him his flame-like quality, his tormented sensitiveness, his resilience in resoluteness. . . . His loneliness was no bar to his ability to charm, captivate those who came in contact with him.'[39] V. K. R. V. Rao, a leading economist and at one time a cabinet minister, says in his book on the Nehru legacy: 'All in all, I would describe Nehru as the most human of all the persons I have known and therefore the most lovable.'[40]

A shrewd critic once wrote, 'The definitive biography of a great man can never be written by one who knew him in the flesh.' But any biographer of Nehru will fail in his task if he does not comprehend Nehru's capacity to charm, to fascinate, to captivate.

My impression when I was in India in the winter of 1978–9 was that there has been a considerable increase in the number of people in India who denigrate Nehru. This is not surprising. Many of the hopes and dreams and visions of a quarter century ago have not been fulfilled and it is tempting to make Nehru the scapegoat. The question which tantalizes me is not so much what people now think of Nehru's record but what Nehru himself would have thought of it if he had lived until 1979 and had realized at the age of ninety that in over thirty years of independence the conditions of life of the poorest people of India had improved little if at all. This would assuredly have broken his heart. How far would he have blamed himself?

Tarlok Singh, a driving force for many years in the Planning Commission, with his love and respect for Nehru, obviously finds it repugnant to criticize him adversely. Yet he has written that Nehru was partly responsible for the failure of the measures of land reform to serve the interests of the rural poor because he did not attach sufficient importance to helping the disadvantaged rural groups to organize themselves to demand their rights against the opposition of the politically powerful, richer peasants. He did not, Tarlok Singh says, place as much emphasis as he might have on strengthening such organized, secular and national forces as the trade union movement, the co-operative movement, organizations of landless labourers and poorer peasants and of other groups and classes whose interests are not safeguarded by the present system, and on bringing all the progressive forces together into a creative working partnership. In order to get the necessary social structural changes in India there had to be strong pressure from the disadvantaged groups. Nehru's 'very ideals and the confidence he aroused held back these pressures'.[41] Another former senior public servant told me that Nehru's fault was that he did not insist on the implementation of land reform in the first half of the fifties when his power within India was at its peak, symbolized by his being at the same time president of the Congress Party and chairman of the Planning Commission as well as Prime Minister, Foreign Minister, and head of the atomic energy department. At that time Nehru could, he believed, have overcome the opposition to land reform of the vested interests within the Congress Party. P. C. Joshi, a member of the President's committee on land reform, believes that the 'opportunity for sweeping changes was lost in the 1950s, and it will be much more difficult to finish the task today'.[42]

My impression is that there is now general agreement that India would have made greater economic and social progress in the last thirty years if it had not in the fifties and the first half of the sixties concentrated so high a proportion of its limited resources of intelligence and administration, and of external and internal finance, on investment in heavy industry and in large irrigation projects, at the expense of agriculture and middle-sized and small industry and middle-sized and small irrigation projects. Lawrence Veit in his scrupulously careful book on India's development published in 1976, under the auspices of the Council on Foreign Relations in New York, stated:

If instead of investing in heavy industry, India had concentrated on mining, light manufacturing, economic infrastructure, and agriculture, its economy probably would have had greater resilience; it would have resumed its growth sooner; there would have been more current output to satisfy the poor during the recession, and the foreign exchange situation would have been easier.[43]

On agriculture Tarlok Singh has written: 'In retrospect, we have to concede that in the past [under the Nehru regime], agriculture did not receive its due share of scarce resources like foreign exchange, and the scale of investment in agriculture was less than adequate.'[44] Nor, I would add, did agriculture receive its due share of first-class cabinet ministers and first-class public servants. Nehru clearly has to bear a good deal of the burden of responsibility for these mistaken priorities. But the responsibility is not his alone. His cabinet ministers and the senior public servants who advised him do not appear to have urged him to change his priorities.

The World Bank's record was better. In its economic report on India in 1956 it was mistaken when it stated without qualification that there was 'inherent conflict between the pursuit of economic equality and the pursuit of rapid economic development', but it was far-sighted when it warned against India's 'extremely ambitious' projects for expanding production of capital equipment. India, it said, was still relatively inexperienced in this field and its resources were not 'naturally adapted to the production of heavy plant and machinery, which make heavy demands on capital and technical skill. From a strictly economic point of view it would almost certainly make better sense to concentrate more on lighter and less complex metal products.'[45] In 1960 the special World Bank mission of Abs, Franks and Sproule stated in its report:

The need for effort to ensure success in agricultural policy cannot be over-stressed and we have found it difficult to be certain whether the implications of this have been fully realized in all quarters. . . . Success will involve . . . ensuring that the overall policy of the Union Government is effectively implemented by the individual States with whom the executive responsibility for agricultural policy rests.[46]

This translated from the diplomatic language of understatement means, 'We are convinced that the Indian Government does not realize what must be done to ensure success in its agricultural policy and in particular that it is not putting the necessary pressure on the governments of the individual States to implement its policy.'

The Planning Commission in the early fifties did not only give Nehru extraordinarily inaccurate forecasts of the growth of population in India, it also in the first five-year plan (1952) made a statement about the population problem so restrained as to be misleading. It said: 'A rapidly growing population is apt to become more a source of embarrassment than of help to a programme for raising standards of living.' Nehru, therefore, did not know in the first half of the fifties how serious India's population problem was. He must, however, have known by the mid-fifties that it was serious. Even so, as Sarvepalli Gopal has put it in his biography of Nehru, he had

> no feeling of urgency about the need to curb the rise in population. He considered the rate of increase to be by no means abnormal, and in fact less than in most countries of Europe; and he was willing to rely on long-term forces, such as the spread of education, the development of a health service and industrial progress, to mitigate the problem.[47]

This presumably explains, though it does not excuse, his putting in charge of the family planning programme in the fifties two ministers of health, Amrit Kaur and Susheela Nayer, who had been leading members of Gandhi's immediate circle of devotees and shared his lack of enthusiasm for artificial methods of contraception. They certainly did not display zeal for family planning. They failed to spend the money allocated to them for that purpose.

I have already said that part of Nehru's tragedy was that he stayed on as Prime Minister for a year or two after he had lost his grip. I found when I was in India in the winter of 1978-9 that some leading politicians were prepared to be precise about when he should have resigned. One, in talking to me, set the date as 1962, two years before Nehru's death. This would have enabled his successor to lead the Congress Party in the general election that year. Asoka Mehta goes further. He believes that Nehru should have resigned in 1958. He contends that by then Nehru 'had laid solid foundations for all that he had wished to achieve—integration of the [princely] states, new constitution, democratic set-up, two successful general elections, economic planning, linguistic reorganization of states, secular mood in the administration. The remaining [six] years of power showed no further surge of creativity. The resplendent and iridescent phase of his career was over.' And, he adds, by clinging to power he inadvertently helped to establish the 'dynastic concept of succession'.[48]

Related to the criticism that he hung on to power too long is the criticism that he did not in the fifties select the best possible successor and train him to succeed him. He himself had been selected by Gandhi as the leader of independent India. It would have been in the Gandhian tradition for Nehru in turn to have selected his successor. He did not need to go as far as Mackenzie King who selected not only his successor, St Laurent, but his successor's successor, Pearson. Prime ministers do not like selecting a successor, for an heir-apparent can become a rival and he is also a constant reminder of political mortality. He is the skull at the feast of power. There was in the early fifties an obvious successor for Nehru to have selected, Jaya Prakash Narayan, who was then the leader of the Praja Socialist Party. Nehru did try in 1953 to get him into the cabinet, but looking back now it seems probable that he did not try hard enough. Part of the profound affection and respect with which Jaya Prakash Narayan is held by the people of India arises from his renunciation of active politics in 1953 to trudge with Vinoba Bhave along the dusty lanes of India's villages on behalf of the bhoodan land-gift movement; for Indians are apt to hold in higher regard those who renounce than those who achieve. Perhaps if Jaya Prakash Narayan had become deputy Prime Minister in 1953 and Prime Minister in 1958 or 1962 he would have demonstrated that his strength was in criticism, not in the constructive tasks of government. It is, however, hard to believe that the gamble of making him deputy Prime Minister in 1953 was not worth taking. If he had turned out to be a failure as deputy Prime Minister Nehru could have eased him out of the race for the succession just as he eased Morarji Desai out. Nehru can be criticized for not spending at least as much energy on trying to get Jaya Prakash Narayan to be deputy Prime Minister as he spent in getting Krishna Menon into the cabinet.

Asoka Mehta makes two other criticisms of Nehru. He weakened the delicate balance inside the Congress Party by establishing the supremacy of the legislative wing of the Party over the organizational wings and of the Supreme Command of the Party over the Party's provincial committees. He established bad precedents by too frequent amendment of the constitution (17 times in 17 years) and by too frequent use of the power of the Central Government to take over the government of a State.[49] These errors made easier the establishment of Indira Gandhi's dictatorship.

Taking all these criticisms into consideration and also the criticisms of Nehru's foreign policy, his failure to attach sufficient importance to administration, and his trust in Krishna Menon, where are we left when we try to assess Nehru's role as Prime Minister? We are left, it seems to me, with a man whose accomplishments greatly outweighed his failures. Accomplishments and failures have to be seen against the daunting problems he had to deal with when he became Prime Minister. There were the problems of partition, communal violence, refugees and the princely states; but far transcending all these in importance was the fact that 'on the eve of Independence, India was still stamped with the sharp disparities of the most deeply stratified society in human history',[50] stratified by caste, economic class, language, religion and region, and that it was a society where grinding poverty was the lot of most of its people and had been their lot for centuries. India may be in a parlous state today, but if Nehru had been assassinated in 1946 how much more parlous would India's state be? For Nehru fought for the things which are most likely to hold India together and to bring its people in time out of the morass of their poverty—secularism, protection of the rights of minorities, respect for democratic parliamentary institutions, insistence on the necessity of social reform, faith in the essential goodness and intelligence of the people of India, contempt for lavish expenditure by the rich, sorrow and anger because of the misery of the poor, pride in India's past, visions of India's future greatness.

Future Prospects

An Indian economist friend said to me at the beginning of 1979, 'If you look at India's record over the last thirty years you are depressed. If you look at the record of the last four years or so you are encouraged.' At the end of 1979, he would probably have added, 'If you look at the record of this year you are plunged into gloom.' In India there is sometimes only the trembling of a leaf between hope and despair.

The statistics of agricultural and industrial production which I cited earlier in this chapter substantiate my friend's claim that the record of the four years or so up to the spring of 1979 was encouraging. A break-through in agricultural production had begun in 1973 aided by a succession of good monsoons. The long sluggish period in industrial production seemed to have ended in 1976. Foreign exchange reserves rose rapidly from 1975 on, largely as the result of remittances from Indians who were working in the oil-producing Arab countries. By the spring of 1979 the reserves of foodgrains and of foreign exchange were at an all time high. Inflation had been brought under control; the consumer price index rose by only 2 per cent in 1978. The year ending 31 March 1979 was the fourth consecutive year of above average performance for the Indian economy.

Before the year 1979 ended the high hopes of the spring were shattered. The drought which India experienced was one of the worst in this century. Sharp increases in the price of oil added greatly to India's burdens. These difficulties were compounded by political instability and consequent uncertainty about the policies which future governments were likely to follow. The annual rate of inflation was edging up to about 20 per cent. While this was happening in India the recession in the rich countries was deepening. This would reduce the demand for Indian exports and increase the pressures on the governments of rich countries to raise even higher the barriers to the entry of such goods as clothing, textiles and footwear. The recession would probably also result in a lowering of both the volume and the quality of aid.

In spite of all this my belief when I write this in mid-January 1980 is that the longer-term outlook for economic growth in India is good, mainly because there are excellent prospects of substantial further increases in agricultural production and agriculture supplies 45 per cent of the national product and greatly affects the performance of other sectors of the Indian economy. It seems to me, however, that there are three possible developments which would negate this encouraging longer-term forecast. One is beyond the control of India; it is that there may be a serious deterioration in average rainfall as the result of very long swings in rainfall cycles. The second possible serious adverse development is a failure to curb the growth of population. The third is that political leaders in India may prove to be incapable of pursuing policies which will carry the benefits of economic growth to the poor and that this will plunge India into a period of anarchic violence; this possibility is discussed in the concluding section of this chapter.

One reason for optimism about the future of Indian agriculture is the recent increase in irrigated area. Irrigated area increased in the years 1977–8 and 1978–9 by record amounts: 2.6 million hectares in 1977–8 and 2.8 million hectares in 1978–9 compared with only 1.4 million a year in the preceding three years, and it seems likely that future rates of increase will be even higher. What is not so clear is whether there will be substantial improvement in the effective use of the water made available for irrigation. Some experts maintain that in recent years the efficiency of the use of water in irrigation has been only half of what could reasonably be expected under Indian conditions and that India has been slow in developing practical research on the use and management of water. The encouraging increase in the area of land under irrigation has been accompanied by a likewise encouraging increase in the use of fertilizers. In 1977–8 the use of fertilizers increased by 26 per cent, and in 1978–9 by 19 per cent. Whether there will be a more efficient use of fertilizers depends largely on the development of agricultural extension services and of practical research in agriculture. Some Indian agronomists believe that the additional output from a given quantity of fertilizer can be double what farmers are now achieving. Fortunately a more effective agricultural extension service, the training and visit system, will by the mid-eighties cover about a third of India's farm families and may eventually cover virtually all of them; and first-class scientific research in agriculture, notably at such impressive institutions as the Punjab Agricultural University, is not only producing improved strains of grain, of cattle and of buffalo but is also providing farmers with detailed practical advice on how to improve their farming practices. There is hope that at long last the extension services, agricultural research, and agricultural co-operatives will devote at least as much attention to the poorer two-thirds of the farmers as to the wealthiest one-third. Another important hopeful development is the probability that the green revolution on irrigated land may be followed in the first half of the eighties by a green revolution on non-irrigated rain-fed areas as the result of the development of new dry-farming technology, and the rain-fed areas constitute 75 per cent of India's cropped area. All this, as the official *Economic Survey* for 1978–9 concluded, 'gives cause for hope that Indian agriculture is entering into an era of steady and reasonable growth'.[51] Some experts go further. They believe that these developments make possible a raising of India's foodgrain yields from their current low level of one to one and a half tons a hectare to their realizable potential of around four tons a hectare, and a raising of other crop yields in a similar proportion.

It is important, however, to realize that these optimists qualify their conclusions by stating that the vast potential of Indian agriculture can be realized only if there is agrarian reform. Without agrarian reform there can be great increases in agricultural production but not the full potential. What B. G. Verghese said of Bihar in a lecture in December 1977 applies, though in a lesser degree, to the other states of India for Bihar is notoriously the worst-governed state in India, the most impoverished and the most caste-ridden:

A highly oppressive, iniquitous and inefficient land system and agrarian relations that perpetuate feudalism . . . are clearly inimical to agricultural progress and social change as these would threaten the established order. Land and caste are the warp and woof of politics in Bihar and thwart the agricultural transformation that could make it a granary. . . . High priority must be given to the honest implementation of agrarian reforms including existing legislation for consolidation [of scattered holdings of land], fixity of tenure [for tenant farmers], and fair rents for sharecroppers, the enforcement of minimum agricultural wages, the distribution of ceiling surplus lands, debt relief, the grant of homestead plots to all eligible persons, and the prevention of alienation of tribal lands.[52]

The great potential of agricultural development in India is encouraging. What is also encouraging is the possibility that the Central and State governments of India and the Government of Nepal are beginning to realize the extent of the damage caused by the criminally reckless deforestation of the Himalayas since Independence—erosion, silting up of dams and reservoirs, floods—and will be taking steps to stem the damage. (The Mayurakshi dam in West Bengal which Lester Pearson opened in 1955 is a horrible example of the effect of deforestation. Its

rate of siltation is 450 per cent higher than had been assumed.[53])
The improvement in relations between India and Nepal, and
between India and Bangladesh which took place under the
Janata Government will, if maintained by succeeding governments, ease the task of reaching agreement on joint measures
by the three governments to stem erosion and to make the best
use possible of the immense resources for power and irrigation
of the Greater Ganges.

An even more encouraging augury for the future of India is
that the draft sixth five-year plan for 1978–83 published in 1978
says virtually all the right things about how India should go
about speeding up healthy economic and social development.
It emphasizes the necessity of ending under-employment and
mass poverty by concentrating attention on massive programmes of small, highly-productive, labour-intensive, rural
public works and by building up efficient, productive, labour-intensive, small-scale industry in the villages, towns and cities.
The draft plan says so many of the fashionably right things
about development that the most authoritative international
journal on development, the *International Development Review*
published by the Society for International Development, devoted 25 pages in its final issue for 1978 to articles on the plan
and extracts from it.

But most of the right things about Indian development have
been said in previous five-year plans and, nevertheless, the conditions of life of the poorest two-fifths of the people of India have
improved scarcely, if at all. The authors of the sixth plan,
conscious of this, urge that in order that the poor may receive
the benefits of development they must be organized. They stress
this theme three times in the first volume of the Plan—at the
beginning, the middle and the end. The statement at the beginning is, 'And, finally, the rural and urban poor have to be
organized. Their vigilance alone can ensure that the benefits of
various laws, policies and schemes designed to benefit them do
produce their intended effect.' In the middle of the report is
this passage: 'Organized tenants have to see that the tenancy
laws are implemented. Organizations of the landless have to
see that surplus lands are identified and distributed to them in
accordance with the law within five years. Local leaders of the
poor have to ensure that all area plans and sectoral plans

designed for the benefit of their localities and target groups are effectively administered.' And the authors of the Plan return to this theme in the second to last paragraph of the volume: 'The poor and the dispossessed will not come into their own only by plans and programmes, however well conceived, [or] by declarations of intent. . . . they have to be helped to organize themselves to claim as a right the benefits that should flow to them. . . .'

But the draft five-year plan fails to make practicable proposals on how these recommendations might be carried out. Moreover, not all the members of the Planning Commission who drafted the plan consider that the recommendations that the poor should be helped to organize themselves are realistic. One said to me, 'You can't organize the sheep against the wolves.'

In the thirty-two years of Independence two groups have become politically dominant in India: the better-off peasants, who belong mainly to the lower peasant castes, the kulaks of India; and the urban middle and lower-middle classes. The bourgeois governments which they have dominated in New Delhi, the State capitals and the cities, towns and villages have pursued policies which have failed to improve the conditions of life of the poorest two-fifths of the people who continue to live in misery. It is greatly to India's credit that the draft sixth five-year plan constitutes a public confession of the errors of omission and commission which have resulted in this national shame. Almost all the other poor countries of the world have likewise failed to improve the conditions of life of their poor but few of them have, like India, publicly confessed their failure.

World Bank experts believe that in the world as a whole the rural poor (who constitute 85 per cent of the billion poorest people in the world) 'have received little or no benefits from economic growth over the past decades'.[54] An expert on Latin America stated in 1978 that in Latin America, 'although the statistics are in dispute, the situation of the poorest one-quarter or one-third of the population may actually be worsening'.[55] 'After thirty years of consistent economic growth [in Brazil] the richest 10 per cent of the people take nearly half the income, while the share enjoyed by 90 per cent of the Brazilians actually fell between 1960 and 1970.'[56] In their failure to ensure that economic growth led to a lessening of the misery of the poor, the poor countries are repeating the experience of Britain in the first half of the nineteenth century when 'the working class as a whole gained no increase in standards [of living] from the new system and the poorest, perhaps 20 to 30 per cent of the population (displaced cottagers, starving weavers) were actually worse off'.[57]

In May 1960 I wrote a commentary on the report of the Abs–Franks–Sproule mission which had been sent to South Asia by the World Bank. (I sent the commentary to the Canadian government and to Nehru and the Canadian authorities sent it to the President of the World Bank.) In it I said:

The heart of the problem of the economic development of underdeveloped countries in the nineteen sixties is India. If this nation of four hundred and fifteen million people cannot, by using democratic means, succeed within the next ten years in making a substantial advance towards its economic and social goals, none of the other non-totalitarian countries in Asia—or indeed Africa—are likely to have confidence that they can succeed. But with adequate help from the more advanced countries India can, I am convinced, save itself by its exertions and save Asia and Africa by its example.

What changes would I now, twenty years later, make in this assessment? I would not say that none of the non-totalitarian countries in Asia or Africa would be likely to have confidence that they could succeed if India couldn't. I would say none of the *larger* non-totalitarian countries (thus excepting Singapore, Malaysia and Hong Kong). And, instead of speaking of India's economic and social goals, I would be more precise. I would say, 'If India cannot improve the conditions of life of its 250 million very poor people, most of the other 750 million very poor people in the world have little to hope for.'

There is grave potential political instability in India but, compared to almost all the other large or middle-sized Asian countries south of the Soviet Union and China and to almost all the countries of black Africa, India has been remarkably stable. India has had fair general elections. Its armed forces have not intervened in politics. It has had no military coup d'état. No Prime Minister has been executed by his successor. India is the dominant power in South Asia. India with armed forces of over a million ranks fourth in the world in the size of its armed forces, being surpassed only by the Soviet Union, China and the United States. India has great potential for development in agriculture and industry. 'The diversity and volume of India's endowment [of natural resources] is quite adequate to sustain a standard of living much higher than now prevails.'[58] Once India has succeeded in raising the income of its poor it will have a vast internal market for its agricultural and industrial production, for its population of 655 million is almost the same as the combined populations of the whole of Africa and South America (about 700 million). Indians have an immense capacity to endure adversity. Almost all the people of India, other than the tribal people, feel that they belong to a common culture, a culture which is ancient and rich, and this feeling holds India together in spite of the deep stratifications in Indian society.

Conclusion

At the beginning of the eighties it is clear that the principal *internal* obstacles to India realizing its potential are political and social. It is likewise clear that the principal *external* obstacle to India realizing its potential is the failure of the rich and the poor countries to establish a partnership in which the rich countries would make profound changes in their policies in order to help those poor countries which are determined to improve the conditions of life of their poor. (I set forth my views on this in a memorandum I wrote in New Delhi in January 1979. See Annex B, pages 286–7 below.)

Raj Krishna, who was the member of the Planning Commission chiefly responsible for the emphasis in the draft five-year plan on the necessity of organizing the poor, wrote at the beginning of 1979 a series of three newspaper articles on the performance of the Indian economy. He began by describing 'the recent positive performance of the Indian economy without authoritarianism and in spite of floods and labour unrest'. He concluded by contrasting this 'with the performance of the Indian polity, particularly in respect of the maintenance of unity at the top and the physical protection of the weak at the bottom of the polity'.

Disunity and disorder originating purely in politics can grow to a point when economic growth is damaged. Politics can wreck (as it is already eroding) resource mobilization so much that real investment fails to grow. And while mere growth can perhaps remain immunized against politics, radical redistribution will be impossible without enlightened and vigorous politics designed to carry the benefits of growth to the poor. A democratic leadership capable of such politics is nowhere in sight.[59]

If political leaders in India should prove incapable of carrying the benefits of growth to the poor, what is likely to be the result? While I was in India in the winter of 1978-9 I came across five attempts to answer this question. Pran Chopra, a former editor of *The Statesman*, and V. K. R. V. Rao, a former cabinet minister and now the chairman of the Institute for Social and Economic Change in Bangalore, had articles in the issue of the *International Development Review* which contained lengthy extracts from the draft five-year plan.[60] Douglas Ensminger wrote a series of eight articles for the *Indian Express*.[61] He was the representative of the Ford Foundation in India from 1951 to 1970 and had just made a seven-week return visit to India. The other two forecasts were in impressive books on India published in 1978, one by R. H. Cassen, a British development economist,[62] and the other by Francine Frankel, an American political scientist.[63]

Pran Chopra forecast a powerful upheaval in India within five years. The upheaval would come either when the promises in the draft five-year plan

begin to be implemented, or it will come when it begins to be clear that they are not going to be implemented. . . . The transfer of even minor privileges from the rich to the poor is sparking off riots. Trying to transfer land will do that much more, and so will the disappointment of the poor if efforts to transfer land are not made or do not succeed.

V. K. R. V. Rao, after referring to 'the existing power, class, and caste structure in rural India that has thwarted all attempts so far to bring about social justice and a more egalitarian growth in the rural areas', asserted:

We cannot let the present situation continue. The poor and the dispossessed will not remain acquiescent and inarticulate and will sooner or later precipitate a violent change that may only throw the country into a state of anarchy . . . an era of anarchic violence.

Douglas Ensminger's conclusion was that the rural poor were going to be organized.

The government can either decide to provide the leadership for this sector of the population to develop constructively, or wait until they organize themselves to carry out revolutionary programmes.

R. H. Cassen's conclusion was that if the problem of rural poverty

is not solved or even relieved ... [and] if discontent continues to intensify, fostered by underground political movements or even the unfulfilled promises of politicians, the forces of repression will gradually become incapable of containing it.[64]

This does not, however, in his opinion mean that a successful revolution of the poor in the next decade or two is likely. One condition, he writes, of a revolution is some belief in the possibility of a credible alternative to the existing order; this is not apparent in India. A revolutionary movement confined to a single locality would easily be put down by the police or the military. 'The only way a revolutionary movement could overcome the physical power of the centre—unless the military were itself converted to the revolutionary cause—would be by a simultaneous uprising over very large areas of the country.' But a revolutionary movement to be more than local 'must transcend not only the micro-social differences of caste and economic interest ..., but the very considerable linguistic and other differences that separate one part of India from another. ... No regime could resist a simultaneous rising by the people of India. But what can produce that?' In order that the unrest which seems highly possible in India should turn into revolution, there must be a revolutionary organization capable of providing leadership for a mass uprising. 'So far the Indian Left has not given much sign of its capacity for this task.' He is therefore driven to the conclusion that the 'political evolution of India in the next decade or two is not presently imaginable in terms other than the possible forms of development of the existing system of government.' But though this is the conclusion to which his analysis forces him to come he confesses that he is 'left with a feeling that somehow or other, as India's problems pile up, there must be growing prospects for violent overthrow of governments by organized movements of the poor and oppressed. If we are wrong in our belief that this is a long way off, we are at least in good company. Lenin himself at the end of 1916 thought the success of the Russian Revolution was something he might not live to see.'[65]

Francine Frankel's conclusion was that unless effective political parties sent workers into the villages to organize the poor on class lines there would probably be no hope for a gradual revolution of India's society.

At present, the greatest dangers to long-term political stability do not appear to come from any attempt to build up effective political parties that can mobilize the poor peasantry and institutionalize their demands. Rather, the most serious threat to political order can be expected from the progressive loss of legitimacy of traditional power relationships, without putting any substitute structure in its place. Adversary groups, confronting and colliding with each other in the absence of any accepted rules, can trigger cycles of violence and repression that destroy the ability of existing democratic institutions to function, while failing to create the conditions for reconstruction of a more effective political order.[66]

A 'powerful upheaval', 'an era of anarchic violence', 'revolutionary programmes', the forces of repression gradually becoming incapable of containing discontent, 'cycles of violence and repression'. Such are the developments which these five writers believe are likely to take place if the leaders of India fail to pursue policies which will result in improving the conditions of life of the poorest two-fifths of the people of India. Such developments are likely to create a situation where each of the three great powers (the United States, the Soviet Union and China) would fear that one or both of the others would take advantage of the upheavals in India to secure influence or control over the whole or parts of India and each would be tempted to take pre-emptive action. Perhaps they could reach agreement on non-intervention but it is more likely that the competition between them for influence or control would create serious international crises and might touch off a world war. The fate of more than India is bound up with India's efforts to end the poverty of its people.

Annex A

THE POOREST FORTY PER CENT OF THE PEOPLE OF INDIA

The population of India in 1980 is about 670 million. Forty per cent of this is 268 million. The World Bank in its Development Report for 1978 (p. 3) stated that 'about 800 million people in the developing world still live in absolute poverty, with incomes too low to ensure adequate nutrition, and without access to essential public services' and that about a quarter of these live in India. The World Bank's estimate of 800 million was based on population figures which are some years out of date. Taking this into account and changing somewhat the definition of absolute poverty, the number of absolute poor in the world could be put at a billion. Assuming that the Indian proportion remains a quarter, this would mean 250 million absolute poor in India. This was indeed the figure which the World Bank gave in its annual report for 1979 (p. 51) when it stated that some 250 million people in India 'continue to be deprived of minimum necessities in terms of nutrition, unpolluted water, clothing and shelter'.

The Draft Sixth Five-Year Plan 1977–83 published in 1978 stated that, according to 'a recent estimate, using norms of calorie consumption, the percentage of population below the poverty line in 1977–8 may be projected at 48 per cent in rural areas and 41 per cent in urban areas. The total number of the poor, so defined, would be about 290 million.'

The poorest 150 million of the people of India were called 'destitute' in the *Quarterly Economic Report*, No. 92, 1978; the destitute in rural areas had in 1973–4 a monthly per capita total consumer expenditure of 43 rupees or less at 1973–4 prices; the destitute in urban areas 55 rupees or less. Translated into U.S. dollars at 13 cents to a rupee this means $67 or less a year in rural areas and $86 or less in urban areas. A more realistic translation of rupees into dollars would give something in the neighbourhood of $100 a year in rural areas and $130 in urban areas (at 1973–4 prices) for per capita total consumer expenditure by the 150 million poorest people in India.

The Draft Sixth Five-Year Plan stated that in over a quarter of a century of planning, that is since 1951, 'the most important objectives of planning have not been achieved . . . : full employment, the eradication of poverty and the creation of a more equal society. . . . The prevalence of poverty and inequality [has been] virtually unchanged over the years. ... So far [the Scheduled Castes and the Scheduled Tribes which make up a fifth of the population] have been only marginally involved in the process of development.' (Vol. 1, pp. 2–3)

According to preliminary results of the Rural Labour Inquiry for 1974/5 there is some evidence that the average daily earnings of rural labourers declined in real terms during the preceding ten years and that the number of days that rural labourers had been unemployed had increased.

The index of per capita consumption of foodgrains increased by only 1 per cent from the average of the period 1970–5 to the average of the period 1975–8, from 163.3 kilograms to 164.9 kilograms. This increase of only 1 per cent took place in a period when average per capita income went up by 6.3 per cent. Another study stated that per capita consumption of foodgrains had remained essentially unchanged since 1961 while per capita income had increased in real terms by about 18 per cent.

More than 80 per cent of the 250 million absolute poor of India live in rural areas, and in rural areas in 1971 there was one doctor to 12,000 people while in urban areas there was one to 1,500. In 1971 only 30 per cent of hospital beds were in rural areas. The Minister of Health stated in September 1979 that of a total of 184,000 doctors in India 68 per cent were working in the cities to serve only 22 per cent of the population while nearly 78 per cent of the population were being cared for by the remaining 32 per cent of the doctors. (*Overseas Hindustan Times*, 6 September 1979)

R. H. Cassen in his impressive book on India published in 1978 concluded his detailed examination of studies of Indian poverty as follows:

> It seems that wherever one looks it is difficult to find any evidence of a trend of improvement for the poor. ... Everything we have so far looked at gives inconclusive evidence about the change in the living conditions of the mass of the Indian people, although we have little reason to believe in any improvement during the last decade and a half in either the proportion above a minimum level, or the level of the lowest deciles, and some reason to believe in a worsening. (R. H. Cassen, *India: Population, Economy, Society* (New York: Holmes & Meier, 1978; New Delhi: Macmillan), pp. 255–6)

If, to simplify the calculation, we take the population in 1957 as 400 million and the population in 1979 as 650 million, and assume that 40 per cent of the people have continued to live below the poverty line we get:

	1957	1979	Increase
Population	400	650	250
40% below poverty line	160	260	100
60% above poverty line	240	390	150

One can say that this means that 150 million people have crossed the poverty line in 22 years and also that the number of people below the poverty line has increased by 100 million.

Although the distribution of income in India is highly unequal, 'India's situation is considerably more egalitarian than that of many other nations. According to one study based on a sample of 44 developing countries, India's poorest 20 per cent earned 8 per cent of the national income. This compared to 5.6 per cent for the sample as a whole. Moreover, the study showed that India's richest 20 per cent had a 42 per cent share of its income compared to 56 per cent for the sample as a whole.' (I. Adelman and G. T. Morris, *Economic Growth and Social Equity in Developing Countries* (Stanford, Calif.: Stanford University Press, 1973), quoted in Lawrence A. Veit, *India's Second Revolution* (New York: McGraw-Hill, 1976), p. 81)

The Draft Sixth Five-Year Plan gave the following indications of the failure of land reform. In 1971–2 the potential surplus of land above the ceilings prescribed by the guidelines for land reform was about 21 million acres but only 1.29 million acres had been distributed. Between 1961–2 and 1971–2 there had been no change in the ownership of rural property (mainly agricultural land) by the poorest 10 per cent of rural households and the richest 10 per cent; in both years the poorest 10 per cent owned one-tenth of one per cent and the richest 10 per cent, more than half. These figures, the Plan stated, 'show that up to the 60's the land reform measures had no visible impact on the distribution of rural property'. (Vol. 1, pp. 29–30)

Malcolm S. Adiseshiah, Director of the Madras Institute of Development Studies, has asserted that 'inequality in asset-holdings is also on the increase, with 20 per cent of rural households accounting for less than 1 per cent of rural assets, while 4 per cent own more than 30 per cent'. ('Mixing Continuity and Innovation', *International Development Review*, 1978/3–4, p. 19)

Annex B

A NEW PARTNERSHIP BETWEEN RICH COUNTRIES AND POOR COUNTRIES*

By Escott Reid

Of the billion poorest people in the world probably about 250 million are adults who could work full time if work were available. Mass poverty can be abolished if these 250 million people are employed in productive work which will enable them to purchase the basic necessities of life for themselves and their dependents.

Not all the poor countries of the world have governments which are prepared to commit themselves to policies which will result in productive work for the poor in their countries. Some governments are controlled by groups which fear that measures calculated to give the poor the possibility of acquiring the basic necessities of life will endanger their dominant position in society, in economic life and in politics. These governments will not be willing to join in an organized inter-governmental effort to provide productive work for the poor.

Such an organized international effort will therefore consist of governments of poor countries which are prepared to commit themselves to policies which will result in productive work for the poor and governments of rich countries which are prepared to help them in this endeavour. What is required is a multilateral inter-governmental agreement between these countries setting forth the obligations of the signatory governments. The main obligation of the rich member countries will be to increase their help to the poor member countries. The main obligation of the poor member countries will be to devote this help and a reasonable proportion of their own resources to policies, programmes and projects calculated to provide productive work for their poor.

Very considerable changes will be required in the policies, programmes and projects of almost all the poor member countries, since in the past these have resulted in little or no improvement in the standards of living of their poor citizens. Large changes will be required in the policies of the rich member countries; they will have to

* Published in the *U.N. Development Forum*, May 1979, and in the *International Development Review*, 1979/3.

increase greatly the flow of real resources from them to their partners in the new inter-governmental agency by changes in their policies on such matters as aid, trade, investment, commodities and transfer of technology.

The inter-governmental treaty or agreement establishing the new agency will have to be very specific on the obligations of the member countries if the scepticism of both sides is to be allayed to the extent required to make the agreement workable. This scepticism is profound. It is rooted deep in the history of the past twenty to thirty years. The poor countries believe that the rich countries have failed to carry out their past promises to help them. The rich countries believe that the failure of almost all the poor countries to improve the conditions of life of their poor demonstrates that they have misused the aid that has been given them.

The poor countries eligible for membership in the proposed new international agency might be those with a per capita gross national product of less than $500 a year (in 1978 U.S. dollars). Almost all the billion poorest people in the world live in those countries. The international agreement would set forth the penalties for failure by a member country to carry out its obligations under the agreement. The penalties might include suspension of its membership. Votes in the governing body of the agency might be divided equally between the rich and poor member countries. The vote of a rich member country could be proportionate to its share of the total flow of resources from the rich member countries to the poor member countries. The vote of a poor member country could be based in large part on the proportion which its population bears to the total population of all the poor member countries.

The negotiation of the new international treaty or agreement will be extremely difficult. It would be expedited if the government of India, which contains about a quarter of the poorest billion people in the world, were to put forward a tentative and provisional draft of the treaty or agreement as a basis of discussion. To begin with, the Indian government might submit a draft in confidence to half a dozen or so key governments. When it has revised the draft in the light of their comments, it might publish it.

New Delhi,
15 January 1979

NOTES

Almost all the statements and quotations in this book, apart from those in the epilogue, are from the communications which I sent to the Department of External Affairs in Ottawa while I was High Commissioner to India. These communications constitute part of the Escott Reid Papers in the Canadian Archives. The sources of other statements and quotations are given below.

CHAPTER ONE   I CHOOSE INDIA

1. Dean Acheson, *Present at the Creation* (New York: Norton, 1969), p. 336.
2. My memorandum of August 1947 is discussed by Don Page and Don Munton in 'Canadian Images of the Cold War 1946–47', *International Journal*, Summer 1977, pp. 577–604.

CHAPTER TWO   THE SPECIAL RELATIONSHIP BETWEEN INDIA AND CANADA, 1947–1952

1. Alastair Buchan, *The End of the Postwar Era* (London: Weidenfeld and Nicolson, 1974), p. 19.
2. Ibid., pp. 3, 18.
3. Subimal Dutt states that in the summer of 1950 Nehru said to the Central Committee of the World Council of Churches: 'For the first time after 30 or 40 years of civil war and domination of the warlords, China has a strong centralized Government and internal order.... China is a great power within its domain and is likely to become stronger' (Subimal Dutt, *With Nehru in the Foreign Office* (Calcutta: Minerva Associates, 1977), pp. 75–6).
4. *The United States in World Affairs 1952* (New York: Harper (for Council on Foreign Relations), 1953), p. 16.
5. Lester B. Pearson, *Mike: The Memoirs of the Rt. Hon. Lester B. Pearson*, Vol. II (Toronto and Buffalo: University of Toronto Press, 1973), p. 166.
6. Ibid., p. 184.

CHAPTER THREE   INTRODUCTION TO INDIAN DIPLOMACY—AND VILLAGES

1. Pearson, op. cit., p. 328.
2. Sarvepalli Gopal, *Jawaharlal Nehru: A Biography*, Vol. II, 1947–1956 (Delhi: Oxford University Press, 1979), p. 144.

CHAPTER FOUR THE ARMISTICE IN KOREA
1. Chester A. Ronning, 'Canada and the United Nations', in King Gordon (ed.), *Canada's Role as a Middle Power* (Toronto: Canadian Institute of International Affairs, 1966), p. 42.
2. Acheson, op. cit., p. 700.

CHAPTER FIVE CHINA
1. Geoffrey Barraclough and Rachel F. Wall, *Survey of International Affairs, 1955–1956* (London: Oxford University Press, 1960), p. 7.

CHAPTER SIX INDO-CHINA
1. Sir Anthony Eden, *The Memoirs of Sir Anthony Eden: Full Circle* (London: Cassell, 1960), p. 90.
2. Ibid., p. 82.
3. Ibid., pp. 96–9.
4. Ibid., pp. 133, 139, 142.

CHAPTER EIGHT AMERICAN ARMS FOR PAKISTAN
1. Michael Brecher, *India and World Politics: Krishna Menon's View of the World* (London: Oxford University Press, 1968), p. 208.
2. Barrie M. Morrison, 'Canada and South Asia', in *Canada and the Third World*, ed. Peyton V. Lyon and Tareq Y. Ismael (Toronto: Macmillan of Canada, 1976), p. 17.
3. David D. Newsom, Under Secretary of State for Political Affairs, Address to the Council on Foreign Relations, New York, 18 October 1978.

CHAPTER NINE KASHMIR
1. B. N. Pandey, *Nehru* (London: Macmillan, 1976), p. 313.
2. Gopal, op. cit., Vol. II, p. 185.

CHAPTER ELEVEN HUNGARY AND SUEZ
1. Gopal, op. cit., Vol. II, p. 291.
2. K. P. S. Menon, *The Flying Troika* (Bombay: Oxford University Press, 1963), pp. 172–3.
3. James Eayrs, *Canada in World Affairs: October 1955 to June 1957* (Toronto: Oxford University Press, 1959), pp. 168–9.
4. Pearson, op. cit., p. 255.
5. M. O. Mathai, *Reminiscences of the Nehru Age* (New Delhi: Vikas, 1978), p. 173.
6. Gopal, op. cit., Vol. II, p. 293.
7. Pandey, op. cit., p. 346. Nehru to Mrs Pandit, 13 February 1957. Quoted also in Vijaya Lakshmi Pandit, *The Scope of Happiness* (London: Weidenfeld and Nicolson, 1979), p. 287.
8. This account of the reports of K. P. S. Menon and J. N. Khosla is based

on Nehru's statement in the Lok Sabha on 13 December 1956 and reports from the Canadian Ambassador in Moscow of conversations with Menon.

CHAPTER THIRTEEN SOME PUBLIC FIGURES

1. T. N. Kaul, *Diplomacy in Peace and War* (New Delhi: Vikas, 1979), p. 75.
2. The quotation is from Subimal Dutt, op. cit., p. 290.
3. M. O. Mathai writes that in 1951 or 1952 Nehru said, 'If you calculate the amount of time I have spent with him [Menon] it will not be more than a few hours' (op. cit., p. 167).
4. Ibid., pp. 26–8.

CHAPTER FOURTEEN INDIA'S PROSPECTS

1. The estimates of national income per capita from 1900 to 1947 come from K. Mukerji, 'A Note on the long-term growth of national income in India, 1900–1 to 1952–3', *Papers on National Income and Allied Topics*, Vol. 11, 1962, pp. 15–24. According to this study the average national income per capita at 1948–9 prices for the three years 1900–3 was 223 rupees; for the three years 1919–22, 268 rupees; and for the three years 1944–7, 264 rupees. The population in 1902–3 was 235 million, in 1921–2, 251 million, and in 1946–7, 337 million.

CHAPTER SIXTEEN RECONSIDERATION: EPILOGUE

1. D. L. Sheth, 'Politics of Caste Conflict', *Seminar*, January 1979, p. 29.
2. Memorandum from the Planning Commission transmitted in letter of 18 August 1978, from H. M. Patel, Minister of Finance, to E.R.
3. Memorandum from the Planning Commission transmitted in letter of 6 July 1978, from H. M. Patel, Minister of Finance, to E.R. The Draft Sixth Five-Year Plan states that per capita agricultural production remained stagnant from 1951 to 1978.
4. *Indian Express*, 30 March 1979.
5. R. H. Cassen, *India: Population, Economy, Society* (New York: Holmes & Meier, 1978; New Delhi: Macmillan), p. 210.
6. Based on data of manufacturing shares in gross domestic product for both developed and developing countries as reported in *The World Tables 1976* published for the World Bank in 1976 by the Johns Hopkins University Press.
7. The figure of 5.9 per cent was given in the memorandum from the Planning Commission transmitted to E.R. on 6 July 1978. The rate of increase in industrial production was 9.5 per cent, 3.9 per cent and 7.8 per cent in the years ending 31 March 1977, 1978 and 1979 respectively.
8. An indication of this is the statement in the Draft Five-Year Plan for 1978–83: 'The share of the small-scale sector, excluding household industries, fell from 19.5 per cent of the income arising from all industrial production in 1968 to 16 per cent in 1976' ('India: the Sixth Plan', *International Development Review*, 1978/3–4, p. 29).

9. Dharam Vira, *Shri Ram Memorial Lecture*, 12 January 1979.
10. *Overseas Hindustan Times*, 24 May 1979.
11. Tara Ali Baig, 'Our 300 Million Children', *The Illustrated Weekly of India*, 11 February 1979.
12. *Primary Education in Rural India—Participation and Wastage* (New Delhi: Agricultural Economics Research Centre, Delhi University, 1971). Cited in Cassen, op. cit., p. 234.
13. B. G. Verghese, *Monthly Public Opinion Survey*, September 1978.
14. Letter of 23 December 1978. *Times of India*, 29 December 1978. *Hindustan Times*, 31 December 1978.
15. Cassen, op. cit., p. 335.
16. Dharam Vira, op. cit.
17. Ajit Bhattacharjea, *Jaya Prakash Narayan* (New Delhi: Vikas, 1975), p. 132.
18. George Brown, *In My Way* (Harmondsworth: Penguin, 1972), pp. 48–9.
19. Menon himself cited half of this statement in an interview about three years later. According to Menon, Kennedy said, 'Whatever we do, you think we are wrong' (Michael Brecher, op. cit., p. 184).
20. Gopal, *Jawaharlal Nehru: A Biography*, Vol. I, 1889–1947 (Delhi: Oxford, 1976), p. 336.
21. Kuldip Nayar, *India: The Critical Years* (New Delhi: Vikas, 1971), pp. 3 and 68.
22. Brecher, op. cit., pp. 301, 304, 309.
23. Ibid., pp. 154, 167, 171, 197.
24. The statements in the preceding four paragraphs are based on Gopal, op. cit., Vol. II, pp. 141–7, 224, 293, 297, 298.
25. Frank Moraes, *Witness to an Era* (New Delhi: Vikas, 1973), p. 180.
26. Gopal, op. cit., Vol. II, pp. 140, 225.
27. Ibid., p. 67.
28. M. S. Rajan, 'The Indo-Canadian Entente', *International Journal*, XVII, No. 4, Autumn 1962.
29. Barrie M. Morrison, op. cit., p. 16.
30. Ramesh C. Thakur, 'Change and Continuity in Canadian Foreign Policy', *India Quarterly*, Vol. 33, No. 4, October–December 1977, p. 414.
31. David Van Praagh, 'Canada and Southeast Asia', in *Canada and South Asia*, pp. 329, 333.
32. Sandra Gwyn, 'We Need You, Mr Pearson', *Saturday Night*, Toronto, April 1978.
33. Escott Reid, *Strengthening the World Bank* (Chicago: University of Chicago Press (for the Adlai Stevenson Institute), 1973).
34. Cassen, op. cit., pp. 309–17.
35. A. S. Abraham, 'A Tale of Two Countries', *Times of India*, 26 March 1979.
36. *Encounter*, June 1964.
37. Walter Crocker, *Nehru* (London: Allen and Unwin, 1966), p. 11.
38. Ibid., pp. 10, 144, 170.
39. Asoka Mehta, *Reflections on Socialist Era* (New Delhi: S. Chand, 1977), p. 403.

40. V. K. R. V. Rao, *The Nehru Legacy* (Bombay: Popular Prakashan, 1971), p. 88.
41. Tarlok Singh, *Towards an Integrated Society* (New Delhi: Orient Longmans, 1962), p. 362.
42. Quoted by Ho Kwon Ping, 'Revolt of the Landless Peasants', *Far Eastern Economic Review*, 12 January 1979.
43. Lawrence A. Veit, *India's Second Revolution* (published for the Council on Foreign Relations by McGraw-Hill, New York, 1976), p. 345.
44. Tarlok Singh, 'Reassessing Nehru's Perspective on Planning', in *Jawaharlal Nehru and Public Administration* (New Delhi: Indian Institute of Public Administration, 1975), p. 31.
45. Report of World Bank Economic Mission 1956, pp. 118, 62.
46. Report of the Franks–Abs–Sproule Mission, March 1960, p. 14.
47. Gopal, op. cit., Vol. II, p. 309.
48. Asoka Mehta, op. cit., p. 452.
49. Ibid., pp. 447–52.
50. Francine Frankel, *India's Political Economy, 1947–1977: The Gradual Revolution* (Princeton: Princeton University Press, 1978), p. 18.
51. Government of India, *Economic Survey for 1978–9*, p. 53.
52. B. G. Verghese, *Gift of the Greater Ganga* (Coromandel Lecture, 10 December 1977), pp. 4, 22.
53. Ibid., p. 6.
54. Leif E. Christoffersen, 'The Bank and Rural Poverty', *Finance and Development*, December 1978, p. 19.
55. Richard R. Fagen, 'The Carter Administration and Latin America: Business as Usual?', *Foreign Affairs*, Vol. 57, No. 3, America and the World, 1978, p. 664.
56. Barbara Ward, *Progress for a Small Planet* (New York and London: Norton, 1979), p. 225.
57. Barbara Ward, foreword to Mahbub ul Haq, *The Poverty Curtain* (New York: Columbia University Press, 1976), p. xi.
58. Lawrence A. Veit, op. cit., p. 59.
59. Raj Krishna, 'Performance of Economy', *Times of India*, 10, 11, 12 January 1979.
60. Pran Chopra, 'A Brave New Plan—But Will It Work?' and V. K. R. V. Rao, 'The Seeds of Radical Change', *International Development Review*, 1978/3–4, pp. 18–23.
61. *Indian Express*, March–April 1979.
62. Cassen, op. cit.
63. Frankel, op. cit.
64. Cassen, op. cit., p. 338.
65. Ibid., pp. 293–4, 298, 300.
66. Frankel, op. cit., p. 582.

INDEX

Abdul Hamid, 212
Acheson, Dean, 3–4, 23, 29, 44–5, 183
Aksai Chin, 248
Allen, George, 46–7, 48, 61, 123, 124
Ayyangar, Gopalaswami, 12

Baghdad Pact, 140
Bajpai, Girja Sankar, 11–13, 33, 194
Bao-Dai, 5–6, 7
Beauvoir, Simone de, 167
Bevin, Ernest, 6, 64–5
Bhabha, Homi, 257
Bhave, Vinoba, 174
Bowles, Chester, 11–12, 30, 48, 56, 145
Braden, Spruille, 25
Brecher, Michael, on Krishna Menon, 254, 255
Brockington, Leonard, 199
Brown, George, 253
Buchan, Alastair, 17, 21
Bulganin, N. A., 133–43; warns Eden and Mollet about aggression in Egypt, 163
Bunker, Ellsworth, 145

Canada: and international affairs, 14–15; and Commonwealth, 15–19; and Colombo Plan, 18–19; and Indian immigrants, 19–20; supplies uranium oxide to India, 20; special relationship with India, 23, 51, 85, 258–65 (erosion of, 100, 264); and recognition of Chinese Communist Govt., 23–4, 65–6, 68; her apprehensions about U.S. policies in Asia, 24; diplomatic features of, under St Laurent and Pearson, 26; and armistice in Korea, 43; and Indo-China, 69–70, 82–3; and U.N. peace-keeping activities, 81; and U.N. General Assembly, 145; and Suez crisis, 145, 152, 165–6; and Hungarian revolution, 151, 162, 166; assessment of Indo-Canadian relations, 259; *see also under* Pearson, Reid, St Laurent
Cassen, R. H., 280, 281
Chanda, Anil, 141, 142, 184
Chiang Kai-shek, 62, 63
Childs, Marquis, 134–5
China: formation of communist govt., international reaction to, 22–3; and Korean War, 23–4, 65; and p.o.w. issue at U.N., 30–4; Nehru on, 54–5; and Burma, 55–6; and Soviet Union, 56–7; boundary issue between India and, 59–61; and imprisoned American airmen, 61–2; Formosa and coastal islands, 62–3; and recognition of communist govt. by Commonwealth countries, 64–5; and U.N., 65–8; and Indo-China war, 70–1; *see also* Chou En-lai
Chopra, Pran, 280
Chou En-lai, 22, 23, 33, 61; visits New Delhi, 55–6, 57–8, 76
Churchill, Winston, 111
Clutterbuck, Alexander, 37
Cohen, Benjamin, 25, 26
Colombo Plan, 18–19
Commonwealth, 15–19, 100, 131; and Suez crisis, 154–5, 166
Communist Party of China, 142
Communist Party of India, effect of Krushchev–Bulganin visit on, 141–2
Congress Party of India, 202–3, 208, 252
Connally, Tom, 77
Cooper, Sherman, 145
Corbusier, Le, 87
Crocker, Walter, 36, 123, 266

Das, Durga, 42
Desai, M. J., 124; discusses Kashmir issue with author, 128–31

Desai, Morarji, 12–13, 204–6, 271; on Nehru, 205–6
Deshmukh, C. D., 12
Dharam Vira, 245
Diefenbaker, John, 185–6, 189
Diem, 84–5
Dien Bien Phu, 70
Dulles, J. F., 45, 46, 62–4, 70, 71; and China, 72–3; and SEATO, 73–4, 78; and Nehru, 91
Dutt, Subimal, 138–9, 150, 198

Eayrs, James, 162
Eden, Anthony, 29, 45, 70; and Locarno-type pact for S.-E. Asian countries, 71, 73–4
Egypt, 144; invaded by Israel, 149; Anglo-French aggression in, 152–4, 157–9, 161, 163
Eisenhower, D., 11, 46, 47, 136, 148, 160–1, 185
Ensminger, Douglas, 280, 281
Entezam, Nasrollah, 33

Food and Agricultural Organization, 14
Formosa, 67, 71
Foster, William Z., 46
France, 72, 146, 147, 149, 150, 152, 153, 155, 156, 157, 161
Frankel, Francine, 280, 282
Freedom First, 50

Gaitskell, Hugh, 149, 179
Galbraith, J. K., 25, 145
Gandhi, Indira, 91, 196–8, 208–9, 253; and Krushchev–Bulganin visit to India, 134–5; and Vijayalakshmi Pandit, 197; and K. Menon, 198
Gandhi, Mahatma, 205; his influence on Nehru, 225
Geneva settlement on Indo-China, 69–70, 181; and SEATO, 73; collapse of, 82–5
Ghazanfar Ali Khan, Raja, 119, 123
Goldschlag, Klaus, 95
Gomulka, Wladyslaw, 148, 150
Gordon, Lincoln, 25

Great Britain: and recognition of Chinese Communist Govt., 64–5; and Kashmir issue, 128, 129, 131; and steel plant in India, 137; and aggression in Egypt, 144–6, 149–50, 152, 155, 156

Hammarskjold, Dag, 50, 184–5
Herter, Christian, 25
Ho Chi Minh, 5–6, 7, 20, 70, 82
Hungary: Stalinist Communist regime imposed on, 146; backdrop of, 146–7, 150–2, 153; *also see under* Nehru

India: and the Commonwealth, 17–19, 100, 131; Korean crisis and U.N., 30–3; and Korea, 43, 51–2; and China, 54–5, 219, 265–6; border dispute with China, 59–61; recognition of Chinese Communist Govt., 64–5; and Indo-China problem, 71–3, 76; and SEATO, 73; as chairman of International Control Commission on Indo-China, 79; and U.N., 100; and U.S. military aid to Pakistan, 101–15; assessment of foreign policy, 131–2, 190; and bad relations with U.S., reasons for, 136–7; Hungarian crisis and Anglo-French invasion of Egypt, *see under* Nehru; economic, political and social prospects of, 209–19; population and stagnant economy of, 209, 239–40, 269–70; climate of, 209–10; caste in, 210–11; common culture and political unity of, 212; feudalism in, 214; divisive forces in, 214; corruption in, 214–15; peasants in, character of, 216; economic growth of, 216–17, 279–80; agriculture in, 217–18; poverty and national income of, 239–40, 283–5; social advance and education in, 218–19, 241–5; administration in, 245–6; foreign policy of, 246–52; and Kashmir, 247; and Pakistan, 247, 248–9, 250–1; and secession of Bangladesh from Pakistan, 250; and Soviet invasion of Afghanistan, 251;

future prospects for, 272–82; and five year plans, 276–7; *also see under* Kashmir, Nehru, Pakistan

Indo-China, 69–85; situation discussed at Commonwealth Conference, 5–7; Geneva Conference on, 69–70, 73, 79–80, 181; and China, 70–1; Locarno-type pact proposed on, 74–6; and International Control Commission, 79–80; collapse of Geneva settlement, 82–5; *see also* Vietnam

International Control Commission on Indo-China, 79–81

International Civil Aviation Organization, 14

International Monetary Fund, 14, 264

Israel, 149

Janata Government, 236; its foreign policy, 249, 250, 276

Jammu, *see* Kashmir

Jinnah, M. A., 212

Joshi, P. C., 268

Kadar, Janos, 148, 156

Kamath, H. V., 177

Kashmir, 49, 100, 117–32; plebiscite in, 120, 121–4, 126; and U.S. military aid to Pakistan, 123–5, 130; and U.N. Security Council, 128–9, 130; India's views on, 128–30; and Indian foreign policy, 247

Kaur, Rajkumari Amrit, 36, 208, 270

Kennedy, Donald, 123

Kennedy, J. F., 257

Kher, B. G., 38

Khosla, J. N., 179

King, Mackenzie, 7–8, 14–15, 271

Korea, 43–52; and Chinese p.o.w. issue, 43, 46–7; Dulles on armistice, 45; and Indian membership in peace conference, 49–50

Korean War, 23–4, 25; and Chinese prisoners, 26, 30–2; and peace negotiation, 30–3

Kripalani, Acharya, 175, 177

Krishnamachari, T. T., 12, 174, 189–90

Krushchev's visit to India, 133–43; preparations for, 133; reaction of West to, 135, 137, 141; and Pakistan, 136; effect of, on Communist Party of India, 141–2

Laos, 69

Laski, Harold, 253

LePan, Douglas, 3

Lloyd, Selwyn, 29, 45, 186

Locarno-type pact for S.-E. Asia, 73–81

Lodge, H. C., 50

MacArthur, Douglas, 21, 23

MacDonald, Malcolm, 5–6, 152, 168–9, 195–6

Macdonnell, R. M., 79, 81

McCarthyism, 21, 23–4

Mao Tse-tung, 22, 46, 56, 64

Martin, Paul, 30, 51

Mayhew, Robert, 18

Mayurakshi dam, 87–8, 275

McMahon line, 60, 248

Mathai, M. O., 176, 198–9, 255

Mehta, Asoka, 177, 267, 270, 271

Menon, K. P. S., 154, 159, 178

Menon, V. K. Krishna, 25, 29, 31–2, 35–8, 81, 100, 146, 158, 181–90, 199, 260; and Korean armistice, 29, 43–5, 50, 52, 181; and Geneva Conference, 69, 71, 79; and Indo-China, 71–3, 74, 79, 80, 83–5; on quantum of U.S. arms to Pakistan, 108; and Kashmir issue, 128; and Hungarian crisis, 148–9, 151, 161, 162, 167, 170–2, 176, 187; and Suez crisis, 173; and Pearson, 181–2; his antipathy to U.S., 182–3, 254–5; in U.N. General Assembly, 182, 183; and Indian foreign policy, 183, 188; and Nehru, 183–4, 186–9, 198–9, 254, 255–8; as member of cabinet, 186–7; as minister of defence, 187; and External Affairs Ministry, 187; and damage to India's interests abroad, 188–9; and Vijayalakshmi Pandit, 193–4; and Panikkar, 195; and Radhakrishnan, 202; and Russians,

Index

Menon, V. K. Krishna (*continued*) 253–4; and international affairs, 253–8; and Indo-U.S. relations, 254–5; and Pakistan, 255; *also see under* Nehru, Reid
Middleton, George, 110
Mohammad Ali, and Kashmir, 119–21, 122
Moraes, Frank, 179, 257
Mountbatten and Kashmir, 117–18, 223
Mukherji, N. K., 246
Murphy, Robert, 61

Nagy, I., 147–8, 153
Narayan, Jaya Prakash: and Hungary and Suez crises, 174–5, 271; and Kashmir, 247, 257
Nasser, A. G., 172–3
Nayar, Kuldip, 254
Nayer, Susheela, 270
Nehru, Jawaharlal: visits U.S.A. and Canada, 3–4; his speeches, 5, 230–2; on Indo-China situation, 6–7; on democracy, 17; and formation of communist govt. in China, 22–3; and U.S. foreign affairs, 25–6; and Chinese prisoners of Korean War, 30–3; and Panikkar, 34; and V. Pandit – K. Menon relations, 38; and Korean armistice, 45, 46, 47; on China and Chinese character, 54, 55; and Sino-Russian split, 56–7; and Chou En-lai, 57–8; visits China, 59; intervenes in Peking over release of American airmen imprisoned in Korea, 61–2; and problem of Formosa and Chinese offshore islands, 62–4; and representation of Communist China in U.N., 67–8; appeals for cease-fire in Indo-China, 69–70, 71; and proposed Locarno-type pact on Indo-China, 74–5; discusses such a pact with Chou En-lai, 76; reaction to SEATO, 78; talks with: Pearson, 90, St Laurent, 90–1, Dulles, 91; manner with visiting statesmen, 91, 221; on difference between governments of India and Pakistan, 94; and arms aid to Pakistan, 101–3, 105–7, 114; and Kashmir, 117, 123, 124–5; and Mohammad Ali, 119–20; and Hungarian revolt, 131, 144, 148, 151–2, 153–4, 158–9, 161–2; and Krushchev–Bulganin visit, 134, 138; and Egypt (Suez) crisis, 149, 152–3, 158, 164–5; replies to Bulganin's warning to Eden and Mollet about aggression in Egypt, 163–4; opposes in A.I.C.C. meeting proposal of India severing relations with the Commonwealth on Egypt issue, 166; speech in Calcutta on Hungarian crisis, 166–8, 174; briefed on happenings in Hungary by Swiss govt., 170; condemns Soviet intervention in Hungary, 172–3, 175–8; and Krishna Menon, 176, 178, 183–4, 186–9, 198–9, 254–8, 270, 271; debulganization of, 179; and Morarji Desai, 205–6; assessment of, 220–35, 266–72; and Patel, 220; an 'arrogant aristocrat', 222, 266–72; his impatience, 222–3; a lonely man, 223–4; Gandhi's influence on, 224–5; and Communism, 225; his 'good man', 225; his westernization, 225–6; a liberal, 226–7; judges the West and Russia by different moral yardsticks, 227; foreign policy and diplomacy under, 227–8; an optimist, 228; his way of life, 228–9; in danger of assassination, 229; his sense of mission, 232; loves being Prime Minister, 232; as leader, 232; great in spite of many weaknesses, 233; his vision of India, 233–4; and the peasant, 233–4; and China, 247–8; his last years, 252
Nehru, R. K., 12, 29, 31, 37–8, 52, 60, 195; and U.S. arms aid to Pakistan, 108–10
Nixon, Richard: visits New Delhi and Karachi, 102–3
Noel-Baker, Philip, 111
North Atlantic Treaty, 14, 140, 141

Ostrorog, Stanislas, 34, 101, 111, 174

Pakistan, 247; Nehru on, 212–13; Pearson's impression of, 93–5; American military aid to, 101, 123–5; and Kashmir, 117–18, 127, 247
Pandey, B. N.'s *Nehru*, 118
Panchsheel, 77, 158
Pandit, Vijayalakshmi, 29, 31, 34, 193–4, 258; and Krishna Menon, 35, 37–8, 50, 52, 162, 178, 193; as President of U.N. General Assembly, 193; her influence on Nehru, 193–4; and Indira Gandhi, 197
Panikkar, K. M., 34–5, 183, 187, 194–6; and SEATO, 78
Pant, Apa, 86
Pant, Pandit, 203, 208, 258
Patel, Sardar, 205
Pearson, Lester, 4, 8, 10, 15, 18, 22, 25, 26, 35, 38, 259; and Krishna Menon and Chinese p.o.w. issue, 29–32; and Korean armistice, 43, 46–7, 49, 50, 52; on Formosa and offshore islands, 62–3; and recognition of Chinese Communist Govt., 64–5, 66, 67; at Geneva Conference on Indo-China, 69; visits India, 86–95; in Sikkim, 86–7; visits Mayurakshi dam, 87–8; in Banaras, 88–9; talks with Nehru, 90; his interviews with Indian statesmen, 91–2; his impression of India, 92; compares Indians with West Pakistanis, 94; comments on India's ambiguous political stand, 100–1; and U.S. arms aid to Pakistan, 113; makes statement on India, 137–8; on Krushchev–Bulganin visit, 140, 259; and Suez crisis, 145, 149; his speech in U.N. General Assembly quoting Nehru's condemnation of Soviet intervention in Hungary, 178; and Krishna Menon, 181–2
Philippines, 78
Pillai, Raghavan, 11, 29, 33, 34, 37, 45, 48, 49–50, 52, 59, 60, 63, 75, 78, 140, 170, 198; and Kashmir, 120–1; and Hungarian revolution, 151, 154; and aggression in Egypt, 163–5; and Krishna Menon, 183–4, 186–7

Prasad, Rajendra, 202

Raghavan, N., 33
Radhakrishnan, S., 59, 117, 123, 201–4, 258
Raj Krishna, on performance of Indian economy, 279–80
Rajagopalachari, Chakravarti, 7, 155, 199–201; letter to St Laurent on Commonwealth Club and aggression in Egypt, 165
Rajka, L., 146–7
Rao, V. K. R. V., 267, 280–1
Rankin, Bruce, 12
Rau, Benegal, 25
Rezzonico, Clemente, 170
Reid, Escott: sees Nehru in Ottawa, 3; reports on Nehru, 5; becomes High Commissioner in India, 7–8, 10; on East–West tension, 8–9; arrives in Bombay, 11; defends Nehru and India's foreign policy to U.S. officials, 25–6; his arrival in Delhi and introduction to Indian diplomacy, 29–38; calls on Nehru, 30, 55, 56; and Krishna Menon, 35–8, 44–5, 71–3, 80, 83–5, 178, 181–90; tours Indian villages, 38–42; and Chou En-lai's visit to Delhi, 57–8; and release of American airmen imprisoned in Korea, 61–2; and recognition of Chinese Communist Govt., 65–6; talks with K. Menon about U.S. policy in S.-E. Asia, 71–3; reports on Indo-Chinese problem, 73; and proposal of a Locarno-type pact on Indo-China, 74–8; and International Control Commissions on Indo-China, 79–80; and collapse of Geneva settlement on Indo-China, 82–3; in Sikkim with the Pearsons, 86–7; discusses Pearson's Indian visit with Nehru, 89–90; his impression of Pearson, 92–3; on cultures of Hinduism and Islam, 94–5; on Nehru's 'neutralist' policy, 99; and U.S. arms aid to Pakistan, 110–13; on principles behind U.S. and

Reid, Escott (*continued*)
Indian foreign policies, 115–16; and Kashmir issue, 118, 120–1, 123, 126–7; discusses India's views on Kashmir with M. J. Desai, 128–31; assesses Indian foreign policy, 131–2; and Krushchev–Bulganin visit to India, 133, 134, 135–7; discusses with Subimal Dutt lack of Indian appreciation of U.S. aid and K.–B. visit, 138–9; and Hungarian revolution, 144–5, 151–2, 155–6, 156–7; and invasion of Egypt, 150, 155–6; talks with Pillai on Hungarian revolution, 151–2, 154, 155–8; talks with Nehru about Russian aggression on Hungary, 159–60; plans to give Nehru true account of happenings in Hungary, 160–1; talks with Pillai about Anglo-French aggression in Egypt, 163–4; reaction on Nehru's Calcutta speech on Hungary, 168–9; discusses Hungarian situation with Nehru, 169–70; sends Nehru Pearson's telegram about K. Menon's behaviour in U.N., 171; sends Nehru St Laurent's speech about mobilization of world opinion against Soviet intervention, 172; discusses with Nehru Nasser's objection to Canadians in U.N. force for Middle East, 172–3; on Nehru's speeches in Parliament condemning Soviet intervention in Hungary, 173–9; his assessment of Indian foreign policy, 190; his farewell talks with Nehru family, 208; his farewell meeting and discussion with Nehru, 209–13; his assessment of Nehru in 1957, 220–35; several visits to India of, after 1957, 236; his visit in 1978–9 and reconsideration of India's prospects, 236–82; *also see under* India and Nehru

Reid, Escott: extracts from his messages, notes and memoranda on: East–West tension, 9–10; Indian expectations from Canada, 10; relationship between Canada and India, 25–6; U.N. resolution on Korean crisis, 35; his first meeting with Krishna Menon, 36; relations between some Indian officials, 37–8; Indian countryside, 41–2; talks with George Allen, 47, 48; proposal of appointment of Thimayya in Korean conference, 50; talk with Nehru on China, 56; Nehru–Chou En-lai meeting, 57; dispute over imprisoned American airmen, 62; Canadian recognition of Peking regime, 66; Indian anxieties about Indo-China crisis, 73; Indian reaction to SEATO, 74–5; proposed Locarno-type agreement on Indo-China, 77; Krishna Menon, 80, 178, 184, 185, 187–90; collapse of Geneva settlement on Indo-China, 82; work of supervisory commissions in Indo-China and Krishna Menon, 84; St Laurent–Nehru meeting in New Delhi, 91; Pearson, 92–3; Nehru's 'neutralist' policy, 99; Indian reaction to U.S. arms aid to Pakistan, 108, 111–12, 116; Kashmir issue, 121, 126–7, 131, 132; Krushchev–Bulganin visit, 133, 134, 137, 139; India's decision to remain in Commonwealth, 154–5; Nehru's attitude to Hungarian revolution, 160; Vijayalakshmi Pandit, 194; O. M. Mathai, 198–9; Rajagopalachari, 201; Radhakrishnan's assessment of political situation in India, 203; Morarji Desai, 204–5; Indian peasant, middle-class, and development, 216–17; advancement of India in political, economic and social matters in ten years, 218–19

Reid, Patrick, 10
Reid, Morna, 10–11
Reid, Ruth, 10–11; her impression of Indian villages, 39–40
Reston, James T., 150–1
Robertson, Norman, 11
Robertson, Walter, 46
Ronning, Chester, 43

Sahay, Vishnu, 124
Salisbury, Lord, 11
Sartre, Jean-Paul, 167
Sen, Boshi, 207
Sen, Tinoo, 36
Singh, Tarlok, 267, 269
Smith, Sidney, 186
Socialist Party, 208
South-East Asia Treaty Organization (SEATO), 73–4, 78
Soviet Union: and Reid's memorandum on East–West conflict, 8–9; supports India in Kashmir dispute, 136; and steel plant in India, 137; and Bandung Club, 137; and Chinese Communist Party, 142; and India–U.S. relations, 142; and India's foreign exchange requirements, 143, 144–8; and Anglo-French invasion of Egypt, 163; invasion of Afghanistan, 251; *also see* Hungary *and under* Nehru, Reid
St Laurent, Louis, 3, 4, 7, 8, 15, 18, 22, 63, 74, 165, 271; supports Nehru's cease-fire appeal in Indo-China, 69; on Middle East and Hungarian crises, 165–6, 172; his reaction to Nehru's statement on U.S. arms aid to Pakistan, 114, 259; and Nehru, 189, 259
Stevenson, Adlai, 11
Suez, 146; *see also* Egypt
Swiss Legation in Hungary and Nehru, 170

Thailand, 78
Thimayya, G. S., 50, 52
Toynbee, Arnold, 266
Truman, Harry, 23, 24
Trumbull, Robert, 102–3
Tyabji, Badr-ud-din, 121

U.N. General Assembly: and Korean crisis, 43, 50, 51; and Pearson, 66; and recognition of Chinese Communist Govt., 65–7; and Kashmir, 128; and Suez crisis, 145, 155; and Hungarian revolution, 162

U.N. Security Council, 65; and Formosa, 67; and Kashmir, 128–9; and Hungary, 147
Unesco conference in Delhi, 156–9; and Hungary and Suez issues, 164
Unesco seminar on Gandhian outlook, 4–5
U Nu, 55–6
United Nations Relief and Rehabilitation Agency, 14
United States: and help to India, 12; and Korean War, 23–4; and Chinese p.o.w.'s 29–30, 46; and armistice in Korea, 44–50; oppose Indian membership of Korean peace conference, 49–51, 183, 254; and Krishna Menon, 50, 182–3, 254; and Formosa, 62–3; and recognition of Chinese Communist Govt., 65–7; and Indo-China, 69, 70–1, 78, 82, 84; and arms aid to Pakistan, 101–15; and Kashmir, 124–5, 129; and bad relations with India, reasons for, 136–7; India's lack of appreciation of aid by, 137–8, 140; had no ambassador in India during Egypt crisis, 145; and Hungarian revolt, 151; India's misgivings about foreign policy of, 182–3; and Pakistan, 249

Veit, Lawrence, 268
Vercors, 167
Verghese, B. G., 275
Vietminh, 73, 82
Vietnam, 5–7, 20–1, 69, 73, 76, 82, 83–5; *see also* Indo-China
Vivekananda, Swami, 207

Ward, Barbara, 54
World Bank, 14, 217, 264, 269; on the rural poor, 277–8

Yugoslavia, 167

Zinkin, Maurice, 105, 204; on corruption, 215; on Indian bureaucracy, 245
Zorin, V. A., 159